EDUCATION IN MORALITY

Moral education is high on the agenda of most Western societies, but the contemporary climate of moral confusion and sometimes panic is not necessarily conducive to considered judgements about what teachers and schools should be doing in this area, and about which forms of moral education deserve the support of parents, citizens and governments.

This volume offers a collection of philosophical chapters that address various aspects of moral education and seek to illuminate some of the central issues arising in this area. The collection covers a broad range of fundamental questions at the forefront of contemporary philosophical debate about moral education and contains a range of contrasting points of view on many of the issues at stake.

Part I considers the nature of morality and moral education. In Part II a debate is developed about citizenship and moral education in a liberal democracy, and about the importance of wider social considerations. Part III examines the notion of education in the virtues and offers a critique of the currently popular concept of 'character education'. Part IV focuses on pluralism and postmodernism, which provide some of the most powerful challenges to familiar concepts of moral education. Finally, Part V raises the question of moral motivation.

J. Mark Halstead is Reader in Moral Education at the University of Plymouth and Director of the Centre for Research into Moral, Spiritual and Cultural Understanding and Education (RIMSCUE Centre). A former school-teacher and journalist, he has written several books on values in education.

Terence H. McLaughlin is University Lecturer in Education at the University of Cambridge and Fellow of St Edmund's College Cambridge, where he is Director of Studies of Philosophy. He has written on many areas of the philosophy of education, and is currently the Vice-Chair of the Philosophy of Education Society of Great Britain.

ROUTLEDGE INTERNATIONAL STUDIES IN THE PHILOSOPHY OF EDUCATION

EDUCATION IN MORALITY

*Edited by J. Mark Halstead
and Terence H. McLaughlin*

London and New York

First published 1999
by Routledge
11 New Fetter Lane, London EC4P 4EE

Simultaneously published in the USA and Canada
by Routledge
29 West 35th Street, New York, NY 10001

Routledge is an imprint of the Taylor & Francis Group

© 1999 selection and editorial matter,
J. Mark Halstead and Terence H. McLaughlin;
individual chapters, the contributors

Typeset in Garamond by
The Running Head Limited, Cambridge, UK
Printed and bound in Great Britain by
Biddles Ltd, Guildford and King's Lynn

British Library Cataloguing in Publication Data
A catalogue record for this book is available from the British Library

Library of Congress Cataloging in Publication Data
Education in morality / [edited by] J. Mark Halstead and
Terence H. McLaughlin.
p. cm. — (Routledge international studies in the
philosophy of education : 8)
Includes bibliographical references
1. Moral education. I. Halstead, J. Mark.
II. McLaughlin, Terence. III. Series
LC268.E357 1999
370.11'4—dc21 98–44183   CIP

ISBN 0–415–15365–4

CONTENTS

CONTRIBUTORS

David Best is Professor in the Department of Philosophy, University of Wales at Swansea.

David Carr is Professor of Philosophy of Education at the University of Edinburgh.

Brian Crittenden was Professor of Education at La Trobe University Victoria, and is a Fellow of the Academy of Social Sciences in Australia.

J. Mark Halstead is Reader in Moral Education at the University of Plymouth.

Graham Haydon is Lecturer in Philosophy of Education at the University of London Institute of Education.

Paul H. Hirst is Emeritus Professor of Education at the University of Cambridge.

Ruth Jonathan is Professor of Education at the University of Edinburgh.

John Kekes is Professor of Philosophy at University at Albany, State University of New York.

Will Kymlicka is Professor of Philosophy at the University of Ottawa.

Michael Luntley is Senior Lecturer in Philosophy at the University of Warwick.

Alasdair MacIntyre is Arts and Sciences Professor of Philosophy at Duke University, Durham, North Carolina.

Terence H. McLaughlin is University Lecturer in Education at the University of Cambridge.

Amélie O. Rorty is Emeritus Professor of Education at Harvard University.

Roger Straughan is Reader in Education at the University of Reading.

Marianne Talbot is College Lecturer in Philosophy at Brasenose College, Oxford.

ACKNOWLEDGEMENTS

Chapter 1 was originally published as 'The Many Faces of Morality' in *Midwest Studies in Philosophy*, volume XX, edited by Peter A. French, Theodore E. Uehling, Jr. and Howard K. Weltstein, © 1996 by the University of Notre Dame Press. It is used by permission of the publisher. Chapter 4 is an abridged version of an article entitled 'Education and Moral Development: The Role of Reason and Circumstance', published in the *Journal of Philosophy of Education*, volume 29, edited by Richard Smith. It is used by permission of The Philosophy of Education Society of Great Britain and Basil Blackwell. Chapter 7 was originally published by the Centre for the Study of Cultural Values at the University of Lancaster, and is reprinted by permission. The other chapters were written especially for this volume.

INTRODUCTION

Moral education is high on the agenda of most Western societies, but the contemporary climate of moral confusion and sometimes panic is not necessarily conducive to considered judgements about what teachers and schools should be doing in this area, and about which forms of moral education deserve the support of parents, citizens and governments. There is no shortage of new initiatives and strategies in many parts of the world, but sometimes these simply add to the confusion.

This volume offers a collection of philosophical chapters that address various aspects of moral education and seek to illuminate some of the central issues arising in this area. Although the collection does not aspire to provide complete coverage of all the major aspects of the domain of moral education, it covers a broad range of fundamental questions at the forefront of contemporary philosophical debate about moral education and contains a range of contrasting points of view on many of the issues at stake.

The essays in Part I, 'The nature of morality and moral education', contain some reflections on general matters relating to the subject of the collection as a whole. In Chapter 1, Amélie O. Rorty develops some suggestive observations on the complex and sometimes hidden 'ecology' of the terrain of morality. For her, morality is regionally and functionally diverse, but is essentially oriented – in a wide variety of different ways – to practice. Practical morality is, in her view, an 'educational institution' 'designed to produce certain types of persons, with specific virtues, mentalities, habits and skills directed to affect the world in a certain way'. The role of moral theory in bringing morality to a 'well-ordered place' must, she considers, be conducted in close relationship to politics, education and the imperatives of practical decision. David Carr, in reviewing the area of moral education both historically and philosophically in Chapter 2, draws attention to the difficulties liberal theories of ethics generate for any programme of moral education, and insists that any adequate basis for such a programme requires a commitment to education in virtue derived from certain established ideals of human growth and flourishing.

Part II, 'Rationality, society and the morally educated person', begins with Chapter 3 in which Brian Crittenden outlines the principles that should govern moral education in a pluralist liberal democracy, with particular reference to the common school. Ruth Jonathan's argument in Chapter 4 is in significant tension with a position of the kind developed by Crittenden, because of her insistence that social considerations should be given a greater salience in our understanding of moral education than is typical in liberal accounts. In Jonathan's view, these considerations relate to the self-defeating practical consequences of liberal neutralism in moral education and the need to give due weight to the significance of contingency and circumstance. Jonathan advocates the development of a conception of moral autonomy that is more socially sensitive in various ways, and which seeks to move beyond neutrality and proceduralism in critical reflection and an undue emphasis upon rights-based moral individualism towards an acknowledgement of our enmeshment in the social world. One of the central themes in Jonathan's chapter is that 'the educational enterprise requires a well-grounded social purpose, with the transformation of social structures understood as a prerequisite to individual emancipation, as well as one of its hoped-for consequences'. Continuing a focus upon social considerations, in Chapter 5 Will Kymlicka addresses the specific question of education for citizenship, and analyses the capacities and dispositions required for citizenship, properly understood, and the range of educational aims and tasks to which their development gives rise.

Part III shifts the focus of attention to 'Virtues, practices and the education of character'. In Chapter 6, Paul Hirst argues that moral education should not be primarily about cultivating reason or a set of virtues or personal autonomy. Moral thinking, motivation and living are necessarily dependent on participation in a vast array of already developed and developing social practices. It is only through progressively discovering in active participation the personal value of morally structured practices that students can develop fulfilling, satisfying lives. In Chapter 7, Alasdair MacIntyre argues that there can be no theory-neutral account of the virtues; what one moral tradition defines as genuine virtues will be defined by a rival tradition as counterfeit. MacIntyre argues that because of the existence in modern societies of a number of distinct and competing accounts of the virtues, with no single account able to refute the claims of its rivals by appeal to generally shared criteria, there can be no rationally defensible shared form of moral education in such contexts, but only a number of rival and conflicting forms. In Chapter 8, Terence McLaughlin and Mark Halstead offer an analysis and critique of two broad conceptions of education in character and virtue: 'non-expansive' conceptions that embrace forms of 'character education' currently popular in the USA, and 'expansive' conceptions that include proposals for the development of forms of liberal democratic civic virtue.

Some of the most powerful challenges to familiar conceptions of moral education come from pluralism and postmodernism, and these challenges are considered in Part IV. In Chapter 9, John Kekes describes the plurality of often-conflicting values people face as they try to develop their conception of the good life. Moral imagination is important, he argues, because it helps people to discover what it would be like to live according to the various possibilities available to them, and it helps them to avoid falsification and self-deception. This suggests three aims for education: the recognition of limits set by the deep conventions of a tradition; the adoption of possibilities according to which it would be good to live; and the development of character. In Chapter 10, Michael Luntley develops a conception of character education compatible with many of the radical assumptions of postmodernists. In the absence of the metaphysics of timeless truth and universal reason, moral education cannot be thought of as an instruction either in the true propositions of morality or in the general principles of reasoning as the foundation of moral decision making. Moral education is a more cumbersome and protracted affair, in which young people acquire the character and sensibilities they need to negotiate their way through the particular contingencies of life. In Chapter 11, and in a contrasting argument, Marianne Talbot offers a number of explanations for the current fashionableness of moral relativism, and argues that moral relativism is false because it offers an impoverished view of moral error, which is a notion deeply entrenched in our moral intuitions. Talbot argues that the belief that every person is intrinsically valuable is an absolute moral truth, rejection of which involves moral error, and that this belief should form a crucial part of moral education. In Chapter 12, David Best explores the relationship between the arts, culture and moral education, offering a critique of postmodernist conceptions of the self, language and thought. He challenges some of the notions of value implicit in postmodernist theories, and concludes that if we see moral education as concerned with the development of personal integrity and responsibility, then the arts continue to have a vital part to play.

The essays in Part V raise the question of whether morality involves some special kind of motivation and, if so, whether it is a kind of motivation education should be trying to encourage. In Chapter 13, Graham Haydon suggests that some philosophers have jettisoned the concept of morality completely because it is often expressed as rational and absolute rather than as manifest in people's feelings and motivated by compassion. He argues that moral motivation involves the capacity to think 'This is what I morally ought to do as a point of principle', but it is also tied to a sense of human community. The challenge for teachers is to make morality in this sense intelligible to pupils. In Chapter 14, Roger Straughan argues that an interpretation of moral education in terms of 'teaching children the difference beween right and wrong' is inadequate because people sometimes fail to do what they know or believe they ought to do. He examines the concepts of moral weakness and weakness of will, and their connection with self-deception; he argues that moral education, rather than seeking to 'strengthen the will', should promote the cool and detached review of various options. The first step may involve encouraging students to engage in an open and honest self-appraisal of their own wants and motives.

Philosophical considerations alone are insufficient to provide a complete illumination of all the issues arising in relation to moral education. Other academic disciplines and forms of research, together with the practical insights and experience of those engaged in the task, have an indispensable role to play. However, philosophy has an important contribution to make in bringing about a clearer understanding of the task of moral education, and it is hoped that this collection is evidence of this.

J. Mark Halstead
Terence H. McLaughlin

Part I

THE NATURE OF MORALITY
AND MORAL EDUCATION

1

MORALITY AS AN EDUCATIONAL INSTITUTION

Amélie Oksenberg Rorty

There are not now, nor were there ever, any specifically moral concepts. Morality is everywhere . . . or nowhere in particular. Our proper admirations, our proper indignations and contempt range widely: they cannot be neatly classified as aesthetic, moral or prudential. Normativity − the directions of ideals, commands and obligations − ranges equally widely. The grounds for our obligations − and our reasons for attending to those grounds − vary widely: the proper answer to the question 'Ought I . . .?' cannot be found by turning to a specific set of considerations or to a specific structure of reasoning. Sometimes the answer has the form 'You'll betray what is centrally important to you if you don't'; sometimes it is 'You'll be in deep trouble if you don't'; or 'You'll be dangerously irrational if you don't'. Nor does narrowing the question to 'What does morality require of me in this circumstance?' limit the field. The claims of reason (however they may be found!) or those of our fundamental identity-defining ground projects and commitments each present distinctive grounds for determining what morality requires; the pains of exclusion from the human community or those of an ill-formed and ill-spent life each provide distinctive counsels against immorality. None is sufficient, none absolutely necessary; they are not reducible to a more fundamental ground; there is not even a clear taxonomic hierarchy among them.

I want to explore some of the distinctive functions that the practices we are pleased to call 'moral' play in our lives. Practical morality is constructed to solve some of the problems that arise from the complexity of our natures and the diversity of our central connections to the world. The great variety of directions in *practical* morality arises from the problem of constructing the 'best possible human world' in which the distinctive (and often competing) life-projects of individuals and groups find their fulfilment (see Rorty 1992). I shall argue that differences among *theories* of morality − differences about how to characterise 'the moral domain' − reflect historical changes in our primary practical and philosophical preoccupations. As one or another of the variety of tasks that practical morality is designed to address becomes focally prominent, philosophic theories of morality offer different analyses of the category of 'the moral domain'. To be sure, many of our concerns overlap with the issues Aristotle (for example) discusses in his ethical works: what are the most general aims of our activities? In what does human excellence consist? What role does reasoning play in leading a good life? What can be blamed or praised, as falling within our power? But Aristotle does not designate a specific domain as *moral*. His ethical writings analyse the character structure of 'the best' among us: they combine perfectionist, prudential and social-functional considerations, without drawing distinctions among them. Grounded in both metaphysics and psychology, they are addressed to *oi politikoi* who construct the institutions that form character. By contrast, a good deal of contemporary ethics is designed to continue the apparently endless task of answering Hobbes while nevertheless retaining much of the directions of Hobbes's basic psychology. Moral theorists from Butler to Adam Smith and Hume introduced the category of the moral: but in their usage, the moral sciences encompassed what we would classify as *human psychology*. They attempted to find a natural purchase for beneficence and other social concerns that are compatible with enlightened self-interest. That search both culminates and ends with Kant's locating the grounds for (what he saw as) the unqualified, absolutely binding claims of duty. The morality of a free, self-legislating rational being is contrasted with the post-Hobbesian psychology that remains our natural equipment. And it is there – in a primary contrast to what remains an essentially naturalistic Humean psychology – that the contemporary category of morality has its first full self-conscious articulation.

But we do, after all, live in a post-Hobbesian, post-Kantian world, whose practices have in part been formed by the categories and distinctions we have inherited from Hobbesian and Kantian moral theory. Though we might have excellent reasons for emphasising our Aristotelian or our Humean inheritance, we cannot construct our practices or our theories wholly from their plan. For us, *morality* remains a lively category (see Rorty 1988). We would be well served by construing apparently conflicting theories of morality on the model of practical conflicts – whose distinctive interests are open to negotiation, arbitration and accommodation – rather than on the model of competing scientific theories that must be judged as true or false, adequate or inadequate.

The diverse functions of practical morality

Practical morality – morality as it lives and breathes – is an educational institution: it is designed to produce certain types of persons, with specific virtues, mentalities, habits and skills directed to affect the world in a certain way. Even when it takes a detour into the terrain of philosophic theories and systems, morality is directed to activity, however internal or spiritual, however self-perfectionist it may be. Independently of its theoretical and ideological commitments, practice-oriented morality has always improvised on the Marxist injunction: the point is not (only) to understand the world but to improve it.

Like other educational institutions, morality is directed and constructed to perform a large range of independent functions: to prohibit destruction and harm, to promote harmony and stability, to develop what is best in us. The rationale and psychology of these functions are so diverse as to raise the question of whether morality forms a single unified system. Taken together, the various functions of morality are – like those of other educational institutions – precariously balanced against each other. They protect individuals and develop what is best in them while also serving the social and political communities that – in a profoundly ambiguous way – both limit and enhance individual lives.

Before exploring the complex ecology of the moral terrain, we should ask: to whom is it addressed? Who are its agents and beneficiaries? The practical question that morality is designed to answer is: 'What should I – what should we – do?' The grammar clearly points to the first person, but is it the first person singular or the first person plural? In one way, of course the answer appears to be the first person singular. It is 'I' who ponders and sometimes decides; it is these hands that reach or refuse; it is 'I' who grieves or rejoices at what has been done. But the first person quickly multiplies, both externally and internally. In truth, our choices and projects would be in the free fall of empty space if they were not supported and opposed by our fellows. Our deliberations are implicitly sustained by our beliefs about the interests and penchants of our fellows, often also internalised in the many voices, the various personae – philosopher, immigrant, parent, householder – that constitute us as the so-called individuals we are. Our multiple personae each have distinctive needs, rights and obligations, different habits, priorities and virtues (see Rorty and Wong 1990). They struggle with one another for the control of our allegiances and actions. Each has a special set of preoccupations in the field of practical reason . . . if indeed there is *one* such domain. The dream of individual integrity is rarely a solitary achievement: it is largely a by-product of the successful – and often accidental – cooperation among the intersecting and tensed associations that are the sources and the projections of our multiple personae. And that is just speaking intrapsychically. 'We' are primary agents of morality: it is 'we' who – in an unstable pattern of intrapsychic and social alliances and oppositions – decide and act. Morality is not the enterprise of isolated individuals who, as it happens, contingently depend on one another for their welfare. It is, rather, the enterprise of a complexly divided community of complexly divided individuals who nevertheless can, and often should, act independently of one another (see Rorty 1992).

If moral agents are members of a community, practice-oriented morality might seem to be culturally specific: each culture defining a moral system and vice versa. But in truth any viable culture is dynamically subdivided, encompassing radically distinct action-guiding priorities. As it lives and breathes, the morality of a culture's military corps is functionally different from that of its mercantile class, just as both differ from the morality of the High Priests (whoever they may be). There may be some highly general – not to say vague – consensus about the basic style and directions of a culture, but these are likely to be ambiguous, usefully open to distinctive interpretations by those with opposed interests. Determining the primary directions of a culture's morality sets the scene of a political battlefield: claiming to describe a culture's morality is a way of claiming the high ground (see Rorty 1994a).

We should beware of being prematurely egalitarian in identifying moral agents and beneficiaries. Morality is not always addressed equally to every citizen or intrapsychic persona, each deciding for all (see Rorty 1991). Even if the capacities for morality were equally distributed, practice-oriented morality requires active abilities and habits. Since working moral character is specified and developed by a wide range of social institutions, the primary audience and agents of morality are the happy few – whoever they may be – who (whether they realise it or not) structure the institutions that transform mere capacities into active abilities, the institutions that form our moral profiles.[1]

Like other educational systems, morality is enlarged by the institutions that serve as its instruments. Workplaces, banks, court, armies and hospitals all generate a vast range of internal bureaucratic regulations, flow charts of duties and virtues, rights and obligations. The regulations that sustain the work of these institutions are not typically openly acknowledged to carry moral weight, but in truth their infractions carry the same sorts of sanctions as violations of officially designated moral obligations. Non-conformists are regarded with suspicion; they are charged with irrationality; they have difficulty eliciting cooperation and they suffer the pressure that is intended to produce guilt or, at the very least, shame. Social institutions structure the directions of basic motives and ambitions, provide the models for public deliberation and accountability; they set norms for the tenor of broader social interactions, as egalitarian or hierarchical, formal or informal, adversarial or arbitrational. They form the patterns and the habits exercised in resolving ordinary conflicts, and they define the terms of utility and fairness. A surprising amount of the content of practice-oriented morality – as well as its recent emphasis on obligations and duties – derives from the flow-chart regulative practices of institutions (see Bourdieu 1992). Their claims on us are – for all practical purposes – as far-reaching, as demanding, as over-riding, as those we are pleased to call 'morality'.

Implicitly, then, morality is addressed to the bureaucrats – parents and kindergarten teachers, judges and prime ministers – who articulate and effectively enforce the policies that in turn structure the salient habits of moral agents. It is only in those rare circumstances when egalitarian, political and

10

social institutions are firmly and effectively in place that morality can be directly addressed to presumptively autonomous individuals. Indeed, individual autonomy cannot be – it had better not be – presupposed by morality: it is an idealised aim and a fragile achievement of specific political systems.

Still, however far we may be from being fully qualified self-legislative moral agents, we are nevertheless all moral bureaucrats, siblings, neighbours and colleagues, attempting to influence one another's moral mentality in all our encounters. So while the primary audience and initial agents of morality are the bureaucrats who frame the institutions that form agency, it turns out that it is after all directed to us all, not because we are all equally autonomous, but because we are all principled moral meddlers. Adapting the immortal words of Walt Kelly, 'I have met the moral bureaucrat and le bureaucrat c'est moi.'

One more twist on the hidden demography of moral agency. The 'we' who articulate moral ideals are the vanguard visionaries of morality – the prophets, poets and philosophers – who influence the educators who influence legislative bureaucrats who form us. We might ask: where does this vanguard get its ideals and indignations? The moral visionaries who are the ultimate legislators of the world themselves improvise on themes taken from the diverse history of our practices and directions. Our morality is composed of motifs originally heard in Jerusalem, Athens, Rome, London and Paris . . . not to mention those that arose from their complex interactions with Constantinople, Kashmir and Cathay. Virtually all we think and all we do is composed of a palimpsest history of conquest, trade and exile that has formed our practices and evaluations. This by no means assures the possibility of our constructing a normative moral Esperanto. No matter how strict their Qur'anic interpretations may be, the literal understanding and observance of the Law in Isfahan does not coincide with that in Afghanistan or Malaysia. Even purist fundamentalists are affected and internally divided by local geopolitics.

Having first divided and then multiplied the demography of moral agency, we can turn to its varied tasks and functions. Like other educational institutions, morality performs a wide range of independent but interlocking – and, in practice, sometimes mutually conflicting – functions, each with its own directions and directives, with its own rationale and criteria for adequacy. Here is the beginning of a list of the problems that morality is intended to solve: its various functions are, of course, neither exhaustive nor mutually exclusive.

1   The minimal negative morality of righteousness preserves and protects individuals and the primary groups that form and constitute them; it defines wrong doing and sets its sanctions.
2   The minimal positive morality of decency defines the fundamental principles of justice and rights; it promotes the political conditions for resolving

11

conflicts and the social conditions for basic coordination; it defines and promotes responsible agency and educates basic decency, as it extends to strangers and enemies.

3   The tasks of the constructive morality of virtue are far more varied:

-     it promotes the social and economic conditions that sustain mutually beneficial trust and cooperation;
-     it characterises flourishing and the norms of normality, and promotes the virtues that express or serve them;
-     it sets norms for the tenor – the attitudes and affections – of a vast range of social and personal attachments and enmities: for friendship, rivalry, dissent, collegiality, citizenship and compassion, as these might go beyond the minimal demands of liberal mutual respect and towards the intrinsic good of *philia* and *agape*, what we might call the Russian novel aspect of morality;
-     it articulates ideals and excellences, sets priorities among the activities that constitute our lives.

The minimal negative morality of righteousness tends to be egalitarian; it sets constraints and obligations that are presumed to be realisable by everyone even in the worst of circumstances. The minimal positive morality of decency sets the terms of basic cooperation and responsibility presumably available to everyone under relatively benign circumstances (whatever these may be). The constructionist morality of virtue and goodness directs the fulfilment of ideals, the habits of inventive benevolence and affection that may not be equally realisable by everyone.[2] Because many of these functions are interdependent and substitutable, criteria for their identity and differentiation are elusive.[3] Nevertheless, initially at least, each of the functions of morality defines a distinct terrain: each is prompted by, and specifies a distinctive domain of relevant considerations; each requires its own virtues and habits (see Williams 1981: ch. 5; Taylor 1985: ch. 4; Hampshire 1989; Rorty 1992). To be sure, the virtues are, at a basic minimum level, interdependent, each requiring due concern for the considerations of the others. (Generosity that violates justice and prudence only bears the name of generosity in quotation marks.) So connected, the basic level of virtue sets the necessary but not sufficient precondition for the possibility of morality. But beyond that minimal level, the virtues are specialised. High generosity cannot be derived from the principles and psychology of justice. The rationale for their development, the motives that typically prompt them, the criteria for their successful performance, the political and social institutions that support and govern them, the detailed practical reasoning internal to their exercise, are local to their concerns. Although practical reason conforms to the general context-invariant laws of logic, it is further specified by domain-specific rules of relevance. In determining what justice requires in a particular situation, we raise a set of considerations – we ask specific questions and refuse the relevance of others – that are radically different from those appropriate to determining the prudent or generous thing to do. The commands of justice diverge from the counsels of prudence or of generosity largely because they have been marked by a different set of relevance includers and excluders.

Expanding morality – generating its local requirements – in this way might seem to weaken the force of its obligations, and certainly to trivialise the claim that its heterogeneous functions regionalise practical reason. If morality expands to include the rhetoric of etiquette, it should come as no surprise that it has distinctive functions with distinctive criteria for relevance and satisfaction. It might seem more elegant and perspicuous – not to mention kinder and gentler – to limit the domain of morality to the requirements of decency that can generally be fulfilled by virtually everyone, and to relegate the admirable excellence to the domain of the supererogatory. But condemnation and praise, the informal practices and attitudes of moral sanctions, do not observe such sharp boundaries. On the one hand, we treat failures of generosity in much the same way that we treat failures of decent cooperation, by distancing ourselves, by substituting scorn and disdain for trust and affection. For serious moral agents, failures of goodness or virtue engender the same sort of guilt, shame and self-recrimination that follow failures of righteousness. On the other hand, morally-laden judgements and reactions are subtle and discriminating: as the force of obligations varies from the passing light to the deadly serious, informal sanctions and penalties for their infraction vary as they are applied to a sleaze or a fiend, with graceful stopping places demarcating the loathsome, the shameful, the despicable and the contemptible, each open to its finely differentiated social sanctions.[4] And so too with morally laden admiration as it ranges from the stalwart to the saint, from the well-intentioned to the resourceful problem solver. Hume puts it well: 'Each of the virtues, even benevolence, justice, gratitude, integrity, excites a different sentiment from the spectator' (1972: 607–8). The habits and skills of knowing when and how to place friendship before science, science before patriotism, art before prudence are differentially morally laden. With all these distinctions in working order, the sharp delineation of *the* domain of morality is exposed as an unreflective inheritance of the theological need to distinguish the saved from the damned.

Despite its regional and functional diversity, the substantive morality of goodness and virtue is nevertheless imperialistic: it extends to whatever might be required to serve its original directions. In all its uplifting and downgrading forms, moralising pervades every aspect of our lives, intruding on the minutiae of the smallest gestures. We attempt to regulate and direct one another even in our most affectionate, unguarded playful moments. The Table of Commandments expands to the detailed regulations of Exodus and Deuteronomy; the sermons of Jesus are essentially supplemented by the letters of Paul; and the Constitution of the United States remains a schema for a possible polity until it is articulated in a body of legislative and judicial decisions. What is more, all these pointers remain words in the air until they are expressed in the practices of institutions, the behaviour of legislators and judges, and the tonality and gestures of our ordinary interactions. Practical morality is a bootstrap operation: it attempts to create the educational conditions that promote the minute habits that are its realisation in practice.

But a moment's reflection on the bitter factions within educational institutions makes it clear that we have hardly brought morality to a well-ordered place. The multiple functions of educational institutions notoriously have a divided clientele: they prepare an elite for highly specialised intellectual achievements; they are the cruel instruments of the socialisation of a trained labour force; and they provide a safe haven for radical social critics of all kinds; they are organised to promote autonomy . . . and to develop the civic virtues of constructive cooperation (see Larmore 1987; Rorty 1994b). The territorial ambitions of the various functions of morality, each ramifying to control whatever might affect their successful performance, force issues of priority. Like other educational institutions, morality gives us too much guidance from too many directions: it sometimes generates the very uncertainties and conflicts it was meant to resolve. It is the practical problems of dealing with these uncertainties and conflicts – rather than the postulated *a priori* unity of practical reason – that impel us to attempt to construct philosophic systems of morality.

In any case, the demography and sociology of morality do not explain, let alone justify, its normative force. They do not account for the authority of moral reasoning and moral obligations. When *should* justice take precedence over the claims of affection and affiliation? Under what circumstances *should* inventive benevolence properly lay aside the morality of decency? When should considerations of general welfare over-rule ideals of human perfectibility? (see Walzer 1973). No anatomy of moral sociology, no genealogical history of its fragmentation and changing directions can help us understand how best to answer the question 'What should we do?' Resurrecting Durkheim, giving him a Marxist purpose and an ironic Nietzschean expression dramatises the plight, rather than resolves the problems, of moral agency. Distinguishing the various functions of morality, differentiating their respective regional virtues and localised practical reason without assigning them an order of priority reintroduces the kind of chaos and conflict that morality was invented to resolve.

Differing characterisations of the moral domain

Enter philosophical systems of morality. We turn to moral theory for criteria to determine when basic justice should outweigh friendship, when generosity is more important than decency. The practical necessity of organising regionalised virtues and localised practical reason into an 'all things considered system' prompts the construction of philosophic theories of morality. They assume the task once assigned to divinity: that of constructing the best of all possible worlds, one that assures the compossible realisation of the varied directions and directives of morality. They are designed to explain, to rationalise and reconstruct the phenomena of morality. The fears of arbitrariness and irrationality that generate philosophic theories also set their agenda: they press for disambiguation and attempt to structure the diverse functions of educative morality within a single domain, rationalising and justifying a normative order of constraints and priorities among them. Indeed, a good deal of moral philosophy from Plato to Hegel and Mill has tried to assure us that despite all appearances to the contrary, morality is guided by a specific set of general aims, principles or motives; that regionalised practical reason is integrated within a single, unified field; that the virtues – and their respective rationales and rewards – are interconnected.

Philosophic theories of morality are Janus-faced: as directed to their contemporaries, they work within the frame of inherited assumptions and an inherited idiom. They express or presuppose views about the pre-moral structure of human psychology – the raw materials with which the craft of morality must work – as well as views about what is best and worst in that raw material, an account of what can be used to bypass or transform the worst to develop the best. In locating moral capacities and abilities, they define both the conditions and the scope of responsibility as egalitarian or hierarchical. Although they depend on empirical generalisations of all kinds, they tailor their arguments to address the specific concerns of their audience, often beginning in indignation and outrage, and sometimes in the hope of reconciling apparently opposed insights. But in the interest of convincing any and all comers, moral philosophers typically abstract from their immediate concerns to offer what they take to be objective arguments that any rational person must accept as valid. Disguising their origins and even the questions that form their agenda, moral philosophers attempted to justify their ideals and principles in the most general terms possible, presenting relatively local normative claims about the priorities that ought to obtain among the various functions of morality in an impartial, presumptively universally binding form (see Bourdieu 1992). But the more generalised morality becomes, the less immediate guidance it provides; the more it has distanced itself from its original concerns, the less directly motivating are its directions.

In any case, distinctive measures of priority generate different configurations, different ways of systematising the relations among the various moral functions. Transcendental arguments that establish the priority of a free rational will as a precondition for the possibility of morality establish neither its developmental priority nor its moral supremacy. Nor does the developmental priority of such psychological attitudes as attachment bonding, fear, pity, or sympathy establish anything about their normative ranking order. Showing that an attitude or an ability is first or last in a developmental sequence does not by itself – without the addition of many further premises and arguments – prove anything about its rank as a moral value. In a similar way, the various functions of morality can stand in quite different orders of priority to one another: minimal negative morality may provide the political conditions of security and trust that permit the development of the decency; and the general practice of decency or justice may conduce to the development of more complex virtues. But nothing about the respective moral value of justice and generosity follows from that order of dependence.

It should not be surprising that there is a strong correlation between traditional philosophic theories and the various functions and aims of morality. And it should not be surprising that they accord distinctive priorities to the various functions of morality. With outrageously crude simplification, we can characterise the focused priority of some traditional moral theories. Concerned to assign priorities among human excellencies, Aristotelians describe the virtues germane to the activities that constitute well-lived and fully achieved lives, attempting to analyse the political systems that sustain, structure and express those excellencies. Augustine, Maimonides and Aquinas attempted to derive the directions and the systematic order among our primary activities from (what they saw as) divine law. Hobbes gave priority to the rational necessity of assuring the political conditions for individual security. Focusing on the psychological and social preconditions for developing civic and civil virtues, Humean theories trace the genealogy of the morality of decency: they track sympathy and the operations of the calm passions as they enlarge narrow self-interest to form the social virtues and the sense of justice. Kant concentrates on establishing the conditions for the minimal morality of righteousness, attempting to derive the structure of their obligations from the conditions that make rational agency possible. Focusing on criteria for evaluating priorities among public policies, utilitarian theories concentrate on formulating the requirements of individual and social welfare. Each of these theories has its own form of territorial ambitions: each undertakes to locate and derive the multiple functions of morality from its own favoured standpoints.

Attempting to combine the perspectives of these approaches, many recent philosophic theories of morality construct the architecture of postmodern philosophic systems, each attempting to incorporate the successful designs of their predecessors. But the various primary directions of such eclectic theories can be configured in a number of quite different ways: the deontological constraints of righteousness can, for instance, be set within a utilitarian frame; or utilitarian aims can be built into the morality of decency; perfectionist ideals can be enlarged to encompass personal affections.[5] Postmodern attempts at eclectic philosophical systems multiply the number of viable theories: every bit of our layered, interconnected and conflicted moral history seems equally available to be placed anywhere or everywhere as an arch or as a cornerstone of our moral practices. As the history of moral philosophy all too clearly attests, the conflicts that arise within moral practice reappear as conflicts between philosophic theories. Such theories reintroduce the same benefits and tensions, the same jockeying for primary positions within their integrative systems that occurred between the diverse functions of morality. We are presented with all too many reasonable proposals, all too many maps of the structure of the system of morality. We find ourselves with more potential conflicts between different ways of ordering our priorities than ever.

The new emphasis on civic virtues

Recognising irreducible and irreconcilable differences among reasonable conceptions of morality, recent revivals of Enlightenment theories – ranging from Rawls to Habermas, from Scanlon to Korsgaard – take a constructivist turn. Where the early Enlightenment proposed to define criteria for rational moral evaluation, the new Enlightenment concentrates on formulating the principles that should regulate fair rational deliberation about just political institutions, among mutually respecting citizens who may differ about their substantive moral commitments.[6]

But for all their significant differences, the new Enlightenment philosophers share some of the ambitions – and some of the assumptions – of the early Enlightenment: the hope is that the civic virtues of respect – the virtues germane to deliberation – might also provide the models and, under benign circumstances, elicit the motives for practical cooperation. Philosophy might show us how to replace the power struggles of unregulated moral conflict with constructive moral deliberation. Perhaps the rationality that evaluates the various dimensions of morality might also be capable of controlling and guiding – perhaps actually forming – a person's psychology. Philosophers and citizens alike might cease being sneering adversaries; we might somehow acquire the mutual respect, patience, the good will and the skills required for shared deliberation, resolving conflicts without relocating them.

It is certainly true that in acquiring the civic virtues germane to shared deliberation we would actualise an important ideal, that of forming a community of mutually respecting persons. But if (by the varied standards of each philosophic theory of morality), we become more just, more subtle, more loving, more creatively imaginative – perhaps even more like the compassionate presences of Russian novels – was it really philosophy that improved us? It would be surprising if we became kinder, gentler citizens by virtue of having become more rigorously precise philosophers, engaged in shared mutually respecting deliberation. It seems more likely that whatever moral and philosophical improvements we manage to achieve are co-related by-products of other changes, many of them arising from unforeseen and unintended economic and political movements.

Of course the projects of the new constructivist Enlightenment never supposed that philosophic deliberation could by itself issue in well-formed policies directed to assuring the basic material conditions without which morality remains a notional, and even an inhumanly demanding project. No one thought that philosophy at the round table could replace street politics and street education. Nor did the new Enlightenment pretend to assure the development of the abilities and skills that the substantive morality of virtue requires. No one thought that the conditions for mutually respecting deliberation could be sufficient to assure the complex set of psychological and social habits of genuine respect, habits of courtesy and empathic attentiveness of ordinary civic life.

Consider the problems set by genuinely shared, participatory deliberation. Even if we manage the virtually insuperable task of ignoring differences in power, we still face the difficulty that the dispossessed and disestablished are not always well equipped to argue their case. It is, after all, one of the most serious consequences of disempowerment that the eloquence of need is not always matched or supported by precise, effective analysis and argument. What does genuine respect for one's fellow citizens require? That we recognise their needs and provide the best rational arguments to address those needs? And what does respect require when the disempowered refuse our diagnostic interventions on their behalf? 'That's not what we meant,' they may say, 'that's not what we meant at all.' Does genuine respect always allow the last word to a victim? Presumably it is just such questions as these that are to be assigned to (presumptively) fair, equal philosophic and public deliberation among free and equal participants.

Although the new Enlightenment avoids some of the Utopian hopes of early Enlightenment theories, they manifestly face similar bootstrap problems: the civic virtues – the abilities and the dispositions required for appropriate participation in constructive deliberation – are typically only developed by the political and educational structures that such practices are directed to define and establish. The most genuinely respectful shared deliberation remains talk without the political and psychological conditions that move the conclusions of conference table to the minutiae of daily life. Without that, the most elevated and good willed cooperative moral deliberators become fair targets for an Aristophanic comedy.

This is one reason that Rawls and Habermas, among others, are eager to cooperate with economists and educators. They recognise that a detour into philosophic theories of morality brings us back to the varied practical, educational tasks of morality, now provided with a moral form of Robert's Rules of Order for fair deliberation and practical accommodation. But since we are unlikely to follow these guidelines unless we are relatively safe and secure, with our mutual respect at the conference table sustained by sound social arrangements in town, we are in a way back where we started. Illuminated, encouraged and more articulate, we must return to morality as an educational institution.

We are now in a better position to see the power – and the limitations – of philosophic theories of morality. However closely they may be linked, philosophic theories of morality and practice-oriented educative morality have quite different aims. Philosophic theories present themselves as competitors, at best open to synthesising incorporation; the various functions of practice-oriented morality are in principle complementary, allowing mutual accommodation and compensation.

The strength and utility of philosophic theories of morality are those of middle-management bureaucracy; they goad us to specify our aims and refine our practices, to identify and correct our inconsistencies, to articulate and disambiguate the assumptions that stand behind our conflicts. They direct us to the tasks of reconciliation and shared deliberation (see Scanlon 1982; Richardson 1990; Korsgaard 1996). They press us to explain and to justify ourselves to our fellows, to reconcile apparent conflicts by sensitively translating distinctive vocabularies, attempting to specify shared general values and principles, agreeing to compartmentalise and contextualise irreducible differences by mutually respectful negotiation and accommodation. Their limitations are also those of middle-management bureaucracy: in favouring clarity of definition over productive functional adaptability, they risk losing sight of the aims of the enterprise. They can issue sensible orders but not assure the conditions that promote their satisfactory execution.

Moral imagination and moral deliberation

It is for this reason that many moral philosophers have recently turned to applied ethics, to the philosophy of law and the philosophy of education. Often without fully acknowledging and analysing the shift, such philosophers find themselves developing new types of deliberative virtues. Instead of treating moral conflicts on the model of competing scientific theories, attempting to achieve an overlapping consensus about general principles, they construe them as practical disagreements. A certain discreet talent for ambiguity in the formulation of principles and a certain vagueness in characterising values and ideals can avert potentially disruptive and harmful conflict. Moral conflicts are most often appropriately addressed by the arts and skills of labour arbitration – by accommodation and compensation – rather than by determined disambiguation, adjudication or generalised theory construction. But while arbitration and accommodation – the best sense of compromise – do not suffer the same circularities that beset theory construction, they nevertheless also presuppose a wide range of cooperative abilities and habits. They, too, depend on the very psychological and political conditions of substantive cooperation that their successful exercise is intended to achieve.

It is also at this point, and for similar reasons, that many philosophers – Iris Murdoch, Martha Nussbaum, Judith Shklar, Stanley Cavell – turn to literature for further moral guidance. If the architectural plans of moral philosophers and the negotiating strategies of arbitration are not sufficient to assure moral practice, perhaps Sophocles, Jane Austen, Tolstoy and Toni Morrison might succeed in showing us how to endure the conflicts we cannot resolve.

Perhaps we can acquire or at least refine moral abilities by vicariously, imaginatively participating in the lives of fictional characters. Perhaps following Emma in her dreams of love, Raskolnikov in his nihilistic experiment, Gradgrind in his determination to rule with facts, could enliven a resolution to our dilemmas.

But if philosophic theories of morality cannot resolve the conflicts of practical morality, neither can the projects of the new moral Romanticism. Our responsive mimetic identification with fictional characters may well make us more sensitive to modes of suffering that we have not ourselves experienced. But vividly envisaging cruelty at work does not necessarily make us more alert to our own forms of cruelty; nor does it necessarily make us more inclined to combat it. There is, after all, no guarantee that we will identify with the victims rather than with the villains. Nor does an attentive focus on individuality and particularity necessarily make us more loving or even more forgiving. A good way to revive envy, rage and hate is to enliven detailed images of particular memories. Propagandists are more adept at using the riches of imaginative fiction to elicit than to quench blood thirst. The moral contributions of the imagination presumably derive from its breaking through the limitations of our own narrowly conceived needs and experiences. But it is precisely the unconstrained power of the imagination that licenses its delight in the brilliant inventiveness of cruelty and disorder: it makes any and every form of viciousness vividly available to us.

Even when it brings the benefits of an enlarged emotional and moral sensitivity, moral Romanticism runs the risks of narcissism, savouring the subtle delicacies of refined guilt and shame that mark the death of both morality and art. That is on the one hand. On the other, we might be concerned that serious, elevated moralising might also wither, if not actually kill the arts. While unhindered wild free play, an impish delight in form and sound are native to the species, they are also fragile. Aesop may have crafted his tale for its moral, Dostoevsky and Tolstoy may have wanted to bring us to their moral obsessions; but we have surely been more profoundly affected by the fantasies those obsessions generated than by the moral lessons they tried to convey. To be sure, the new moral Romanticism never pretended that an empathically sensitive imagination could provide a sufficient condition for morality; it never even claimed that it was a necessary condition. In its modest forms, it only proposed the use of literature as a mode of moral enlightenment and moral enlargement. Yet even in its sober modest forms, the new Romanticism, like the new Enlightenment, presupposes a psychology that is already structured by moral considerations. Like the rules for fair deliberation and accommodation, the morally empathic imagination needs substantive direction.

What conclusions, if any, can we draw from this leisurely tour through the Sargasso Sea of morality and philosophic theories of morality? First, many contemporary moral theorists suffer from the disease of professionalised intellectuals: we treat necessary conditions as sufficient, setting aside the task of analysing the practical, political and educational requirements of morality as if they were either obvious or beyond the scope of our responsibility. The history of moral theory – the work of Plato, Aristotle, Hume, Kant, Mill – reveals quite a different approach. They attempted to address political and educational issues on which the achievements of morality depend.

Second, philosophic theories of morality without politics and education are empty; and the education of an empathic imagination without Enlightenment political philosophy is blind. And both, taken together, presuppose the political and psychological conditions they are directed to achieve. A vast array of benign social and political conditions are required to develop the virtues and abilities of mutually respecting deliberation; the empathic imagination of the new Romanticism requires the moral direction it is intended to supply. The various directions of morality – such as justice, integrity, autonomy, compassion – are not its presuppositions but the fragile outcomes of fragile processes.

Third, mutually respecting deliberation is essential to the process of working out – working through – disagreements about the priorities of the various functions of morality. Such deliberation is best modelled on practical arbitration, guided by reasonable accommodation and compensation. Even when disagreements linger, we are strongly motivated to act on the conclusions of our deliberations: after all, practical morality is initially prompted by immediate and particular concerns that command decisions of some kind.

Finally, our starting point – the sober recognition of the diversity of the projects and functions of practical morality as she lives and breathes – is, after all, not a bad place to be and not a bad place to remain.[7]

Notes

1 In speaking broadly of 'institutions', I intend to refer to formal or informal organisations or practices, whose activities are implicitly or explicitly regulated, that constrain and direct the actions of individuals.

2 It is only after Kant that the morality of virtue moved from its classical focus on moral excellence to the egalitarian morality of decency. Classical virtue theory presents sober problems for liberal egalitarians: problems about the differential abilities of perception and resourcefulness that the morality of high virtue requires. See Scheffler (1993).

3 For instance, although the rationale for evaluating the morality of actions is quite different from that for evaluating persons, the criteria for assessing them are mutually dependent; similarly, although the criteria for evaluating just political institutions differ from those used to evaluate their effects on individual thriving, still the two evaluations often go hand in hand.

4 See Dante's *Inferno* for a subtle exercise in defining the punishments to fit the crimes.

5 Kantians like Onora O'Neill and Barbara Herman attempt to incorporate utilitarian welfare programmes within a deontological frame (O'Neill 1984; Herman 1993); utilitarians like Peter Railton (1984) try to give an account of civic and character virtues; others like Samuel Scheffler (1993) attempt to incorporate

agent-centred restrictions and agent-centred prerogatives within a consequentialist frame.
6 See Rawls (1974–5) on the method of wide reflective equilibrium. See also Richardson (1990).
7 This chapter is descended from an earlier essay, 'Les multiples visages de la moralité', *Revue de Metaphysique et de Morale* (1994) 99(2): 205–21. It was delivered at colloquia at the University of Toronto, Washington University, St. Olaf's College, the Harvard Graduate School of Education and Santa Clara University. I am grateful to the participants of those colloquia and to correspondence with A. D. M. Walker for lively and helpful discussion.

References

Bourdieu, P. (1992) 'Towards a policy of morality in politics', in W. Shea and A. Spadafor (eds) *From the Twilight of Probability*, Canton, MA: Science History Publications.
Hampshire, S. (1989) *Innocence and Experience*, Cambridge, MA: Harvard University Press.
Herman, B. (1993) *The Practice of Moral Judgment*, Cambridge, MA: Harvard University Press.
Hume, D. (1972) *A Treatise of Human Nature*, ed. L. A. Selby-Bigge and P. H. Niddith, Oxford: Oxford University Press.
Korsgaard, C. (1996) *The Sources of Normativity*, The Tanner Lectures, New York: Cambridge University Press.
Larmore, C. (1987) *Patterns of Moral Complexity*, Cambridge: Cambridge University Press.
O'Neill, O. (1984) *Constructions of Reason*, Cambridge: Cambridge University Press.
Railton, P. (1984) 'Alienation, consequentialism and the demands of morality', *Philosophy and Public Affairs* 13: 134–71.
Rawls, J. (1974–5) 'The independence of moral theory', *Proceedings and Addresses of the American Philosophical Association* 49: 5–22.
Richardson, H. (1990) 'Specifying norms as a way to resolve concrete ethical problems', *Philosophy and Public Affairs* 19(4): 279–310.
Rorty, A. O. (1988) 'Three myths of moral theory', in *Mind in Action*, Boston, MA: Beacon.
—— (1991) 'King Solomon and everyman: a problem in coordinating conflicting moral intuitions', *American Philosophical Quarterly* 28(3): 181–94.
—— (1992) 'The advantages of moral diversity', in E. Paul, F. Miller and J. Paul (eds) *The Good Life and the Human Good*, Cambridge: Cambridge University Press.
—— (1994a) 'The hidden politics of multiculturalism', *Political Theory* 22(1): 152–66.
—— (1994b) 'The conflicting aims of education', in B. Darling-Smith and L. Rouner (eds) *Can Virtue Be Taught?* Notre Dame, IN: Notre Dame University Press.
Rorty, A. O. and Wong, D. (1990) 'Aspects of identity and agency', in O. Flanagan and A. O. Rorty (eds) *Identity, Character and Morality*, Cambridge, MA: MIT Press.
Scanlon, T. (1982) 'Contractualism and utilitarianism', in A. Sen and B. Williams (eds) *Utilitarianism and Beyond*, Cambridge: Cambridge University Press.
Scheffler, S. (1993) *Human Morality*, Oxford: Oxford University Press.

Taylor, C. (1985) *Philosophy and the Human Sciences: Philosophical Papers II*, Cambridge: Cambridge University Press.

Walzer, M. (1973) 'The problem of dirty hands', *Philosophy and Public Affairs* 2(2): 160–80.

Williams, B. (1981) *Moral Luck*, Cambridge: Cambridge University Press.

2

CROSS QUESTIONS AND CROOKED ANSWERS

Contemporary problems of moral education

David Carr

What is the problem of moral education?

It would appear to be widely held in this country and elsewhere in the world that Western society is facing moral crisis. Certainly some such view is apparent in the outbreaks of moral panic which seem to occur with increasing frequency – and which are, of course, milked by contemporary media and journalism for all they are worth. To be sure, moral panics have occurred throughout recorded history, and prophets portending final human descent into the troughs of Sodom and Gomorrah have always been at hand to incite them. It may therefore be that more recent instances of the phenomenon need to be seen in proper historical proportion – not as genuine visions of apocalypse now but as due at least in part to the overheated word-processors of contemporary news-hounds. I am not for a moment denying, of course, the horror of the anomic and twisted behaviour of some people in our society, as witnessed by recent news coverage – but such people, like the poor, are always with us and it may be doubted whether human nature as such is generally either less or more inclined to demonic extremes than formerly. Human nature being what it is, the lord of the flies and the heart of darkness are never far from it; but, then, neither are those other qualities that naturally incline humankind to acts of concern, charity and selflessness towards their fellows.

The question of whether human nature as such is nowadays (compared to paleolithic times, or even half a century ago) more or less driven by selfish and cruel rather than kind or altruistic impulses, is not one that I am competent to answer; indeed, if as I suspect, the question makes little sense, it is not one that lies within anyone's competence to answer. A rather more meaningful question might be whether the society in which we live is one whose civil, legal and other institutions conduce more readily to reduction of negative, or promotion of positive, human qualities and dispositions than

24

formerly – and this, of course, suggests a further question of what means might be adopted to control human behaviour or best dispose it to the common good or welfare of others.

Whatever the significance of this question, however, it is of the utmost importance to recognise that it is *not* the problem of moral education, and that one risks falling into serious confusion by supposing otherwise. The temptation to run together these different issues is understandable, of course, because though they are conceptually separable there are connections of a more obvious practical kind between them; it is reasonable to expect, for example, that decisions about the proper direction of moral education would, in all likelihood, have significant implications for the way that individuals come to treat others in society. But it is also crucial to recognise that the issues are importantly distinguishable, since the problem of moral *education* is primarily that of how individual human lives might acquire meaning and purpose through the recognition and appreciation of a significant moral dimension to human experience which can serve to enhance personal life and growth. Natural feeling may well incline a young mother to love her child, and a young man may be well disposed by his social training to respect the property of others – but moral education seeks to integrate such training and sentiments with a deeper understanding of how they contribute to a positive and worthwhile way of living; it aims to articulate what is conducive to individual and social flourishing about such qualities and dispositions and to show how they might be more effectively exhibited in particular human circumstances – in short, to transform feeling and discipline into *virtue*. The basic aim of moral education, then, is to assist young people to live more meaningfully and rightly in the light of a clear recognition of the greater value for positive human development of some principles and qualities over others; that a life lived according to certain dispositions of honesty, self-control, fortitude, fairness, courtesy, tolerance and so on is worthier and more fulfilling than one lived in the vicious grip of dishonesty, intemperance, backsliding, prejudice and spite.

Again, this issue is certainly not *unrelated* to that of how people might, as a matter of fact, come to behave better in practical terms, if only because it may be more reasonable to expect consistently good conduct from those motivated by a love of virtue for its own sake than from those merely so impelled by nature and circumstance. It is no doubt true that we may sometimes have real cause to be grateful for those natural human inclinations that enable people to ignore the teachings of some moralists and philosophers – that having read that God is dead,[1] most of our students do not, like Raskolnikov,[2] proceed to murder their neighbours for gain; but it is nonetheless reasonable to expect that those whose natural benevolence has been reinforced or underpinned by self-accepted moral and religious principles might be more constant and reliable in their allegiance to these inclinations. The point is the familiar Kantian[3] one that whilst benevolent inclinations are perfectly proper and desirable in their way, they are nevertheless liable to be fickle in their attachments; the love a person feels for her family, tribe or nation, if not governed by some larger principle of charity, may quickly turn to cruelty and hate for those not regarded of a kind; and without the true virtue of justice, the loyalty and honesty someone exhibits in his dealings with friends may not be so apparent in his business dealings with strangers – if there is a quick profit to be made and he thinks he can get away with it.

If, then, there is a rather careless and problematic conflation of importantly distinguishable questions about, on the one hand, the proper direction of moral education and, on the other, whether our schooling, training or instruction actually conduces to the production of better public behaviour, it is because of the way these questions are linked through the broadly practical purposes and concerns of morality. It is clear enough that the initiation of individuals into some sort of moral life is of interest to us both by virtue of its potential for assisting people to live more positively and meaningfully and because the influence of morality on interpersonal behaviour and other-regarding conduct is of obvious public concern for the proper civic and political functioning of society.

The two questions become quite seriously muddled, however, when the problem of moral education is brought to focus exclusively on issues of discipline and control – as it so often does in debates about the role of education and schooling in the formation of young people's behaviour. Many, perhaps most, great moral philosophers have regarded discipline and training – the inculcation or reinforcement of certain individually and socially desirable habits or dispositions – as necessary, but not sufficient, for morality. Most serious enquiry into moral education has taken this point to heart and inclined to the view that some progress from behavioural training or conditioning to the appreciation of principle reflects the proper drift of moral development. But many of those whose primary concern lies with questions of social order and control – such as politicians and agencies of law enforcement – appear prey to some degree of intellectual scepticism about the possibility of securing such progress on any large scale, either in principle or in practice. At least since Plato's *Republic*, for example, there have been familiar and persistent worries about whether an education that goes much beyond habituation to rules and routines is a real practical possibility for most members of human societies – and politicians at both ends of the spectrum have been drawn to the verdict of Dostoevsky's Grand Inquisitor[4] on this matter. But from the time of Protagoras[5] there has also been deep and equally persistent scepticism about the very possibility of judgements of value capable of going beyond local custom and convention to the expression of principles of absolute and universal moral significance and application; moreover – though I have argued at some length elsewhere that they are mistaken (see Carr 1991a) – such sceptical perspectives have become even more entrenched in the liberal modern climate of social and cultural pluralism.

26

Recent reflection on moral education

I believe the two questions on which we have touched – of how we might go about arranging circumstances so that certain pressing problems of anomic, anti-social and downright deviant behaviour might be ameliorated, and of how to assist individuals to lead more meaningful lives through an initiation into the realm of moral values – are, despite the evident connections between them, unhelpfully and even dangerously confused in much current educational discussion. It is common enough to run across academic presentations purportedly on moral education which proceed to argue from the claim that contemporary society is rapidly sinking in a rising tide of vandalism, violence and drug abuse to some pet theory of moral formation that might serve to stem this tide. And much the same confusion of issues is discernible on the part of politicians and social administrators when they are wont to turn their attention to the potential of education for remedying one sort of social ill or another – be it illiteracy, shortage of skilled labour or the simple bad manners of the young.

On such occasions, of course, the issue of the alleged moral decline of the young is inevitably made to turn on the presence or lack of imposed authority and discipline in schools; but for various reasons it would be difficult to prove that schools that operate repressive regimes produce more socially responsible and altruistically inclined individuals than those that endorse more permissive policies (or vice versa), and the issue is probably something of a red herring. It is clear enough, for example, that authoritarian school regimes can sometimes 'fail' by producing individuals with bitter antagonistic attitudes to any and all authority, or may 'succeed' only in producing authoritarian, conformist or inflexible personalities. This is *not*, of course, an argument for liberal over authoritarian school regimes in the search for forms of moral instruction which might best conduce to the public standards of behaviour most of us would like to see prevailing among the young; it is simply to say that it is almost certainly a mistake to try to gauge the success of a programme of moral education – *or*, for that matter, a programme of social control – in these sorts of terms at all.

The quite serious muddling of distinguishable questions concerning moral education and social engineering is generally characteristic not only of most public comment on education of a non-professional sort, but also of official and semi-official professional literature as well. Among other recent literature of its kind the National Curriculum Council discussion paper (1993) on moral and spiritual education[6] is a good example – insofar as it exemplifies these and related confusions – of a document conceived and written for the education profession, yet very much in response to more widely aired public concerns. The document has attracted critical, even downright hostile, comment from many quarters – and it is not at all difficult to see why. To begin with, it appeared – hardly coincidentally – in the wake of a surge of public concern about the current social attitudes and behaviour of the young, reinforcing the suspicion that the document is, at least in part, a politically inspired response to a perceived outbreak of moral panic. In consequence, like other documents of its kind, the NCC paper can be regarded as both unhelpful in some respects (in which there might at least have been clarification) and downright counterproductive in others.

As far as unhelpfulness goes, the paper may be criticised for its general vacuity – for parading the usual conventional pieties about the importance of inculcating certain fundamental moral principles in the young, whilst leaving virtually untouched controversial theoretical and practical problems about how this might best be done. Certainly any charge of insubstantiality seems more than warranted in relation to the observations on spiritual education in the first half of the document; in all charity, these are probably best passed over in silence, except to lament that those seeds of critical spirit with respect to the framing of educational aims – which educational philosophers of the past quarter of a century have tried hard to sow – would appear to have fallen here on some very stony ground. The subsequent sections on moral education, however, proceed well beyond vacancy into realms of opacity which only that clear, careful and informed ethical thinking – of the sort in which this document does not engage – could remedy. Much is made, for example, of the importance of teaching moral absolutes, but the paper offers no coherent account of what a moral absolute might be; indeed, so far as one can tell, it would appear to be the main view of the document that it is a principle upon which there is *agreement* among people in a particular social context or among people in general. Here, however, the National Curriculum Council document would appear to fall into a common error (see Carr 1992b) of conflating the distinction between universality and particularity in the realm of moral judgement with that between what may be observed as a matter of common convention or consensus and that which an individual might be inclined to think or do from personal moral motives. But it is arguable that no coherent account of rational moral deliberation is possible once this confusion is in place – from which it follows that there can be no room either for the development of any intelligible conception of moral education and teaching.[7]

It is probably the final section of the document, however, to which most serious exception has been taken in professional educational circles – for it is here, as so often in guidelines for teachers of this semi-official kind, that the heavy hand of paternalism is discernible within the velvet glove of professional advice and consultation. As with the earlier Elton report on school truancy and indiscipline (see DES 1989) to which the NCC paper refers with approval, there is more than a hint of criticism of teachers for failing to maintain those proper standards of conduct which might keep young people on the straight and narrow, and for neglecting to provide them with the right sort of example in terms of dress, speech and devotion to duty. Leaving aside the potentially professionally offensive implication that teachers have, in a large part, been reneging on their proper responsibilities in such matters, there is also a fairly familiar one-sided emphasis on the respects in which schools might have let the side down. This largely ignores the difficult and changing social circumstances and conditions in which schools and teachers have to work – changes, for example, in social attitudes to educational values, authority and discipline which mean that it is simply no longer possible for such agencies, in many places, to command the same respect, allegiance and cooperation as formerly. It may be little more than sanctimonious cant to lecture teachers and schools on drafting mission statements, formulating codes of conduct and applying strict sanctions, in circumstances where pupils and parents have their own value agendas, some of which not only operate counter to those of the school, but are often vigorously supported and reinforced by powerful social, political and economic forces and agencies at work in the larger public domain. Regrettably, then, the NCC paper not only fails to provide us with much illumination or clarification regarding basic questions of moral and spiritual education, it also inclines dangerously (if only by default) to the confusion of such questions with those of social engineering and control.

The cultural roots of the contemporary problem of moral education

The problem of moral education is not as such, then, that of social control or of how we might remedy or ameliorate certain currently distressing social problems of the waywardness of youth; it is, rather, that of how we might assist people to conceive and pursue worthwhile, decent and fulfilling lives with regard to character development and the improvement of interpersonal human relations. We can readily admit, of course, that the latter problem has important consequences for the former – even *causal* consequences – but this does not serve to show that moral education is basically just a form of social engineering; and whether or not we have correctly discerned the nature of moral life and the proper direction of moral education, it is not susceptible to the sort of proof by which we might assess the effectiveness of a technology. That said, it is now time to recognise that the theory and practice of moral education is at the present time vexed by a significant conceptual issue that has, I believe, quite serious implications for the problem of the provenance of that individual anomie and social disaffection widely discerned in contemporary Western society.

The historical determinants of this issue are highly complex and difficult to discern in detail; but the general form of the problem has been rehearsed repeatedly in the extensive recent literature of social and moral philosophy[8] in which it is of considerable current concern. Briefly, however, the story might go as follows. Historically, the progress (or, if one wishes, the decline) of Western civilisation in Europe and elsewhere may be viewed as a matter of evolution from a fundamentally feudal and theocratic social order – culturally homogeneous in terms of its general professed adherence to a particular system of religious doctrines and moral ideals – to a complex post-industrial society, which is clearly culturally heterogeneous in character, which tolerates a plurality of moral and evaluative perspectives, some religious but many not, and whose civil and political institutions are predominantly secular. Whilst the causes of this well-known historical trend call for some explanation in terms of the way in which patterns of social and political life are inevitably influenced and conditioned by human economic developments, it is beyond doubt that they also need to be understood by reference to evolving intellectual and ethical perspectives. For most of the Christian period of European culture and civilisation the proper way for people to live was laid down for them by authority founded on religious revelation and doctrine. In terms of moral and spiritual aspiration the Church exalted the imitation of Christ as the ultimate personal ideal, and the achievement of something like the perfect Christian community was promoted as the principal social goal. Reason and enquiry, at the level of either doctrinal theology or personal moral agency, were regarded as only functioning properly in the service of these goals and ideals.

This overall ecclesiastical hegemony in matters of individual and social morality and conduct was called seriously into question, first, by the Reformation, and second – arguably in its wake – by the development of philosophical ideas about knowledge, authority and freedom in the so-called ages of reason and enlightenment. The Reformation seriously undermined, at least in some quarters, traditional conceptions of authority in matters of faith and morals; it fostered the emergence of a certain individual liberty of conscience that would in due course lead to the development of more thoroughly secular perspectives on the nature of moral and evaluative discourse – not only in Protestant countries, but also among free thinkers in centres of culture still faithful to Catholic Christianity. The philosophical Enlightenment proceeded to develop such embryonic ideas about freedom of reason and conscience with regard to evaluation and commitment towards a less authoritarian and absolutist approach to thinking about faith and values, promoting an unprecedented degree of individual and dissenting opinion; at the same time, the issue of finding some route to the rational negotiation of different opinions was forced, or made more urgent, by the new religious sectarianism that threatened to tear post-Reformation Christendom apart on a tide of violence.

This process of constructing a rational basis for social, cultural and religious tolerance in the face of difference also went hand in glove with the development of a secular conception of civil rights and liberties – and two ideas were of crucial significance for this development. The first of these entailed a departure from traditional or received views of the nature of moral and other values – for, according to the natural law conception of ethics enshrined in the mainstream intellectual traditions of orthodox Christianity, moral values (such as the traditional Christian virtues) were held to be both objective and absolute. During the Enlightenment, however, a new view of values emerges – notably under the influence of empiricist ideas about knowledge[9] – as merely subjective inclinations or preferences, which are given to human beings as the deliverances of experience and with regard to which reason performs no significant constitutive role. This reduced role of reason with respect to practical deliberation is the second significant departure from the traditional view. For whereas, on that view, values – whilst objective and discovered rather than created by reason – nevertheless require reason for their identification, constitution and guidance, practical deliberation is generally conceived in post-Enlightenment terms as little more than an instrument for the satisfaction or gratification of personal inclinations or impulses to which men are heir in various non-rational ways; morally speaking, this reduces to a mechanism for reducing or negotiating actual or potential conflict between the diverse subjective interests and preferences of individuals or social groups. Either way, however, it is regarded as a purely *instrumental* device for maximising individual choices, or reducing conflict between diverse preferences, in the interests of social harmony and cohesion. These two ideas of the subjectivity of values and the instrumentality of reason combine neatly in the ethical doctrine known as *utilitarianism* – at least in its basic form – according to which the rectitude of a moral decision is directly proportionate to its power to maximise preference satisfaction with as little social conflict or frustration of individual interests as possible.

The great moral theories that emerge during the post-Enlightenment period – utilitarianism and its main modern rival, contractualism – lie at the very intellectual heart of modern liberalism: both ethical views regard moral deliberation as instrumental to the achievement of human happiness or fulfilment primarily conceived in terms of the pursuit and satisfaction of individual preferences; both seek to safeguard maximum individual liberty in the course of that pursuit; and so both are inclined to regard undue or unnecessary public interference and intrusion into the privacy or liberty of individuals as the height of moral transgression. Utilitarianism, commonly regarded as an objectivist moral theory, is objectivist only in its insistence on the evidence of human happiness and satisfaction as a relevant objective basis upon which to make right moral decisions; it is *not* objectivist about value preferences – or it is at least agnostic about them – in holding that the only consideration relevant to determining the rightness or otherwise of human preferences and actions is their power to promote happiness or reduce pain, apart from which one value preference might be considered as worthwhile as another.[10] But in the light of these considerations it should be recognised that liberal theories of ethics raise major problems for the development of any contemporary programme of moral education. I believe that this is precisely due to their effective abandonment of axiology or the theory of value as a project of serious concern for moral philosophy in favour of a social theory that interprets the question of what values people should live by almost exclusively in terms of individual choice – whilst simultaneously endeavouring, by means of an instrumental conception of moral deliberation, to reduce the potential for conflict to which such individualism is bound to give rise.

The liberal conception of moral education

Much post-war educational philosophy and theory in the more affluent Western democracies has been concerned to develop a conception of education fundamentally compatible with the largely liberal goals and aspirations of an increasingly secular – albeit culturally diverse – society based on a capitalist market economy. A significant contribution to the construction of this liberal theory of education was made by philosophers of education based at or emerging from the London Institute of Education from the 1960s onwards, and by their counterparts in the United States and other Anglophone countries.[11] These new liberal educationalists saw the principal aim of education as basically that of the promotion of personal autonomy; on this view, education and schooling ought to be concerned with equipping individuals with the rational resources to decide for themselves how they should live, who they should be, what goals to pursue, what to produce, what to consume and so on. All else – any attempt to influence individuals in some particular direction or to determine in advance their spiritual, social or economic destiny – could only count as just so much unacceptable indoctrination or coercion. Indeed, liberal educationalists have also (for the most part) inclined to egalitarianism – at least with respect to educational opportunity – and been vehemently opposed to those traditional conceptions of education which would seek to adapt people, according to the best decisions of others, to particular socio-economic roles or stations in life.

By the same token, the most conspicuous trend in recent work on the philosophy of moral education has been towards the development of views broadly consistent with liberal theory. And perhaps the best and most influential articulation of such a view is to be found in the work of Lawrence Kohlberg (1981) – whose intellectual credentials, through Piaget back to Kant and from Kant back to Rousseau, are impeccably liberal. Kohlberg's basic idea that the individual should be assisted, as far as possible, to progress through a series of developmental stages of more or less heteronomous rule-following, until he is at last able to generate and live by his own self-regulative and logically consistent set of moral principles – in short, in the light of rational moral autonomy – is by now familiar enough. The view is certainly consistent with (indeed, it explicitly draws upon) features of liberal ethical theories such as prescriptivism, contractarianism and utilitarianism, and though it is designed to assist the generation of a system of social and interpersonal rules through which an individual might exercise her own moral decisions and choices (whilst respecting the rights and claims of others), it carefully refrains from advising anyone how to live or what to value in more substantial moral terms. Briefly, Kohlbergian practical deliberation may be construed as a form of instrumental reasoning designed for moral problem solving – and the problem in question is not so much that of how to live, but that of how to let live.

Influential as it was and continues to be, of course, Kohlberg's account also attracted a fair measure of criticism, keeping master and disciples constantly occupied in its defence down the years. And although Kohlberg may be said to have gone some way – via the notion of a 'community of justice' – towards meeting the objection that his account lacked a serious social dimension (though it has not been sufficiently noticed that the contractualism underlying this idea sits uneasily with the prescriptivism at the heart of his theory), it has never adequately met the points that it sidelines, or does not regard as morally salient, certain qualities or virtues related to feelings of care and concern for others,[12] certain ascetic and supererogatory attitudes and motives, and so forth. But, whether or not Kohlberg's theory is correct, it is important to see that it is certainly not *complete* in the respects just mentioned, and that it could not be completed by the inclusion of such features without fatally undermining the liberal tenets of the theory. For the status and appeal of Kohlberg's theory rests entirely upon a liberal understanding of morality as exhausted by considerations of individual rights and interpersonal duties; all other considerations can be regarded as ethically irrelevant. (Love, friendship, charity or chastity, from this point of view, are matters of some aesthetic interest perhaps, but they are certainly of little moral concern.) Essentially, then, the Kohlbergian view of moral education is that of initiation into a system of interpersonal rules predicated on the principle of reciprocity or reversibility – the so-called 'golden rule' of 'do not do unto others what you would not have them do to you'.

Such initiation has nothing to say, however – and cannot have much to say – about the quality of one's value preferences beyond their potential or otherwise for interference or intrusion into the affairs of others; indeed, it is another main purpose of Kohlbergian rules – as well as protecting the rights and integrity of others – to permit maximum freedom of choice of lifestyle to individuals. More radically, of course, the barely concealed assumption at the heart of such liberal theory is in effect that there is no ultimate basis beyond human sentiment or inclination for the rational appraisal of substantive personal commitments or preferences of an evaluative kind; on empiricist premises, values are contrastable with facts as matters of subjective feeling, and one person's feelings merit as much consideration as another's. (I have found it to be widely believed by students that musical preference – for example, the view that Mozart is of more interest and value than Michael Jackson – is just a matter of subjective taste, unsusceptible of serious rational demonstration one way or the other.) But, by that token, reason – or, at any rate, practical deliberation – is merely the slave of the passions;[13] it is an instrument for the rational pursuit of one's own subjective value preferences – or, in the interests of social concord – for the negotiation and resolution of potential conflicts of preference.

In terms of liberal theory, then, moral deliberation is simply the social dimension of enlightened self-interest; it is concerned with imposing a system of checks on our personal inclinations – at most, with the development of some degree of personal restraint via appreciation of the value of social obligation or duty. And so long as wider obligations to others are acknowledged, one is at liberty to conduct experiments in personal living to one's heart's desire. Such a view has been widely and warmly welcomed, moreover, not only as the only one possible or tenable in modern circumstances of social and cultural pluralism, but as immensely liberating from an individual or personal point of view; it frees individuals from various kinds of ideological and doctrinal coercion and constraint to discover and explore a wide variety of possibilities for human growth and development, to encounter new experiences, acquire new sensibilities, and so on.

Others, however, have been able to discern in this purported liberal Utopia only the opposite and adverse effects of personal anomie and social dislocation: we seem to be faced with a bewildering array of choices between often-conflicting personal possibilities in a pluralist postmodern cultural and intellectual climate that seems to teach that all human values and options are only different routes to a single goal of individual fulfilment – that there is no objective rational basis for deciding, for example, between hedonic and ascetic ideals. It is hardly surprising, especially in a political and economic milieu that often seems to encourage the baser human instincts of vanity, material acquisition and consumerism, that many people choose what more traditional moralities would regard as the broad path to hell rather than the narrow gate to heaven. At all events, it has seemed all the more clear to many, that liberalism and liberal theories of education have failed very many of the citizens of Western democratic societies in a way that is revealed in practice in the anomie, rootlessness and boredom of the young, and in the increasingly individualistic and hedonistic directions to which people are generally turning for personal fulfilment.

It is also arguable that what has gone wrong at the level of practical moral life has its origins in philosophical misconceptions about the nature of moral evaluation formed during the so-called Enlightenment and by now deeply entrenched in contemporary popular thinking about such matters; in particular, it is likely that the old-fashioned empiricism underlying much liberal theory misidentified the distinction between factual and evaluative judgements with that between objective states of affairs and subjective feelings. As I have argued before,[14] the older Aristotelian distinction between theoretical reasoning and practical deliberation provides a rather deeper insight into the nature of evaluation than the crude empiricist distinction between subjective non-rational values and objective rational facts. In these terms, values are to be seen not as subjective preferences but as principled dispositions or rational commitments, rooted in certain established practices conducive to human flourishing, and tested by their power to sustain and vindicate such practices. Values, in short, are generally matters of practical aspiration which require for their true appreciation and acquisition a large measure of commitment, devotion and engagement. The worth of an established and enduring form of human endeavour, such as the practice or appreciation of a form of art or music, cannot be discerned from the outset by an untutored mind, but requires the serious application through which proper understanding of value may come in time; thus, while young, we take on the word of trustworthy or reliable adults that *this* human enterprise is worthier of dedicated pursuit than *that*. It would also appear that young people are crucially dependent upon such guidance for their proper personal growth, and we cannot be confident that they will move forward in a positive and constructive way if this is denied them under the delusion that their powers of free choice are not to be constrained or prejudiced by non-liberal interference.

A view of the acquisition of moral and spiritual values more characteristic of traditional thinking, then, is that it is precisely a function of personal commitment to certain established ideals of human growth and flourishing – not merely a matter of the suppression of those of one's own personal inclinations which might conflict with public order. The contrast between a traditional and a liberal conception of morality emerges quite sharply, for example, with regard to the putative virtue of chastity, which is – or certainly was – regarded in some cultures as an ideal to which at least some people might aspire in the light of a certain conception of human flourishing. In the terms of a liberal morality, of course, any idea of chastity as a moral virtue as such can make little or no sense at all, since moral considerations enter into the practice of sexuality only to the extent that they are implicated in such possible social consequences as violence upon the person, the spread of disease or unwanted pregnancy. Whereas, then, a liberal conception of morality and moral education is one that seeks to allow maximum freedom of individual expression whilst simultaneously encouraging the observance of certain social constraints on that freedom for the common good, on a more traditional conception, which has of late been widely replaced by the liberal one, moral and spiritual life has a definite form and content, to which the young may be strongly advised to aspire, for the promotion of certain objectively specifiable goals lying beyond the subjective sphere of personal preference.

Moral aspiration: what price a modern restatement?

But, then, the crucial issue facing contemporary moral education is, I believe, that of whether young people are, in schools or at large, better educationally served by a liberal or a non-liberal conception of moral education –

by the teaching of what we might call a postmodern ethics of obligation or a traditional ethics of aspiration. This question lies at some conceptual distance from the one with which, as we saw earlier, it is often confused; it is not, that is, the same as the question of which form of moral discipline might best conduce to less crime, drug abuse, sexual promiscuity and disrespect of law and order among young people. And though any answer to the question of moral education may be expected to have implications for good or ill with regard to such social evils, it is nevertheless not a question to be settled in terms of such outcomes; one can easily envisage the adoption of certain methods of social control which might effectively reduce anti-social behaviour in certain circumstances – for example, vigilantism or capital punishment – which would not necessarily conduce to a more morally enlightened or decent society. It should also be observed that anything worthy of the name of morality must also be a matter of individual voluntary choice, leaving young people free to reject either a liberal morality of obligation or a traditional morality of aspiration. Indeed, many past and present social evils may well be due simply to the deliberate and perennial rejection by some people of any sort of moral considerations whatsoever; we cannot choose between views of morality and moral education on the highly unstable and difficult-to-determine statistical grounds of which might most readily be endorsed by young people.

That said, it would seem reasonable to suppose that there *are* criteria upon which one might base a decision between different moral perspectives for moral educational purposes, and that such criteria must – since morality is at heart a practical matter – have something to do with the way in which human individual and social life stands to be enhanced in practical terms by one choice or another. This leaves us with a choice which is itself, of course, a *moral* one; as such, what we may expect to gain on the theoretical and practical swings of one option, we should also expect to lose on the roundabouts of the other. A liberal ethics of rights and duties seems to many reflective people nowadays to be the only intellectually plausible and practically feasible moral perspective in the sort of social and cultural milieu in which we presently find ourselves in most Western post-industrial cultures. Moreover, it need not be doubted that a liberal ethics can be entertained as a worthy enough goal, nor that as well as being open minded and tolerant, many liberals are also decent, courageous and idealistic people in more substantial moral terms. But critics of liberalism have no doubt correctly discerned that many people appear ill-equipped emotionally or rationally to cope with the freedom of choice that a liberal ideal exalts – and therefore fall prey to self-indulgent, self-destructive, aimless or demeaning forms of life. Such critics often regret the passing of a traditional ethics of aspiration – for example, the Christian ideal – or call for its return, to restore the perceived erosion of individual moral identity and social purpose. In turn, however, liberals respond that it is vain even to hope to reinstate such an ideal in modern social circumstances – nor are they slow to point out the fanaticism and sectarianism that have often followed in the wake of such ethical ideals and which continue to be responsible for violence on a global scale.

So, in view of potential conceptual and practical gains and losses either way, how is this difficult ethical question to be decided? Once again, I believe that it is important to try to think a little more clearly about the available options. We have already begun by disentangling the question of moral education from the question of social control – for trying to settle the important issue of the proper direction of moral education in terms of which form of instruction best conduces to a reduction in car theft is one way to come up with a skewed answer to an ill-conceived question. But we also need to appreciate more keenly how the issue between a moral education based on a liberal ethics of duty, and one based on a traditional ethics of aspiration, stands with regard to other important conceptual distinctions of relevance to ethics and social theory. First, for example, it is helpful to see that the issue of a liberal versus a non-liberal ethics is not identical to – though it is not infrequently confused with – an issue about whether or not moral education must proceed in a climate of *paternalism*; for, even if I am convinced beyond all reasonable doubt of the truth of a given set of moral principles, I am not logically entitled, by either an ethics of duty or an ethics of aspiration, to require the compulsory initiation or indoctrination of others into these.

This point is of no small importance, since it precisely serves to disinfect a traditional ethics of aspiration from the common accusation of authoritarianism, dogmatism, fanaticism and a general intolerance of contrary points of view. The case here often rests on *de facto* association between the claims of some faiths and ideologies to exclusive truth and their historical deployment of highly repressive and coercive tactics – though it is also worth mentioning that the culprits soonest cited, Marxism and Catholic Christianity, have both developed powerful intellectual traditions of considerable openness to rational criticism. But it is nowadays often just uncritically assumed, due probably to a certain perverse reading of liberalism, that any claim to truth in matters of value poses an instant threat to the right of dissent of those who might be disposed to think otherwise – especially if they are young and have not yet made up their own minds. However, any such claim only needs stating to be immediately seen as highly implausible.

A second distinction to which any difference between liberal and non-liberal views is related – though again it is not identical with that difference – is that between a subjectivist and an objectivist theory of value. Here, whilst it is certainly far from the case that liberals do not subscribe to *any* objective ethical principles, it seems that liberalism as such aspires to a certain agnostic neutrality about the status as true or false of the content of particular moral perspectives; as we have seen, its ethical objectivism is of a formal or procedural rather than a substantially objective sort. It is this error which, I believe, affects the heart of liberal conceptions of ethics – and it is one a traditional ethics of aspiration generally manages to avoid. Indeed, I think that the error in question is of such a serious and debilitating kind as to undermine the possibility of any genuine education in values – moral, spiritual, social, aesthetic or whatever. This should be abundantly clear, for example, in the case of aesthetic and arts education; for if all forms of literature, painting and music are to be regarded as qualitatively on the same level, as equal candidates for attention or praise, then any form of instruction that attempts to go beyond merely acquainting people with available alternatives is ruled out of court – since, of course, teaching genuine appreciation is more or less indistinguishable from persuading or indoctrinating others into one's own subjective point of view. But much the same considerations must also apply to moral education. The view that moral and spiritual values are largely personal and private affairs – that moral education can amount to little more than acquainting people with the views of others in a climate of live-and-let-live omni-tolerance – cannot issue in any serious appreciation of how a life might be enhanced, informed or enriched by meaningful moral and spiritual perspectives, unless significant questions concerning the *truth* of these views (and hence, since such views may be conspicuously inconsistent, of the rightness of some and the wrongness of others) are seriously addressed.

The difficulty of any programme of moral education based on a liberal theory of ethics is that it seems logically impossible for such an account to comprehend or to accommodate a substantial theory of value. Such a theory would have to take seriously the inherently normative character of our substantive discourse of evaluation – of the way in which notions of truth and falsity, rightness and wrongness, of belief and action, enter essentially into such discourse – and need to be capable of offering a plausible account of the operations of rational evaluation. A liberal omni-tolerance of all moral perspectives and aspirations, except those which infringe individual rights and liberties, is simply inconsistent with any project that sets out to discover – as it is the purpose of any substantial form of ethically normative discourse to discover – which human goals are worthier of pursuit than others; and moral education is surely just such a project. In short, at a theoretical level, the prospects of basing a coherent programme of values education of any real substance on a liberal ethics of rights and obligations, appear neither promising nor attractive.

Logically speaking, then, a traditional ethics of aspiration would seem to offer a more promising foundation for moral education, especially to the extent that it appears possible – at least in principle – to exorcise the demon of paternalism from such an ethics. On the other hand, the practical difficulties that beset any attempt to reaffirm a non-liberal ethical perspective in contemporary social and economic circumstances – of, for example, the secular pluralist society and the market economy – are so formidable that one may well be forgiven for regarding any such project as doomed. To begin with, at a theoretical level, it would require a Herculean effort on the part of ethical critics of liberalism to construct a general and widely compelling account of the rationality and objectivity of our moral and other value judgements. Essentially, I believe that the most likely candidate for such an account would be a form of ethical naturalism focused upon an old idea of moral life as concerned not with the internalisation of rules for the rational negotiation of conflicts of interest – as on the liberal view – but with the cultivation and exercise of a range of personal human qualities and dispositions traditionally called virtues. Although there is some present sign of a real turn in the tide of philosophical thinking in this respect, and of considerable interest in more traditional virtue-theoretical perspectives,[15] it is nevertheless only reasonable to anticipate much intellectual, ideological and political opposition to any such project, insofar as it has social and economic implications and consequences that are also liable to be uncongenial to many present-day temporal interests and powers.

An optimistic conclusion?

At all events, it can hardly be doubted that the discourse of serious moral aspiration has undergone considerable recent erosion and decline as the live-and-let-live instrumentalism of liberal and secular conceptions of human association has overtaken general ethical usage. More traditional ascetic modes of moral discourse, clearly acknowledging the extent to which human life *is* capable of positive moral enhancement through the cultivation of such qualities of heart and character as temperance, fortitude, loyalty, honesty and unselfishness – these being not just recognitions of constraints we tolerate in order to benefit from the reciprocal recognition of like constraints by others – no longer seem as compelling as they once were. Much contemporary discourse of human association would seem to be afflicted by a pervasive instrumentality, in which even the recognised moral aspects of interpersonal dealings often play second fiddle to the satisfaction of personal inclination, and in which there is a markedly diminished recognition of the substantial contribution of moral qualities and dispositions to real human growth.

On the other hand, perhaps we should not hasten to embrace an overly dim view of the extent to which traditional human values of community and fellowship are destined to be overtaken by a climate of postmodern cynicism and instrumentality. Here, it might be instructive to draw an analogy between the problem of the erosion of basic values and principles of human moral association, and a familiar problem of philosophical psychology regarding the dangers of colonisation of ordinary folk-psychological discourses by scientific languages of mental life developed on the basis of neurophysiological researches into the functions of the brain. It appears that many philosophers of a so-called materialist or physicalist bent are strongly inclined to believe that with the inevitable progress of science there must come a day when a scientific language of psychology replaces popular psychological usage in talking for any useful practical purposes about the life of the mind. This view has been plausibly criticised, however, on the grounds that no matter how advanced or sophisticated any new scientific language of the mind might become, it must inevitably continue to be largely dependent on the familiar psychological discourse it aspires to replace; indeed, it must forever remain logically in need of thorough explication in such pre-theoretical terms.[16]

Whilst this analogy cannot be pressed too far – since the colonisation of fundamental moral values and attitudes by instrumental conceptions of human affairs is a greater, and more ever present, practical danger – there is nevertheless, I believe, a somewhat similar point to be made about the basic indispensability of folk-moral discourse in relation to anything recognisable as genuine human moral association, and in the face of revisionary threats to that discourse. The point would be, I take it, that the complete erosion of those basic moral categories that inevitably underpin our lives as humans is hardly to be envisaged short of certain unimaginably radical changes in the conditions of that nature; in short, so long as we remain human in nature as well as in culture, however ideologically beleaguered our moral and social circumstances should become, a last redoubt of moral oldspeak must remain to us from which to resist the newspeak of rampant instrumentalism. Moreover, I believe that the discourse of moral aspiration lies at the very heart of that oldspeak.

All the same, the problems that would attend any present-day revival or restatement of an ethics of aspiration as a possible basis for a programme of moral education should certainly not be underestimated – the more so, if such an ethics had to be understood in terms of a form of naturalism focused upon the cultivation of virtues; for, in that case, further difficult and crucial questions of what such virtues might be, and of whether such an ethics might be coherently separable from some or other controversial religious or meta-physical perspective, would also assume considerable urgency. Clearly, how-ever, whatever the difficulties standing in the way of the return to contemporary currency of any such more traditional conception of morality, a large part of the task – should it be possible – would be down to education.

However, I suspect that despite the ravages of modern instrumentalism, many teachers in schools – particularly those committed to some sort of reli-gious ethical perspective – have never actually strayed too far from a basic pre-theoretical conception of moral life as essentially a matter of aspiration. Thus, there are very many schools and other educational institutions, denomin-ational and non-denominational, which persist against all odds in teaching something like the traditional Christian virtues as ideals to be aspired to, irrespective of whether those they teach so choose to aspire. Doubtless teachers in them recognise, intuitively if not at some more theoretical level, that moral education is the very highest of human undertakings, and that any bottom liberal line of doing what one wants so long as it does not frighten the horses is not ultimately conducive to the proper appreciation and acqui-sition by pupils of truly fulfilling moral values. To that end, though such schools and such teachers cannot alone be expected to stem the current rising tide of hedonism, materialism and possessive individualism, for which a liberal climate of thought must take at least some share of the blame, they are at least forces for subversion of some of the more pernicious social and economic influences on present-day life – and, as such, remain potent sources of faith and hope.

Notes

1 The expression 'God is dead' is most commonly associated with the moral philosophy of Friedrich Nietzsche (see Wright 1937).

2 Raskolnikov is, of course, the main character in *Crime and Punishment* (Dostoevsky 1969).

3 This point is to be found in Kant's *Groundwork of the Metaphysic of Morals*, translated under the title *The Moral Law* by Kant (1987: 63).

4 The story of the Grand Inquisitor is recounted by Ivan Karamazov in *Brothers Karamazov* (Dostoevsky 1967).

5 See Plato's *Protagoras*. The alleged view of Protagoras that 'man is the measure of all things' is also exhaustively criticised by Socrates in Plato's *Theaetetos*. Both dialogues are to be found in Huntington and Cairns (1961).

6 *Spiritual and Moral Development: A Discussion Paper* (NCC 1993, reprinted SCAA 1995). See also *Spiritual, Moral, Social and Cultural Development: An OFSTED Discussion Paper* (OFSTED 1994), for another recent official discussion of these questions. Whilst the OFSTED document offers a rather more conceptually sophisticated account of things than the NCC paper, it is still far from free of philosophical problems.

7 I have argued this point more fully in a paper entitled 'Common and personal values in moral education' (Carr 1995b).

8 Whilst the contemporary literature on this general theme is far too extensive to detail here, there cannot be much doubt that various recent works by Alasdair MacIntyre have played a crucial part in defining the terms of current debates. See MacIntyre (1981, 1987, 1992). For another highly influential work in this respect, see Taylor (1989).

9 A classic statement of the empiricist view of values is to be found in David Hume (1969). But see also Ayer (1967: ch. 6). For a more recent useful discussion of the issues between contemporary non-cognitivists and moral realists, see McNaughton (1988).

10 For the sources of utilitarianism, see the works of Jeremy Bentham and John Stuart Mill in Warnock (1970); for the modern debate about utilitarianism, see the essays in Scheffler (1988).

11 The analytical revolution in the philosophy of education, responsible for the postwar reformulation of the liberal theory of education, is generally acknowledged to have occurred in the wake of the work of Peters (see, for example, Peters 1966). A similar lead, however, was taken by Israel Scheffler in the USA and others elsewhere.

12 The point that the Kohlbergian account seriously ignores the elements of feeling, emotion or 'care' in moral life has been developed – not entirely helpfully perhaps – in the context of a feminist critique of 'rationalist' moral educational theory. See especially Gilligan (1982) and Noddings (1984). Earlier criticisms to the effect that Kohlberg's account does not deal well with the problem of moral motivation can be found in the extensive moral educational writings of Peters (1981). For some general discussion of these issues, see Carr (1996a).

13 The view that reason is 'the slave of the passions' was taken by David Hume (1969: 462).

14 See, for example, Carr (1992a). For more detailed discussion of the rationality of evaluation, see Carr (1991a: ch.1, 1991b).

15 The modern revival of interest in the virtues probably dates back some twenty years now. Among earlier works of some importance that might be mentioned are: Geach (1977), Foot (1978) and Wallace (1978). From the 1970s onwards, the literature has proliferated beyond reasonable detailing here. However, the work of MacIntyre (1981) has been influential – as has that of Martha Nussbaum in various works; see, for example, Nussbaum (1993). Other single-authored works of importance are Dent (1984) and Slote (1983, 1992). Krushchwitz and Roberts (1987) *The Virtues: Contemporary Essays on Moral Character* represents an important collection. For further coverage of other work, see Pence (1984) on the virtues; and for efforts to characterise the nature of virtue ethics, see Oakley (1996) and Carr (1995a, 1996b).

16 For a clear perspective on this debate see an Aristotelian Society exchange of 1988 between John Haldane and Paul Churchland. Churchland's spirited defence of the scientific reductionist position is met by Haldane's similarly spirited defence of the indispensability of folk psychology.

References

Carr, D. (1991a) *Educating the Virtues: An Essay on the Philosophical Psychology of Moral Development and Education*, London: Routledge.

—— (1991b) 'Education and values', *British Journal of Educational Studies* 39(3): 244–59.

—— (1992a) 'Practical enquiry, values and the problem of educational theory', *Oxford Review of Education* 18(3): 241–51 (reprinted in W. Hare and J. P. Portelli (eds) (1996) *Philosophy of Education: Introductory Readings*, Calgary, Alberta: Detselig Enterprises).

—— (1992b) 'Moral and religious education 5–14', *Scottish Educational Review* 24(2): 111–17.

—— (1995a) 'The primacy of virtues in ethical theory: Part I', *Cogito* 9(3): 238–44.

—— (1995b) 'Common and personal values in moral education', unpublished paper delivered to the Fifth International Conference on Philosophy of Education (INPE), Johannesburg.

—— (1996a) 'After Kohlberg: some implications of an ethics of virtue for the theory of moral education and development', *Studies in Philosophy and Education* 14(4): 353–70.

—— (1996b) 'The primacy of virtues in ethical theory: Part II', *Cogito* 10(1): 34–40.

Churchland, P. (1988) 'Folk psychology and the explanation of human behaviour: I', *Proceedings of the Aristotelian Society* Supplementary Volume 62: 209–21.

Dent, N. J. H. (1984) *The Moral Psychology of the Virtues*, Cambridge: Cambridge University Press.

Department for Education and Science (1989) *Discipline in Schools: Report of the Committee of Enquiry Chaired by Lord Elton*, London: HMSO.

Dostoevsky, F. (1967) *Brothers Karamazov*, Harmondsworth: Penguin.

—— (1969) *Crime and Punishment*, Harmondsworth: Penguin.

Foot, P. (1978) *Virtues and Vices*, Oxford: Blackwell.

Geach, P. T. (1977) *The Virtues*, Cambridge: Cambridge University Press.

Gilligan, C. (1982) *In a Different Voice: Psychological Theory and Women's Development*, Cambridge MA: Harvard University Press.

Haldane, J. (1988) 'Folk psychology and the explanation of human behaviour: II', *Proceedings of the Aristotelian Society* Supplementary Volume 62: 223–54.

Hamilton, E. and Cairns, H. (eds) (1961) *Plato: The Collected Dialogues*, Princeton, NJ: Princeton University Press.

Hume, D. (1969) *A Treatise of Human Nature*, ed. E. C. Mossner, Harmondsworth: Penguin.

Kant, I. (1987) *The Moral Law*, tr. H. J. Paton, London: Hutchinson University Library.

Kohlberg, L. (1981) *Essays on Moral Development: I–III*, New York: Harper Row.

Krushchwitz, R. B. and Roberts, R. C. (eds) (1987) *The Virtues: Contemporary Essays on Moral Character*, Belmont: Wadsworth.

MacIntyre, A. (1981) *After Virtue*, Notre Dame, IN: Notre Dame Press.

—— (1987) *Whose Justice, Which Rationality?* Notre Dame, IN: Notre Dame Press.

—— (1992) *Three Rival Versions of Moral Enquiry*, Notre Dame, IN: Notre Dame Press.

McNaughton, D. (1988) *Moral Vision: An Introduction to Ethics*, Oxford: Blackwell.

NCC (1993) *Spiritual and Moral Development: A Discussion Paper*, April (reprinted SCAA 1995), York: National Curriculum Council.

Noddings, N. (1984) *Caring: A Feminist Approach to Ethics*, Berkeley: University of California Press.

Nussbaum, M. (1993) 'Non-relative virtues: an Aristotelian approach', in M. Nussbaum and A. Sen (eds) *The Quality of Life*, Oxford: Clarendon Press.

Oakley, J. (1996) 'Varieties of virtue ethics', *Ratio* 9(2): 128–52.

OFSTED (1994) *Spiritual, Moral, Social and Cultural Development: An OFSTED Discussion Paper*, London: OFSTED.

Pence, G. C. (1984) 'Recent work on the virtues', *American Philosophical Quarterly* 21: 281–97.

Peters, R. S. (1966) *Ethics and Education*, London: George Allen and Unwin.

—— (1981) *Moral Development and Moral Education*, London: George Allen and Unwin.

Scheffler, S. (ed.) (1988) *Consequentialism and its Critics*, Oxford: Oxford University Press.

Slote, M. (1983) *Goods and Virtues*, Oxford: Clarendon Press.

—— (1992) *From Morality to Virtue*, New York: Oxford University Press.

Taylor, C. (1989) *Sources of the Self: The Making of the Modern Identity*, Cambridge: Cambridge University Press.

Wallace, J. D. (1978) *Virtues and Vices*, Ithaca and London: Cornell University Press.

Warnock, M. (ed.) (1970) *Utilitarianism*, London: Fontana.

Wright, W. H. (ed.) (1937) *The Philosophy of Nietzsche*, New York: Random House.

Part II

RATIONALITY, SOCIETY AND THE MORALLY EDUCATED PERSON

3

MORAL EDUCATION IN A PLURALIST LIBERAL DEMOCRACY

Brian Crittenden

Dimensions of moral pluralism

There are many ways in which a society can be pluralist. One version (which has a long history in political theory) refers to a division of labour between the central government and sub-groups at various levels throughout society. Such a society could be virtually homogeneous in most other respects (for example ethnicity, religion, moral values). In the present discussion, I am referring to political orders or 'nation states' with a pluralistic pattern of both cultural values as well as political authority, and which include in the former a diversity of comprehensive ways of life or perceptions of the good. In addition, I have in mind societies that are not simply pluralist in moral and other respects as a matter of fact; most of their members also wish to cooperate peacefully in a common political and legal system and to share a common national identity. No such society could survive without agreement on fair procedures for reaching decisions on the essential common practices, nor unless there were the tolerance and freedom necessary for each group to pursue its own way of life consistent with the common welfare of the inclusive society. This does not imply that a society with moral and other forms of cultural diversity must be regarded as preferable to one that is culturally monistic. What it requires is commitment to the conditions that allow for cultural diversity within a common political order. Whether the conditions I have mentioned are sufficient is a matter that will need further consideration.

In theory, the principles of fair procedures, tolerance and freedom could be limited to groups; they would apply to individuals only insofar as they were members of a group. Nor would the political system necessarily be a democratic one. In the contemporary world, however, any society that meets the minimum conditions for a morally pluralist society extends tolerance and freedom directly to individuals (whose conception of the good might not coincide with any of the identifiable groups), and adopts some form of political democracy (in which the preference of each individual is given equal weight

47

in selecting members of government – and, in some cases, in the direct determination of a policy or practice).

A pluralist society as so far depicted can justifiably be referred to as a liberal democracy, as long as 'liberal' does not go beyond the recognition of freedom, tolerance and fair procedures for settling on necessary common practices, and equality as citizens for all the individuals – as well as distinct groups – who are members of the 'nation state'. A crucial point to emphasise in this use of 'liberal' is that it does not imply support for any of the comprehensive visions of the good for human life that go by the name of 'liberalism'.[1] In a liberal democracy these are among the many diverse interpretations of morality that constitute the moral pluralism of the society.

As a practical matter, it is clear that the likelihood of maintaining the delicate balance between unity and diversity required for a pluralist society depends on the extent to which the various dimensions of pluralism are independent. If moral values are closely linked with religion, which, in turn, is tied to ethnic identity, the potential for disintegration into distinct political orders is much stronger than when there is no clear pattern in the relationship among moral values, religion and ethnicity in the society. As I have already noted, the preference for a society that is culturally pluralist is itself a contested value in such a society. The crucial condition is that, whatever the actual degree of cultural unity or diversity, a liberal democracy requires respect for the values that permit cultural diversity – consistent with political cohesion – to flourish.

On the basis of the characteristics of a pluralist liberal democracy I have so far sketched, it is obvious that common schools (i.e. those designed to serve all members of the society) face very difficult – and what might seem intractable – problems in the face of diverse and conflicting moral points of view. Problems arise for such schools from other dimensions of cultural diversity, but moral pluralism is perhaps the most demanding. The school as a social institution inevitably reflects and consciously endorses a certain range of moral values. School discipline includes, as one of its basic components, explicit rules that interpret various moral ideals and apply them to conduct in a school. In the curriculum, even when common schools exclude moral education as a distinct subject, moral issues are inescapable in the adequate treatment of most areas of study. One has only to think of literature, history, social studies, and questions about the uses of science and technology, to realise how pervasive such issues are in the context of formal education. Thus, in both their institutional arrangements and the curriculum, common schools must face the problems that arise from moral pluralism in their society.

Private schools, especially when they reflect a particular moral way of life, clearly are in a rather different position from that of common schools in relation to moral pluralism. However, they do have to take account of the differences that usually exist even within a particular traditional way of life. What is more important is that private schools must give attention to the nature of the morally pluralist society in which their students live, and equip them with the knowledge and attitudes necessary for responsible membership of such a society.

It has been argued that, if all formal education were provided through private schools, each reflecting a particular moral tradition, this would offer the most satisfactory resolution of the problems raised by moral pluralism for education. Apart from the need to consider the actual situation (in which a majority of students attend common schools), I do not believe that the claim is defensible. It does not take account of the many other dimensions of life on which people differ in a pluralist society, and it gives no solution for those students (probably a substantial proportion) who are not identified with any clearly defined moral tradition.

In the course of this chapter I shall concentrate on the bearing that moral pluralism has on the conduct of education in common schools. As I have indicated, this does not imply that there are no issues for private schools as well.

To appreciate the scope of the problem for common schools in dealing with moral pluralism, it is useful to note the variety of ways in which the notion of morality is 'essentially contested' (to use Gallie's phrase). The following does not pretend to be an exhaustive list.

- In addition to what is included in the list of moral values, there are disagreements on how the nature of the content is to be interpreted. For some, moral rules and values are strictly personal guides to one's conduct; for others, they carry an impersonal obligation and have a public character.
- Among those who agree that a moral value imposes a fundamental obligation to act or refrain from acting in a particular way, there are serious differences over the basis of the obligation. Some see it as grounded in radical personal feelings of approval or disapproval. For others, it derives ultimately from the authority of the social, ethnic, religious or other group to which one belongs. Others claim that moral rules are what can be reasonably defended as universally binding on the basis of the common characteristics of human beings and the general circumstances of human life. (Among the latter group, there is argument over what counts as reasonable and what human characteristics are morally relevant.) On the basis of moral obligation – and the details of its contents – the long-standing and pervasive difference is between relativist (or subjectivist) interpretations and those that claim to be objective.
- Even when there is agreement on the nature of a moral value and on a broad range of such values, people often differ on the way they order these values in the shaping of decisions for how they should act in particular cases or conduct their lives generally. Perhaps the main difference here is between those who reject any internal system in the group of moral values and those who argue for a hierarchical order in which one

moral value is regarded as the highest good. Among those who take this view, there is also disagreement on what moral value deserves the first rank. For some exponents of the 'highest good' approach, the system of morality remains complex; for others, it is a highly unified – if not reductive – system. In recent years, this way of thinking about morality has been reflected in some well-known studies related to moral education. One group has focused on a justice-based account of the whole moral domain, while another has interpreted it as care-based.[2]

- At the level of ethics (or systematic reflection on morality), even among those who agree on what count as moral values there can be sharp disagreement on how the moral domain and the claims it makes on our beliefs, attitudes, feelings, and actions are to be justified. I have already mentioned differences of interpretation. For those who are consistent in their thinking there is, of course, a close connection between interpretation and justification. However, it should be noted that the exponents of some interpretations would deny that there is any sense in asking for a justification. Those who do seek to justify moral values are by no means in agreement on the epistemological status of moral claims. Appeals are made variously to characteristics of human life (interpreted at different levels of generality); to intuitive feelings of approval and disapproval; to logical consistency; to enlightened self-interest; to the authority of some group or other; to the will of a Divine Being.

The foregoing points, although by no means exhaustive, illustrate the profusion of diversity that confronts the common schools of a liberal democratic society as they try to take a defensible position on moral values in their institutional features and the practice of formal education.

By its defining ideals, liberal democracy is committed to enabling individuals and groups who support conflicting moral values to live together as peacefully as possible in a common social and political order. As I noted earlier, this does not entail the belief that a pluralist society is preferable to one in which everyone shares the same comprehensive way of life. (The superior merits of each type of society do, of course, have their ardent defenders.) What a liberal democracy requires is that, subject to the conditions on which its coherence as a social order depends, individuals and groups should be free to live according to differing interpretations of the moral and other values that make for a worthwhile human life. To achieve this objective it is reasonable, as John Rawls has argued, to emphasise procedural principles that depend on the minimum necessary range of substantive moral values in reaching decisions that affect the common life of the society. However, the latter is more extensive than the narrowly defined political area in Rawls's theory, and thus the minimum range of substantive values involved is somewhat broader.[3]

In addition, the freedom that is central to liberal democracy must allow the many diverse moral traditions that see the public and non-public aspects of life as closely intermeshed an adequate opportunity to influence policies and practices affecting the common life of the society. The interaction between the conditions for the peaceful coherence of a pluralist liberal democracy and the diverse moral positions that its emphasis on individual freedom allows is much more complex than Rawls's scheme acknowledges. It must also be recognised that the core values that distinguish such a society are inevitably more compatible with some comprehensive moral outlooks than others. There are moral traditions that are radically at odds with such values (most obviously, any that reject coexistence with other such traditions in the same society). While they might be tolerated in a liberal pluralist society, they cannot expect to influence its common policies and practices. It is also inevitable that, while the values of a liberal democracy should not reflect any of the comprehensive liberal ideals of a worthwhile human life, they will be more compatible with such ideals than with those based on other interpretations of the good. In summary, a pluralist liberal democracy entails a commitment to a certain range of moral values and requires decisions that blur the distinction between public and private spheres of morality. Thus, such a society cannot be strictly neutral in relation to the diverse moral systems within its borders. It is an inevitable price to be paid if conflicting moral systems are to coexist peacefully in the same social and political order.

Moral education in common schools: efforts to avoid diversity

Given that the common good of a liberal pluralist society requires a broader range of moral values (and virtues) than Rawls attaches to his procedural principles of justice, it clearly follows that any scheme of purely procedural principles for the public life of such a society must be altogether unsatisfactory. Even if there were no other difficulties, common schools cannot, therefore, escape the problems of moral diversity by working on a neat distinction between procedural and substantive moral principles and concentrating their efforts at moral education on the former. This is not to deny the importance of fair principles of procedure to protect the freedom of citizens in a pluralist society to uphold different moral traditions. The point to emphasise is that they are quite inadequate for reaching moral decisions that affect the common life of such a society.

In the face of radical disagreement over the content of morality, there has been a trend in recent decades to claim that the proper role of schools in moral education is to enable students to develop processes for analysing and arguing about moral issues. This emphasis has fitted with the revival of a more general trend in educational theory and practice to stress teaching and learning *how* to think (scientifically, mathematically and so on) rather than *what* to think. The work of Kohlberg (and others) on stages of moral development, defined mainly by the kind of reasoning used, has also contributed to this approach.[4]

Even if the process and content of moral reflection could be sharply separated, this would not provide common schools in a pluralist society with a solution to the problem of diversity. As institutions, they could not avoid a stand on moral content. In the practice of formal moral education, they would be faced with the diversity that exists over the nature of moral decision making (expressions of feeling, intuitions, deductions from self-evident principles or divine commands, and so on).

To reduce moral education to an intellectual exercise in problem solving (assuming there was general agreement on the process) would lead to a gross misunderstanding of morality. In most, if not all, interpretations it involves a complex relationship of thoughts, feelings, attitudes, intentions, decisions, actions. Even if there were ways of coping with this problem, the fatal weakness of the approach is that morality is not the kind of activity in which it is possible to learn processes of reasoning and decision making independently of content. Whether an argument or the expression of a point of view comes within the scope of morality depends, fundamentally, on the nature of its content. This consists of a range of practices and institutions, along with related normative concepts, ideals and attitudes. These include: respect for life ('murder', 'suicide'); such notions as love, loyalty, justice, generosity, courage; truth telling and honesty ('lying', 'calumny', 'cheating'); promise keeping; institutions such as political authority, property ('stealing'), the family (with special relationships of love, loyalty, respect and concepts such as 'adultery', 'incest'). What counts as acting morally must also refer to the motives of the agent. For example, people may tell the truth for various reasons (for example, self-interest); they act morally in telling the truth when they acknowledge that it is what deserves to be done.

The point I wish to emphasise is clearly illustrated in the cases that Kohlberg used in his empirical work. He could be confident that they were about moral problems and would be recognised as such only because the situations involved conflicts between practices that are commonly accepted as what one does when acting morally (or immorally). People are faced with a moral conflict between saving life and respecting another's ownership of property only if they recognise that both these practices involve fundamental values for ordering the conduct of their lives.

The requirement of content I am defending, while it distinguishes a moral system from one that is immoral or non-moral, does not determine the relative excellence of moral systems. Such systems usually differ in some of the ideals and practices they accept as moral, and certainly in the relative emphasis or value given to the range of ideals and practices they include. Clearly, there are important differences between, for example, Christian and military-style morality, or liberal and socialist morality. We can recognise them all as moralities because they are concerned with a significant range of moral concepts and practices. By this criterion, we distinguish certain systems as 'moral' and to that extent may evaluate them, but the systems that meet the criterion are not thereby graded or ranked. It is not as though there were a complete list against which they were being measured, and in any case such an assessment would not have any bearing on the internal structure of a system.

Essential features of moral learning

How does attention to the content of morality affect the character of reasoning and decision making in moral practice, and thus the nature of moral education? Morality is directly concerned with a certain range of actions: not only the manifest behaviour, but the thoughts, attitudes, motives, feelings, dispositions of the agent. As with any other human practice, concepts form a crucial (and integral) part of morality. If the early moral education of children proceeds satisfactorily, they will come to acquire concepts of love, justice, truth telling, honesty and so on in a particular way: distinctively moral terms are learned in a context of behaviour for which adults, by means of verbal and other gestures, express praise or blame, admiration or contempt. One learns that moral terms do not simply express how this or that person happens to feel, or convey factual reports on what people believe should be done. They express approval of what (it is thought) deserves to be approved. While this 'speech act' should not be identified with the meaning of moral terms, it is a necessary condition if such terms are being used *qua* 'moral'. Depending on the context one may also be recommending, giving a verdict, issuing a kind of command and so forth, in using moral terms. It is also a necessary part of learning such terms that attitudes of approval and disapproval are acquired towards what they describe, that feelings (such as sympathy and disgust) are aroused in relation to certain objects, and that doing or failing to do what we describe in moral terms involves certain emotions (for example guilt or remorse).

I should emphasise an important implication of the account of moral reasoning that I have been giving. It is that the cognitive and the affective aspects of moral experience are not related in a merely contingent way. It is a necessary part of learning such notions as 'truth telling', 'cheating' and 'fairness' that we should have certain attitudes and feelings towards the actions we are prepared to describe in such terms. The affective component is not an incidental appendage in the way that we may associate various emotions with such terms as 'home', 'ice cream', 'winter'. There is no guarantee that people will translate their moral judgements into action. But if attitudes and emotions are necessarily engaged when the procedure of moral judgement making has been properly learned, an impetus for moving from thought to action is built in as part of the process.

If what I have said about the acquisition of moral terms is correct, it seems that moral judgements consist fundamentally in determining how a situation (agent, action and so on) is to be most appropriately described in these terms. The description has the character of an evaluation: when we agree to describe something in such terms we also bring to bear a moral approval or disapproval and a range of related feelings. The perfecting of this activity in all its aspects forms a crucial part of moral education. On some occasions, the task of description may be relatively simple. To act in such and such a way is to tell a lie or to break a promise, and there are no complicating circumstances. In these cases we may argue in a deductive form because we have learned to express some of our moral beliefs as general principles and they already apply in the situation. As I have suggested, such principles are strictly redundant once we have grasped 'truth telling', 'promise keeping' and so on, as moral notions. Much of the time, however, we are faced with situations in which the appropriate description is not obvious. Is withholding the truth in these circumstances to be called a lie? Does my acting towards A in this way amount to treating her fairly? Am I justified in thinking of myself or someone else in such and such moral terms? Does taking the life of a foetus constitute murder? What moral description fits the action of this group of workers going on strike or the policy of a government in relation to, say, unemployment?

Despite the play of feelings and the lack of mathematical or scientific precision, we can still sensibly argue about the correctness or fittingness of a given moral description. We can also improve our capacities for describing morally (that is, making moral judgements). Under one aspect, it consists in a lifelong process; of deepening our understanding of the moral concepts we already in a fashion possess; of modifying or rejecting some of them and adding new ones. Under another aspect, we may speak of it in general as a development of moral insight. To a large extent this is a matter of giving the kind of detailed attention to human beings in a situation that is itself a practice of the virtues of justice and love. Clearly, it also involves the exercise of imagination in a certain way: feeling the stress of a situation or the likely consequences of action from the point of view of other people.

If the mode of reasoning I have been discussing here fairly represents the character of moral inquiry, it is evident that the argument is not primarily a matter of following formal logical rules. It is directly concerned with our evaluative descriptions in using substantial moral terms. It may be a question of whether this or that concept should be held as a moral one, or whether this is a correct (or adequate) moral description. In either case, the process of description cannot be treated apart from the substantial moral concepts that form its context, or from the conclusion reached; the latter is not something we draw out from the description, but it is what the description amounts to. It is also clear that, in this account, moral reasoning is a somewhat untidy and inconclusive matter. There can be serious and unresolvable disagreements in moral beliefs and practices and judgements. It is futile, in the hope of reducing this diversity, to distort moral experience by forcing it into a more precise pattern of logic.

The limits on the demonstrative character of moral argument apply to both the micro-level and macro-level of debate. Concern for the welfare of human beings is by definition part of what morality is about. But in a specific case it may be extremely difficult to determine what course of action shows due regard for human welfare. The notion of welfare is itself rather vague; there are problems in making comparative judgements about the short-term and long-term good or harm; there is the difficulty of weighing the good or harm of one individual or group against another, and so on. At the macro-level I doubt whether it is possible, even in principle, to rank systems of morality or ways of life in an order of merit. Not all virtues and ideals can be realised simultaneously in the one human life. The central characterising practices of morality are only loosely interconnected and can thus be accommodated without contradiction or inconsistency in a wide variety of ways of life. In summary, what I am saying is that moral choices, at whatever level, can and should be reasoned ones, but that there is often a plurality of reasonable choices. In giving an account of moral inquiry, we have to tread a difficult path between arbitrary subjectivism on the one hand and the models of mathematical or scientific proof on the other.

In the face of the formidable diversity over moral values and the interpretation of morality as a whole, common schools in a pluralist society might conclude that the only defensible option is to teach *about* morality and ethical theories. I have already noted that there is a wide range of substantive moral values on which the viability of any liberal democratic society depends. I shall comment further on these values shortly. They provide scope for common schools to engage in moral education (and to function as institutions). Teaching *to be* moral in relation to these values is an obligation, not simply an option, for all schools in a pluralist society.

On questions about the ultimate justification of moral values and the merits of conflicting moral systems, common schools would, for the most part, be constrained to teaching about ethical theories, and working through the various forms of naturalism, intuitionism, emotivism, prescriptivism, existentialism, religious-based morality and so on. This might be of some use in senior years of the secondary school. However, it would not be the same as doing moral philosophy, nor would it be moral education. As we shall see, there are some elements of ethical theory integral to the nature of a pluralist liberal democracy. These may, and should, be defended in the common schools.

The scope of moral education in common schools

Given that process and content are intertwined in moral judgement and action, that no sharp division can be drawn between public and private morality, and that the former cannot be expressed in procedural principles that involve only a very limited range of substantive moral goods, what moral education can be undertaken by schools required to respect the diversity of moral traditions that is protected by a liberal democratic society and is, in fact, a feature of all such societies? The task is somewhat less daunting if we take due account of certain characteristics of a pluralist liberal democracy and of morality.

In relation to the first it needs to be emphasised that a pluralist society includes unity as well as diversity. The maintenance of an appropriate balance between these features is one of the most difficult achievements for such a society. Unless the constituent groups (whatever the nature of their identity) recognise the common inclusive social order, the pluralist society is bound to dissolve into a number of more homogeneous, separate societies. For a pluralist society to flourish, or even survive, there are two conditions that are clearly necessary, and a third that is probably in this category.

First, there must be an adequate range of commonly held ideals, values and procedures. Everyone can be expected to uphold the moral values on which a tolerable life in any society depends: general principles of justice, concern for honesty and truth telling, a willingness to cooperate to secure basic physical and cultural needs. Everyone can also be expected to accept the values on which respect for diversity depends: personal freedom, tolerance of different ways of thinking and acting, respect for the dignity of every human being as a moral agent, commitment to non-violent means of persuasion. I shall return to the common moral content shortly.

Second, a pluralist society requires substantial interaction among its diverse groups (at least at the level of secondary associations), a common political, economic and legal system, and at least some elements of a distinct and evolving common national culture (at the heart of which there is usually a common language). As a pluralist society develops over several generations, many members find their whole ethnic-cultural identity in its evolving common culture. But the critical condition is that, whatever allegiance members have to particular groups, they also respect the good of the society as a whole and contribute to its well-being. Recognition of the common good has to tread a careful path between seeing society as merely an aggregate of individuals (or sub-groups) and seeing it as a kind of higher being to which its members are wholly subordinate.

A third condition for pluralism, not so obviously crucial as the other two, is the general valuing of a certain form of rationality. Put simply, it requires us to base our beliefs about the world and human life on reasons that we regard as relevant and sufficient, and to be willing to change our beliefs in the light of convincing reasons against them.[5] The importance of this condition for pluralism is its connection with non-violent persuasion. As political and commercial advertising so amply show, persuasion that is deceptive, that plays on irrational fears and so on can be non-violent (and effective). What the ideal of pluralism requires is that the effort to persuade should not only be non-violent but one that relies primarily on the strength of supporting reasons.

The third condition is not compatible, of course, with the view that claims about the truth, reasonableness and so on of beliefs and values are strictly relative to particular traditions – if not to the subjective outlook and feelings of each individual. Those who hold such a view often claim that it is the basic justification for the tolerance and diversity that is central to pluralism. Ironically, relativists cannot consistently argue that all systems of belief should be tolerant of one another. If any system believes that it is superior and should be accepted by everyone, relativists have no ground for challenging the claim. Nor can they provide any common criteria for reasoned persuasion among conflicting systems of belief. The grounds for reasoned debate that transcend the boundaries of particular intellectual, moral and other traditions are not only crucial for moral education in common schools but for any serious educational practice. Without such a basis, education is reduced to uncritical socialisation and indoctrination.

In relation to the moral domain directly, I think it can reasonably be described as a collection of the standards and ideals of action that are thought to be fitting for human beings when they are viewed in the broad range of their distinctive characteristics and within the pattern of relationships they inevitably have as members of the physical and socio-cultural world. The existence and specific content of morality depend on certain facts about human beings, for example, that they are capable of rational choice and can be held responsible within certain limits for what they do; that they are sentient beings prone to pain and mortal injury; that they live in a world of limited resources; that the decisions of one generation can have serious consequences for those that follow.

Moral standards and ideals affect the question of what we should do at several different levels. It is a fairly common characteristic of ethical theories to give an unduly narrow interpretation of morality by being preoccupied with only one of these levels. I shall draw attention here to what are probably the most important differences. First, there are the moral standards, principles and so on that refer to what are strict duties and obligations, what is fundamentally required of a person as a moral agent (they are often expressed in the form of negative rules or commands). Then there is the large range of moral standards that express what is good or desirable to do beyond strict duties and varying in their proximity to them. The various principles, taken together, may be accepted in a more or less unsystematic way or they may be interpreted in a definite pattern that reflects a comprehensive theory or ideology. Cutting across the two broad groupings of moral principles, there is a loose distinction to be made in terms of whether they refer primarily to oneself (personal morality) or to others (social morality). In some moral systems, certain values relating to oneself (such as personal freedom or power) have been treated as morally pre-eminent. In regard to social morality, we may distinguish between principles that apply to other specific individuals or groups (one's husband or wife, one's employees) and those that refer to others as members of a whole society or simply as human beings.

While people do adopt some moral ideals that they would not claim are necessarily binding on others, morality, like language, is an essentially public matter. It is only by being initiated into some form of moral life that individuals are in a position to make judgements or express opinions about what is moral. It belongs to the very nature of a society that its members would participate in some pattern of common moral practices. As I have noted, it can be argued that certain specific moral practices are a necessary form of any human society. The range of moral practices and their institutional forms in the society set limits to what moral decisions may justifiably, or even intelligibly, be made. The picture, implicit in some theories of moral education, of children growing up in a kind of moral vacuum and then deciding for themselves whether or in what way they will engage in moral practices is a distortion of psychological and social reality.

I do not wish to imply that we are committed simply to accepting the prevailing moral practices of our society. While there can be no argument or even intelligible claims about morality in the absence of any agreement on what counts as a moral practice, the justification of a moral practice is not a matter of its being commonly accepted. What counts is whether it can be shown to be a worthy standard of human conduct.

I return now to the question of the scope of moral education in the common schools. In relation to the distinctions suggested earlier, the most serious moral disputes in a pluralist society are likely to occur over personal standards (particularly ideals of moral excellence rather than duties or obligations) and inclusive moral systems or ideologies. Perhaps the relatively least controversial area is that of strict duties and obligations affecting interpersonal relationships and the general life of the society. Competing moral systems cannot be completely discrete. If they were, they could hardly be identified as *moral* systems. Although the precise interpretation and relative place given to moral practices vary from one system to another, there is a fair amount of overlap in what are recognised as moral practices. This is particularly so for systems within one society. Moral systems do, of course, embody diverse normative views of human nature. This makes it difficult to assess and compare them without begging the question. However, there are human goods that can be recognised as such independently of any systematic interpretation. These goods include (for example): adequate food, clothing, shelter; sound health; access to the treatment available in the society for injury and sickness; work that contributes to self-fulfilment and the social good; adequate care in infancy, childhood and old age; consideration and respect as a person; relationships of love and friendship; the skills and knowledge that enable people to participate effectively in social institutions and to understand and enjoy the main forms of culture.

Within the category of moral values that affect the general life of the society I think it can reasonably be claimed that there is a core of morality, directly bearing on membership of the inclusive social order, that the common schools of a pluralist society are justified in defending – provided, of course, that this is done in educationally appropriate ways. The reason simply is that without this basic social morality a society would not flourish or even survive; there would certainly be no chance of securing the conditions in which a plurality of moral outlooks could exist. As a minimum, the basic social morality includes practices of justice, truth telling and honesty, concern for others at least to the extent of avoiding the infliction of injury, mutual help in satisfying essential physical and cultural needs, and willingness to recognise the moral claims that others make on us on the basis of these practices. In addition to these values, the policy of pluralism itself involves certain moral values such as personal freedom, respect for persons, and tolerance (within the limits of the basic social morality). If we assume that a fundamental general objective of schooling is the development of a rational, critical understanding in relation to the main constituents of our social and cultural life, it is clear that the practice of education as a whole cannot proceed without respect for certain values – such as integrity, objectivity, impartiality – that have a moral aspect. Within the educational process, it is not possible to be educated in certain fields (for example, history and literature) without further values of a moral kind being developed. There is, therefore, a fair range of moral values (both procedural and substantive) that the school may justifiably defend.

Among other virtues that schools in a pluralist liberal democracy may (and should) cultivate are the following: civility in one's dealings with others, respect for legitimate authority, loyalty to the ideals of the social order, unselfishness in fulfilling various roles (such as that of a parent), conscious engagement in one's work in order to serve the common good, restraint on self-indulgence, responsibility as a citizen in a democracy.[6]

In promoting these aspects of morality, the school could easily encourage the false impression that they form the whole of the moral domain. It is important, therefore, that in various contexts the school should draw attention to personal morality, ideals of moral goodness, and systematic moral theories and how these often affect the specific interpretation of the values and virtues that make up the basic social morality. In the secondary school there should at least be some comparative study of the moral systems in our society. The distinction I have applied in considering what moral values the common school might justifiably advocate in a pluralist society does not provide an entirely satisfactory solution. For one thing, it is both theoretically and practically very difficult to observe the appropriate constraints in treating the complex interaction of diverse moral traditions and the general content of the common social morality. However, among the possibilities, I believe it is the most adequate compromise. A society that coheres as a community and is yet morally pluralistic depends on delicate and complex arrangements that do not respond to simple formulas.

Schools that reflect a particular moral tradition are obviously in a different position from common schools. In their institutional style and their formal educational programmes they can induct students into a comprehensive moral way of life. For many of their students, they are reinforcing the same way of life that is being upheld in other contexts (such as the family or a religious group). However, apart from the educational requirement of encouraging a moral commitment based on critical understanding, such schools (within a plural liberal democracy) have a responsibility to develop in their students the moral attitudes and values required of the members of such a society. In this respect, although private schools may provide a broader framework of interpretation and understanding, their role in moral education is not essentially different from that of common schools.

Notes

1 The moral theories of Kant and Mill are conspicuous examples of comprehensive versions of liberal morality, each with a different emphasis on what constitutes the highest moral good for human beings.
2 Lawrence Kohlberg and most of his followers, while emphasising developmental stages in the form of moral reasoning, have interpreted the content of morality predominantly in terms of justice. Carol Gilligan, although strongly influenced by Kohlberg's approach, has focused on the notion of care or compassion as central to morality. The different emphases have been related to characteristic differences in the moral outlook of males and females. Gilligan acknowledges that a fair proportion of males and females apply the values of both justice and caring (see Gilligan *et al.* 1988: ch. 4). What should be stressed is that the values, virtues and so on that make up morality are far more extensive than justice and caring.
3 The revised form of Rawls's position is set out in Rawls (1993).
4 'Values analysis' and 'values clarification' are among other approaches that emphasise processes. See, as examples, Fraenkel (1988) and Raths *et al.* (1978). In the sections that follow, the account I give of the relation between process and content in morality (and moral education) draws on earlier writing: in particular, Crittenden (1972) and (1981).
5 Alan Gewirth (1994) offers an interesting and fairly expansive account of rational argument about moral issues in a pluralist society.
6 A more extensive account of the virtues required in a liberal democratic society is defended by Galston (1992).

References

Crittenden, B. (1972) *Form and Content in Moral Education*, Toronto: Ontario Institute for Studies in Education.
—— (1981) 'Moral education: some aspects of its relationship to general values education and the study of religion', in G. Rossiter (ed.) *Religious Education in Australian Schools*, Canberra: Curriculum Development Centre.
Fraenkel, J. R. (1988) *How to Teach about Values: An Analytical Approach*, Englewood Cliffs, NJ: Prentice-Hall.
Galston, W. (1992) *Liberal Purposes: Goods, Virtues, and Diversity in the Liberal State*, Cambridge: Cambridge University Press.

Gewirth, A. (1994) 'Is cultural pluralism relevant to moral knowledge?', *Social Philosophy and Policy* 11(1): 22–43.

Gilligan, C., Ward, J. V., Taylor, J. M. and Bardige, B. (1988) *Mapping the Moral Domain*, Cambridge, MA: Harvard University Press.

Raths, L. E., Harmin, M. and Simon, S. B. (1978) *Values and Teaching* (2nd edition), Columbus, OH: Merrill.

Rawls, J. (1993) *Political Liberalism*, New York: Columbia University Press.

4

AGENCY AND CONTINGENCY IN MORAL DEVELOPMENT AND EDUCATION

Ruth Jonathan

Liberal educators have long insisted on a fundamentally moral purpose in fostering understandings and capacities that will enable the young not just to take their place in the world but to respond to it critically and creatively. The aim in moral matters is thus to equip them to reflect critically on the values they meet, and to develop and exercise a capacity for autonomous moral judgement so that they can lead their own lives authentically and play a role in the progressive refashioning of the social world. In recent years, confidence in this neutralist vision has come under attack from two quarters. On the one hand, some philosophers and educational theorists see critical reflection as a necessary but not sufficient response to the cultural pluralism and existential anomie of the modern world, and urge the claims of shared normative frameworks or of virtue ethics in the formation of moral dispositions (see Carr 1991). On the other, politicians and pundits call for directive moral guidance to combat a perceived decline in personal conduct and a claimed erosion of the moral fabric of society. Whilst neither concern reinforces the claims of the other, their twin implication – that there are real current problems of moral motivation and disposition and that these arise in part from a flawed theory and practice of moral education – demands a considered response.

I shall argue here that just as liberal theory's contemporary neutralist interpretation offers an inadequate conception of the development of moral motivation and disposition, so too does its understandings of moral education bring self-defeating practical consequences, lending force in moral development to those very contingencies neutralism aims to transcend. I shall also claim that the relative force of contingency varies with circumstance and that the actual conditions of late-capitalist modernity place the avowed neutralism of liberal educators at a particular discount. If their enduring aims are to continue to be the development of moral autonomy through critical reflection, then they may need to employ a more socially sensitive conception of autonomy, and to pay closer attention to the relative roles of substance and procedure in critical reflection; a revised role for formal education in moral development, conceived as an interaction between the individual and the social, is also required. This would imply a move away from the dominant contemporary view of a rights-based moral individualism, in which ethical relationships are grounded in duties of non-interference with the competing preferences of others and non-infringement of their ethical 'personal space'. It is that view, combined with the fact of cultural pluralism, which persuades liberal educators to conceptualise moral education in a scrupulously agnostic manner, as if the young could evaluate with rational detachment the host of moral messages with which the world bombards us daily. In underplaying our enmeshment in the social world, as its products and producers, this stance does not transcend such messages: it exacerbates their force.

It is not a novel insight to insist that substantive moral values are embedded in our social, political and economic arrangements and institutions, not least those of education, nor to acknowledge that these act as powerful influences on the young. Indeed, the standard response from liberal educators is that this is precisely why the role of education is to equip people to appraise substantive values critically and modify their expression in personal and social life. I shall argue that this received solution to the problem of moral education risks compounding the problem it aims to solve. A first section looks at the intellectual basis for our current concerns of theory and practice, and of our conceptions of the nature of moral development. A second draws attention to a contemporary social context which aims once again to make the moral messages of the social world not only explicit but also psychologically reinforcing and indirectly coercive. A third claims that the embeddedness of the self in its social and material world reinforces certain values and dispositions and places others at a discount, changing the parameters for moral development with time and circumstance. To the charge that these are sociological and psychological matters, whereas the fundamental questions for regrounding our approach to moral education are of a philosophical sort, I would counter that this neat division between fact and value is itself part of the problem which underlies the current inadequate understanding of moral development and moral education. Far from enabling formal education to provide a counterweight to social forces, a self-denying focus on only procedural value ensures the progressive marginalisation of formal education in the moral development of the young. In conclusion I shall turn to possible directions out of this impasse, for both theory and practice.

Moral development and its parameters

Handwringing over the moral attitudes and behaviour of the young calls for a certain scepticism of course, particularly when politicians castigate teachers and parents for falling down on their job as moral educators in the face of rising disaffection and antisocial behaviour among the disadvantaged. Such scapegoating helps to disguise the structural partial causes of our social ills and to legitimise cutting their public costs; and dismay at the moral dispositions and behaviour of the rising generation has been a staple of adult complaint throughout the ages. We must nonetheless ask whether adult fears – however historically hackneyed – have in fact some grounding today, whether the perceived anomie and moral confusion of the young is indeed real and different from the past, and whether today's intergenerational dialogue of the deaf is qualitatively different from the intellectual barriers and emotional rejections that have always been part of bringing up the young. And we must also consider the role the modern liberal ideal of life (and hence of moral education) may have played in whatever crisis conditions modernity exhibits.

The historical process that brought us to the contemporary liberal ideal of the morally self-defining individual, constrained only by the requirements of reciprocity to respect similarly the self-definition of others, has its roots in contingent ontological beliefs and empirical hypotheses that are well documented and will not be rehearsed here (see Bellamy 1992, or Jonathan 1995). Nonetheless, that ideal now grounds neutralist liberal claims to metatheoretical status. Together with the rationale for liberal moral education it underpins, this ideal is now being challenged in the theoretical work of many philosophers and social theorists, mirroring public unease. Growing theoretical interest in the fragmentation of value as an apparently defining characteristic of modernity frequently makes reference to a historical process that was initially liberating but which eventually became self-defeating, in which the same processes that opened cultures and individuals to the richness of a plurality of traditions gradually deprived them of the capacity to engage fully with any moral framework. Many critics (for example Bloom 1987) advocate a return to an earlier point in the process before modernity's painful watershed, thus making a mistake analogous to that of those who urge the reimposition of discipline, control and standards in the sphere of practice. Others claim that the fundamental moral purpose of education has become impossible under modern conditions, in theoretical analyses that offer important insights into the nature of moral commitment but which amount to counsels of despair for educational practice (see MacIntyre 1987). Liberal educators have typically responded by correctly noting that we cannot turn back the clock, and by reasserting the central saving importance of developing moral autonomy in each individual (see Mendus 1992).

In so doing, they sidestep the basic challenge: namely, that to develop in the young the capacity for critical reflection on values cannot in and of itself provide an adequate framework either for the development of individual commitments or for the shared social understandings that both shape and reflect those commitments. Indeed, the rationale for such reflection in individuals presupposes the existence of a surrounding framework of value that both supports and sustains, and against which personal values are elaborated and modified. When this framework is fragmented, in part by the cumulative effect of a past prioritising of individual autonomy, then the construction of personal values (if these are to be more than simple lifestyle preferences) becomes a daunting task, for which critical reflection may be a necessary but not a sufficient condition. In brief, liberal educators continue to back as the prime solution that very process of liberating critical reflection many moral philosophers and social theorists now see as part of the problem. We thus have a theoretical discourse that mirrors and elaborates the plain parent's hunch that there may be more to moral judgement than doing what you think is right, and more to moral education than helping the young to make up their own minds about what values to hold and which lives to lead.

If indeed the further pursuit of rational autonomy may not be a sufficient response to the problem of moral development in modern conditions, we need to focus on those conditions, asking what is peculiar to them and reminding ourselves of how they came about. Although it would be foolish to suppose that the past guaranteed a secure and cosy framework for individual development, it is clear that today an exponential increase in the rate of value fragmentation results in a qualitative change in the social conditions for self-definition. As Williams has noted, this entails not just that we must adapt more rapidly to changing cultural norms, but also that our capacities for response are themselves altered, bringing both an enhanced capacity for reflection and a concomitant 'thinning' of our ethical concepts (Williams 1985: 163). Since we could not turn back the clock even if we wanted to, the liberal educator seems fated to respond by prescribing a homeopathic remedy: that of further enhancing the individual's capacity to push forward the inexorable process of critical reflection from which in modernity there is no escape without bad faith.

In thus attending to only one aspect of modernity's twin defining moral characteristics, the conventional response has three shortcomings, as I have argued elsewhere (see Jonathan 1993). First, by focusing only on individual development, it overlooks the two-way relation between the self and its context. For it is not just cultural pluralism – diversity or even conflicts of values between societies, and between individuals and groups within pluralist societies – which now confronts us, but a new pluralism of the self which brings the very concept of 'framework' under threat. And whereas the fostering of critical reflection may have been a necessary and sufficient response from liberal educators to the first kind of pluralism, it is merely necessary and inescapable to the second. This new fragmentation, in which contending but relatively stable conditions have given way to a pervasive and accelerating process of change, gives rise to peculiar difficulties for moral education, so that what may once have been the road to autonomous commitment and coherence becomes merely the means to preference formation and pragmatism. This process is compounded by the second shortcoming, which arises not from the excessive focus on the individual but from an exaggerated concentration on the cognitive. When the development of moral autonomy is seen as a largely rational endeavour, then in acknowledging modernity's accelerating dual process of growing critical reflection and diminishing ethical commitment, the former gains priority of concern, with the latter seeming a (possibly regrettable) price worth paying, or even perhaps a gain in itself. We might well ask to what ethical position that then commits us, and what grounding we then have for the fundamentally moral purpose of the educational enterprise.

But it is the third shortcoming with the standard response which is the most serious, in its conception of the educational enterprise as self-contained and self-referential, consisting in the cognitive development of each, with no broader transformative purpose for the social context that shapes and reflects that development. There is surely something amiss with this position. For when the good for individuals resides in sufficient cognitive emancipation for each to choose his or her own good, and the good for society is simply whatever facilitates the self-definition of its members, then we have a theory of moral value which relies on playing both ends against the middle. The theorist of moral education can only recommend pressing onwards in the determinate direction of past historical change, and practical moral educators in home or school seem fated to bequeath to the young an exacerbation of their own existential predicament. In conceiving the intentional guidance of moral development as self-contained – as if what is taught were separate from and more powerful than what is caught – we both misunderstand the nature of learning in moral matters, and misconstrue the dialectical relation between individual and social evolution. Since values and dispositions are constituents of the developing self rather than matters for appraisal like the facts, hypotheses, procedures or skills that are intentionally passed on in other areas of learning, the prioritisation of rational development cannot secure the goal of unconstrained self-definition that claims to justify it. And more serious attention is required to the parameters for development which the wider world affords.

Teachers and parents of course have always been aware that 'outside influences' affect the values and attitudes of the young, not just as mere frustrating intervening variables in the development of autonomous judgement, but as an inescapable part of the raw material that goes into the construction of the self. From a wider perspective, that insight suggests a broader transformative purpose for education than the emancipation of the individual, for that emancipation itself depends in part upon the transformation of social structures and practices into forms that can become part of the educative process. It is worth reminding ourselves that to see individual development as separate from social contingencies is a curiously modern perception that would have baffled those philosophers from Plato to Dewey who made significant contributions to educational theory. It is also a quite recent feature of the very world-view that underpins the contemporary ideal of the morally self-defining individual, and one that would not be recognised by liberals such as Mill. Today it is challenged not only by neo-Aristotelian critics of liberalism, but by ethical liberals such as Raz (1986). Of course, to note that the current party line on the legitimate aims and acceptable limits of moral education is historically contingent is to say nothing about its tenability. That requires attention to the prioritised ideal of moral autonomy for individuals and to the dynamic of interaction between agency and contingency in the formation of the self (see Jonathan 1997: chs 6, 7).

Now the received doctrine conceives the morally autonomous individual as one capable of choosing, on reflection, both goals and ways of life as well as means to them. Liberal education is to equip people with the rational autonomy to form preferences and make choices for themselves; deliberate influence in these matters is seen as unacceptably coercive. The implication is that what preferences result is morally indifferent, provided these do not frustrate or undermine the preferences of others. There are therefore two curious results of an apparently agnostic approach to moral education. First, if sincerely held, in effect it prioritises equal liberty and relegates all other values and virtues to the status of preferences of equal standing to be negotiated with the preferences of others. Moreover, it implies a strange inattention, given the consequent importance of preferences, to what the options for preference contingently happen to be, and how choices come to be made between them.

Clearly, if the hallmark of the modern liberal approach to moral disposition and behaviour is that each should be enabled to form and follow personal post-reflective inclination, curbed only when this conflicts with the inclinations of others, then it is crucial to attend to where inclinations come from. Unless we suppose that they emerge in the light of pure reason, seen itself as the key to the good (a doctrine few would now endorse), or that reason and circumstance will inevitably combine to result in sound moral judgement (in the light of a supporting set of metaphysical beliefs and social hypotheses such as those that sustained nineteenth-century political theory), we can only suppose that they come from a dynamic interaction between the reasoning self and his or her contingent circumstances. Thus if educators maintain agnosticism about the reasoning agent's virtues and dispositions, provided only that a procedural allegiance to reason itself is developed, they risk placing the self not in interaction with circumstance, but at its coercive mercy. Indeed, when we understand the development as well as the exercise of autonomy to require public maintenance of a range of worthwhile options, we see that 'the ideal of personal autonomy is incompatible with moral individualism' (Raz 1986: 206) and not, as neutralists believe, its justification.

If then, within education, neutralist liberals refrain on principle from substantively influencing the young, they will be alone in that, and the result of their abstention from influence may well be socially deterministic rather than individually liberating. To put this bluntly: at any given time the contingencies of life for the young, singly and collectively, are largely outside the control of their educators in home and school. Options, not only for satisfying preferences but also for forming them, are in part structured by these contingencies. Supremacy for preference satisfaction, subject only to reciprocity, treats these contingencies as morally indifferent, leaving the self a product rather than a producer of historical change. That is why the educational enterprise requires a well-grounded social purpose, with the transformation of social structures understood as a prerequisite to individual emancipation, as well as one of its hoped-for consequences. More will be said about this in the closing section; we must first look at that contemporary project that sets out to put the cart before the horse, by arranging social structures and institutions to direct the moral development of individuals.

Moral development and the enterprise culture

It is not necessary to rehearse the recent advance across much of the developed world of a strange hybrid of the exhumed social beliefs of nineteenth-century liberalism and the procedural principles of neutralist thought, foreshadowed in the work of theorists such as Nozick and Hayek and variously referred to as neo-liberalism, libertarianism or the New Right. Both the rationale for that political programme, and the moral acceptability of its social consequences, have generated heated debate, not least in relation to education. But there has as yet been little discussion of its existential implications and still less attention to the role of 'the enterprise culture' in the development of moral consciousness in the young. This seems somewhat surprising, when its advocates have made crystal clear that 'Economics are the method. The object is to change the soul' (Thatcher 1988). In the UK, for example, there could be no doubt that neo-liberal policies were in part a moral crusade when their standard-bearer announced on election: 'Our aim has always been more than economic progress; it is to renew the spirit and solidarity of the nation' (Thatcher 1979). Such 'reformers' are thus acutely aware, as were nineteenth-century political theorists, that moral dispositions and social circumstance can be either mutually reinforcing or mutually frustrating. Now as then, the moral development of the public is only marginally to be addressed through explicit educational programmes: the primary task is to structure circumstance so that its lessons are psychologically reinforcing. For markets to flourish, a certain sort of social actor is required, and to promote that kind of agency 'the logic of the market' must be extended into those areas of social life significant for selfhood. To adopt the rhetoric of enterprise, the 'discipline of the market' creates opportunities and even requirements for initiative; it rewards energy and innovation, forces people to think for themselves and stand on their own feet and punishes those who do not conform to its requirements, whether through sloth, indecisiveness, complacency or parasitic reliance on the energy of others. When the rhetoric is less pugnacious, the new culture will give 'individuals more and more control over their own lives' (Baker 1990), offering 'more choice and more opportunity to every member of our society' (Howe 1989). In this more persuasive mode the appeal is populist, claiming democratic – even egalitarian – credentials. For who will gain and who will lose is entirely up to the individuals concerned (as if none of them were socially located), since rewards and penalties are not to be distributed by power elites in political parties, trades unions or professional associations, but by all, acting individually but forming together the hidden hand of the market.

Free choice becomes king: what is endorsed by individuals flourishes, what is not, withers. Preferences are satisfied with maximum effectiveness and without paternalistic intervention. What individuals choose – artefacts, entertainments, ideas, educational programmes – has value, just because it is 'autonomously' chosen; any further questions about worth would smack of authoritarianism, paternalism or vested interest. But maximal individual autonomy does not mean that 'anything goes', for free agency will be disciplined by the market, which prompts individuals to make choices enhancing competitive position, whether this means designer jeans or courses in 'life skills'. After all, 'We can only build a responsible, independent community with responsible, independent people. That is why Conservative policies have given them the choice to buy houses, build up capital and acquire shares in their companies' (Thatcher 1990). Preferences, clearly, are not only to be satisfied by the new culture, they are also to be prestructured by it. And autonomy is understood to operate within a particular set of parameters set by circumstance.

That political programme and its values has met with considerable opposition, not least from many liberal educators who regard its ethos as a denial of humane values and an obstacle to earlier goals of individual emancipation. But a historical perspective might afford scant sympathy for the liberal lament that libertarian rhetoric disguises revisionism in their clothes. It might rather suggest that where moral individualism implies preference-satisfaction as the legitimate goal for individual lives (all preferences seeming to be of equal moral standing provided they are negotiated with other preference-satisfying individuals), the enterprise culture looks like just the kind of world we might expect. If liberals counter that this leaves out the humane values and social goals on which the promotion of individualistic moral autonomy was predicated, we might ask why those values and goals must remain invisible in moral education. The received view, from both libertarians and neutralist liberals, is that the values of the former are in direct confrontation with the ideals of the latter. Be that as it may, either the *explicitly acknowledged* ideals of the latter (as presented to the young in liberal moral education) have provided some of the conditions that have allowed the values of the former to gain a hold over our social consciousness, or thirty years of educational effort – in the area of understanding thought to be most fundamental – are to be judged as a singular failure.

The point to be stressed, however, is that whatever the social roots of the enterprise culture, its champions – and its social consequences – remind us that the construction of individual and social consciousness is neither conceptually nor practicably separable. Whether such a social ethos 'puts a premium on indecent and obscene greed' (Jenkins 1987) or whether indeed thrift and hard work are encouraged, is of course a question of great practical importance, but how we answer it is irrelevant to a more enduring issue to which liberal educators have recently seemed strangely oblivious. Thought and feeling affect circumstance, and circumstance affects thought and feeling. *Changed* circumstance sets changed parameters for thought and feeling, and this is a continuous two-way process. Personal inclinations and preferences, and *a fortiori* moral dispositions and values, arise from a dynamic interaction between the thinking and feeling self and his or her contingent circumstances. If the defining purpose of liberal education is to seek optimal conditions for the development of each self, to the eventual benefit of society, then educational process and content, perhaps most importantly in moral matters, cannot doggedly rely on agnostic procedural principles, irrespective of significant changes in the nature and quality of that dynamic at each particular moment in time. To keep liberal noses clean by having no truck with messy substantive values looks worryingly analogous to the libertarian's disingenuous disclaimer that the aggregate consequences of market choice are no one's responsibility. In practice, education cedes the place to circumstance as engine in the dynamic of development and becomes disempowered as a force for individual and social emancipation. It is therefore urgent to consider how education might play a more positive role whilst still avoiding simple value reproduction. First, we must recall for today what earlier philosophers and educational theorists readily understood: that contingent circumstance, of whatever sort, reinforces some values and dispositions and places others at a discount.

The self and its social world

To insist again on the power of circumstance to mould us is not just to reiterate the old saw that values are more readily caught than taught. For the power of circumstance to shape us depends in part both on its specific nature and on how we understand our relation to it. Thus, today, we are not just at a particular moment of historical evolution, with a certain level of technological development, associated political and economic structures, and related social conditions; we are also disposed to see ourselves as existentially separate from each other and in at least potential control of subsequent change. All of this, in dynamic interaction, constitutes our circumstance. When circumstance is so multifaceted, no single aspect, nor any series of aspects considered in isolation from each other, will reveal to analysis the parameters of moral development which circumstance affords at any given time. But we can get some purchase by looking at some aspects of our present condition.

70

There are salient features of the particular social ethos dominant in many developed societies at this time which make that ethos especially directive in the construction of both individual and social disposition and behaviour. That the economic and social arrangements of late capitalism are psychologically reinforcing and coercive was noted above, instancing a programme for change likened to 'stimulus–response theory in which the stimulus of profit and the fear of failure induce the response of competitiveness' (Cohen 1992: 183). For those who fail, or stubbornly refuse, to respond to stimulus, the penalty is to be material disadvantage and social disapproval. It is often supposed that the power of any such programme must depend on the accuracy of its latent account of human nature, since conformity to a particular understanding of moral motivation is presupposed in the rationale for a set of social arrangements that would only function effectively if this presupposition were true. However, this overlooks the multifaceted complexity of circumstance. Since 'human nature' is itself in part socially constructed, a project and its values may be either self-fulfilling or self-defeating, depending on four factors: the nature of the values it embodies; the kind of social structure it encourages; the evolving dispositions of social actors; and the interaction between these three, mediated in part by educational experience.

To take the instanced socio/political programme as an example, if the enterprisers are right that hedonism and profligacy as well as sloth carry heavy market penalties, then both its economic and its moral projects might bear fruit, whereas if 'the growing role of market-relations . . . may erode society's capacity . . . to protect the forms of virtue on which the market rests' (Plant 1992: 183), then both projects may be undermined. But 'might' and 'may' are the only appropriate judgements here, since neither self-fulfilment nor self-defeat are inexorable for a project in which it is not just that differing values carry different social price tags, but also that social conditions are created through which *the same value* – a single moral disposition – may come into conflict with itself, and be placed at a severe discount. When the basic assumption of a 'reform' programme is that each individual will respond to the carrots and sticks of the market from judicious self-interest, the liberal's first instinct is to see this as its Achilles' heel, on the grounds that moral motivation is more various than this, with many individuals having settled moral dispositions that incline them to place concern and responsibility for others before self-interest. But a culture that extends market principles into the distribution of public and social goods does not present individuals with a straight choice between seeking self-interest or satisfying responsibility to others, for the one choice a social actor does not get in the market is whether to play the social game this way at all. When the revised game amounts to riding a tiger of competition the one with another, certain values become discounted. A familiar example from the market distribution of educational goods illustrates this.

In a competitive context of preference rights in schooling, the parent who combines concern for her own children with concern for the unknown children of others has a most invidious choice: to secure the best for her own to the disadvantage of others, or to neglect the advantage of her own without thereby being able to ameliorate the progressively more inequitable distribution of life-chances which the context of competition entrains. Such an individual has no option that satisfies her moral inclinations, since neither individual choice – to try and secure positional advantage or not – staves off the social conditions and moral climate she deplores, and those with settled moral dispositions to place social responsibility before self-interest must either acquiesce in their children's double disadvantage or join the race, against inclination, as if they were convinced social marketeers. To jump off a tiger is merely risky; to push one's dependants off in the name of social solidarity places concern for others in contradiction with itself.

Moreover, social conditions which have this effect of discounting certain values do not simply compromise their expression in behaviour. They also frustrate the role of those values in the formation of disposition. For parents as moral educators do not merely aim to help youngsters coolly to appraise alternative moral commitments. Liberal parents, whilst trying to avoid *imposing* their own values, still hope that the example of their own behaviour will recommend to their children the values which their demeanour and conduct express. Parental influence in this respect, like that of teachers, has both cognitive and conative elements, and depends on young people's perception of their elders as concerned, benevolent *and effective* moral agents. Thus, when some parents are morally disempowered by particular social conditions, such that either their conduct does not conform to their stated values or those values are seen to be morally ineffectual, the example set seems at worst that of a hypocrite and at best that of a wimp or a fool. The example from schooling choice highlights the plight of those parents who might be potential reluctant winners in the revised social competition but who do not wish to raise the stakes for others. Parallel problems arise for those for whom these new stakes are too high because of their initial conditions. In this way, the lone parent who wishes to set an example of probity, but who cannot meet a child's welfare needs without bending society's rules, is in a different but analogous kind of false position. In these ways, certain social conditions bring an in-built momentum to the interaction between value and circumstance to which a context-sensitive approach to moral education should pay heed.

The social conditions referred to here in relation to an 'enterprise culture' are the result of a complex of political choices that might have been and may become otherwise, although it is part of my case that their social effects interact with the formation of moral disposition and hence with future political choices. That the boundaries of political possibility alter when governing regimes have held power for long periods is ample evidence of this. But there are other kinds of social conditions, resulting from even less reversible historical developments, which, although they cannot be elaborated here, must be briefly indicated. These conditions arise from our chosen exploitation of and adaptations to current levels of technological development, creating a material and social world that also contributes to the parameters for moral development and disposition. I have supported the claim that the 'value fragmentation' of modernity is both real and troubling. The concomitant 'thinning of our ethical concepts', which we seem condemned by today's liberal educational theory to exacerbate, is arguably further fuelled by a range of features of the modern material world. These features, I suggest, make our procedures of intentional moral education *more* decisive in the development of moral disposition than in the past, since changes in material circumstance have weakened both the power of adult example to provide reliable and convincing models for the young and even the role of 'nature' in exhibiting the sticks and carrots which social forces now seek – less even-handedly – to supply.

To make the first point, that adults now function as less convincing role models, sounds like an echo of reactionary laments about a decline in 'family values', but it is more substantial and quite other than that. I have claimed that some sorts of social arrangements, by placing particular values at a discount or in conflict with each other, weaken the power of adult example by rendering them ineffective moral agents, further reinforcing the selective discounting process of particular circumstance. We should also note the way in which technological possibilities have made those who are 'in charge' in the private and public spheres seem increasingly impotent in the eyes of the young, often most particularly in areas of greatest moral consequence. On a growing range of issues – political, economic, ecological, social, bioethical – complex, conflicting and constantly changing data undermine adult confidence in firm opinions and resolute action. This in turn reinforces the younger generation's scepticism of even qualified opinions and circumspect actions from their elders. In an information-rich world where there seem to be few causes without two sides each having claims to legitimacy, little untainted information, and no stories not subject to reinterpretation, the adult who tries to represent reality most faithfully can only seem tentative, hesitant and even vacillating. Adults are often urged to be clear and consistent with youngsters who by definition are still developing the capacities to come to terms with the complexity of experience. But in the modern world, educators can only do so by talking in the misleadingly simple terms the information media themselves encourage and whose tendentious messages the educating adult tries to modify. And it is not just parents and teachers who seem to the young to be impotent in the face of complex reality. Personal responsibility seems placed at a general discount when politicians and the media repeatedly affirm our helplessness in respect of global systems of finance or ecology, while modern technology depersonalises effects by providing the means for more and more action-at-a-distance, systematising and distancing our relations with one another.

To make the second point on material feedback is to draw attention to something perhaps more serious, since our increased control (at least in the developed world) over the brute circumstances of life has unforeseen consequences for the development of moral disposition, placing an increased premium on the precept and example of the older generation just when this is weakened by the same forces. To point out that 'nature' exhibits fewer sticks and carrots as we gain more technological control over it also sounds suspiciously like echoing the age-old complaint that today the young are 'spoiled' – that they have 'never had it so good' or do not know how lucky they are – but it is much more serious than that. For in many respects the younger generation are most *un*fortunate, since many moral 'lessons' (independent of any particular idea of the good) are far harder to learn now than they were in the past. For example, that one's actions have clear consequences for oneself and others, or that in order to achieve a necessary goal, competing personal preferences must be set aside in the interim, must now be cognitively understood and supported by secondhand reports of others' experience. In the past, firsthand feedback made such abstract learning unnecessary, when both acquiring the means to life and sustaining the phases of our life-cycle were activities in which all were unambiguously involved on a daily basis. Briefly, in a material and social world in which some values are placed at a discount, certain basic lessons of moral consequence are harder to learn, and the power of adults to serve as convinced and convincing role models is in inverse proportion to their efforts to respect both the complexity of the world and the development of their charges, it is little wonder that the parameters for moral development today present us with changed problems for moral education.

Clues for reconstruction

So where should we go from here? That our modern condition must inevitably lead to the moral confusion and existential anomie remarked by theorists and public alike is a counsel of despair, and one which most liberal educators, as noted above, have rejected as unduly alarmist. Their rebuttal, however, cannot just rely on the claim that to develop rational autonomy in individuals enables them severally to determine the good, thus leaving the social future open. I have suggested that both sides are in error: the first representing a contingent historical process as socially deterministic, the second seeing the continued enhancement through education of individual rational autonomy as the sufficient means by which we collectively direct our future circumstance. The former position pays too little attention to the power of education to mediate experience and transform circumstance; the latter, in its procedural 'one-club golfing', focuses too narrowly on the individual's cognitive development, abstracted from context. Similarly, the first position cannot avoid pointless and blinkered nostalgia, whilst the latter seems to commit us to a naive social optimism belied by experience.

The upshot is that we should construct a third position, both for the theory and the practice of liberal moral education. That position must acknowledge that how contingency affects the development of consciousness depends upon how we address the interaction between the two, and that any appropriate response must play an active part in the developing dynamic. A new position would still see formal education as the prime site in which any society addresses the interaction between individual and social development, in an attempt to influence both for the good. But it should also consider that as the coercive force of circumstance increases in particular social conditions, and as the power to teach – both of example and of brute circumstance – is weakened, so the role of substantive guidance in moral development becomes more crucial. For where teaching is agnostic in intent, as in the current party line on moral education, it will be the less agnostic in effect as the other combined influences on development are either leached away or skewed in determinate directions. In these circumstances, the 'look, no hands' procedural principles of liberal moral education cannot be deemed adequate to education's fundamental moral purpose unless it is truly supposed that all substantive outcomes are morally indifferent, provided only that they satisfy individual moral preferences whilst respecting the preferences of individual others. Reconstructed aims and procedures for moral education need therefore to be based on firmer foundations than this, for, as MacIntyre has frequently noted, to teach an indeterminate morality is to teach no morality at all.

That search for firmer foundations is part of contemporary attention to the indeterminacy of modern liberal theory, where many political philosophers are becoming concerned that, in its desire to respect pluralism and diversity in conceptions of the good, modern liberalism has forsworn the resources to engage with any who reject its procedural principles, and retained insufficient substantive foundations to guide those who accept them. The problem of moral education for liberal educators can be viewed as this theoretical dilemma in practice and in microcosm. The arguments presented here suggest that its reconstruction in that context has significant implications for those macrocosmic questions. It should be noted that fears that a jettisoning of neutralism amounts to a rejection of liberal ideals themselves are no basis for a defence of the pervasive theoretical *status quo*. Contemporary ethical interpretations of liberalism argue convincingly that personal freedom and the value of autonomy are rather supported than compromised by admittance into the public sphere of those substantive values without which the procedural ideals of liberalism are hollow (Raz 1986).

Further analysis is required to detail how this reconstruction might be approached, and to show that it need imply no abdication in the face of the demands and conditions of modernity. Rather, it might give due attention to their force in setting parameters not just for conduct but for the formation of moral dispositions. To give such due attention requires us firstly to see formal education as *only one* of the sites of moral and social learning, and *only one* of the agencies with an active role in forming disposition and aspiration. That education should pay more heed to the social world in revising its aims and procedures is, as argued here, necessary – if these are not to be marginalised and frustrated. But in itself it is not sufficient, for that still consigns education to a reactive (if more effective) role in the feedback loop of individual and social moral development. What is also central is a reaffirmation of the socially transformative purpose of education itself, with a further acknowledgement that this cannot be approached through individual emancipation alone. Rather, it requires education – in its aims, its procedures and its content – to recognise that the transformation of social structures into forms that are themselves educative cannot remain just a hoped-for consequence of individual emancipation, but is paradoxically also its prerequisite. As Peukert notes, 'The competence to make mature moral judgements . . . seems to be linked necessarily with an intersubjectively reflected, transformative competence of social action' (Peukert 1993: 166). This latter competence should therefore be a primary goal of education.

Of course, a socio-political purpose for education has always been inevitable, but its emancipatory aspect has been conceived in the liberal West in individualist terms. As education became democratised, this aspiration simply extended to more individuals. Thus, over the past fifty years, we have concentrated on freeing individuals from the constraints of their own situation (given sufficient ability and application) and on enabling the more able to move up through a social hierarchy, on the tacit assumption of the early liberals that a moral meritocracy and a more just civil society would ensue, thus recursively enhancing social justice and the well-being of all. Once again, this virtuous circle, with one-way momentum from the individual to the social, has proved a mirage. It is therefore time to recognise this interaction as a continuous feedback loop, with the consequence for educational theory and practice that in order to pursue socio-political goals of transformation – without which educational goals will be constantly frustrated – a less agnostic posture is required. The role of education cannot stop at freeing individuals *from* 'the present and particular', but must also give attention to what it is freeing them *for*. Though currently a heresy, this is not a new claim, but one which echoes classical theories of education and society, and is at the heart of modern critical theory. To flesh it out for our times needs a theory of curriculum, of learning and of the role of the school which is beyond the scope of this chapter, but there are evident implications for moral education.

Clearly from this third position, moral education should be neither conceived nor addressed as if it were limited to the development of personal value-choices for agency in the private, interpersonal sphere. Nor is it enough for the educator to say 'look around you – at the world and at us – and make up your own minds', on the grounds that education provides the resources for the first and last procedures, while the substantive values without which moral agency cannot exist are on view without prejudice as objects of appraisal. Enough has been said here to cast serious doubt on that supporting assumption. To be sure, in recognising anomie and bewilderment, we still wish to avoid a cure worse than the disease. There should (and most likely could) be no return to telling people what they should believe or how they should act, where their beliefs and actions do not harm others. But a recognition of the social construction of the self, through the expression of moral dispositions in the social world as in their formation, needs to underpin both how and what we teach. And this alters how we construe and present to the young the limits of what can safely be claimed as 'self-regarding' in the moral sphere, modifying the process of moral education and extending its focus. For in a material and social context in which, like it or not, we are 'all members of one another', atomistic individualism cannot retain the plausibility it once had for some early liberals and which is now crudely celebrated by libertarians. With a more complex understanding of the inter-action between agency and contingency, individual reflective preferences subject only to the restraints of reciprocity become a principle for moral agency whose effects exacerbate the conditions it aims to address (see Jonathan 1997: ch. 7).

In brief, if we see the achievement and expression of moral autonomy not as an *individual right* but as a *social value*, a major consequence follows for the educational enterprise in general and the process of moral education in particular. Firstly, as above, the emancipation of each becomes inseparable from and contingent upon the collective emancipation of others. And hence, the enduring ideal of the emancipation of self from circumstance becomes inseparable from a broader transformative purpose for education. For it is only if the structures and conditions of circumstance themselves become edu-cative that general emancipation is possible. Since social structures and conditions are modified and reformed by social actors whose expectations and commitments are mediated by their education, a considered survey of those structures and conditions and of the parameters they offer for enhancing or frustrating personal development must be a central part of formal learning. It is true that liberal educators have sought to interpret the world around them to the young in as 'objective' a manner as possible, to avoid undue influence and to keep the future open. But if 'objectivity' is seen to require strict value-neutrality, then when neutral procedures have non-neutral effects, avoidance of undue influence amounts to abdication to the forces of circumstance and is a far cry from keeping the future open. When material and social circumstances are saturated with value, 'objectivity' must include appraisal of those values, of their power to mould us and our world, and of their consequences for our future possibilities and relations with each other. It is surely educational hubris to be so fearful of unduly influencing the young that we do not address with them the existential implications of particular moral dispositions and conduct and of the social arrangements which arise from them and hedge their further expression and development.

References

Baker, K. (1990) 'No return to stifling socialism', *The Times*, 14 March.

Bellamy, R. (1992) *Liberalism and Modern Society*, Oxford: Polity Press.

Bloom, A. (1987) *The Closing of the American Mind*, London: Penguin.

Carr, D. (1991) *Educating the Virtues*, London: Routledge.

Cohen, A. (1992) 'The personal right to identify: a polemic on the self in the enterprise culture', in P. Heelas and P. Morris (eds) *The Values of Enterprise Culture: The Moral Debate*, London: Routledge.

Howe, G. (1989) 'Annual Disraeli Lecture', London.

Jenkins, D. (1987) 'God, bishops, Tories and the election', *The Times*, 5 June.

Jonathan, R. (1993) 'Education, philosophy of education and the fragmentation of value', *Journal of Philosophy of Education* 27(2): 171–8.

—— (1995) 'Liberal philosophy of education: a paradigm under strain', *Journal of Philosophy of Education* 29(1): 100–2.

—— (1997) *Illusory Freedoms: Liberalism, Education and the Market*, Oxford: Blackwell.

MacIntyre, A. (1987) 'The idea of an educated public', in G. Haydon (ed.) *Education and Values*, London: Institute of Education, University of London.

Mendus, S. (1992) 'All the king's horses and all the king's men: justifying higher education', *Journal of Philosophy of Education* 26(2): 173–82.

Peukert, H. (1993) 'Basic problems of a critical theory of education', *Journal of Philosophy of Education* 27(2): 159–70.

Plant, R. (1992) 'The moral limits of the market', in P. Heelas and P. Morris (eds) *The Values of Enterprise Culture: The Moral Debate*, London: Routledge.

Raz, J. (1986) *The Morality of Freedom*, Oxford: Clarendon Press.

Thatcher, M. (1979) Speech to Conservative Party Summer School.

—— (1988) Speech quoted in *Sunday Times*, 7 May.

—— (1990) 'Address to the 10th Conservative Party Conference', reported in *Daily Telegraph*, 15 October.

Williams, B. (1985) *Ethics and the Limits of Philosophy*, London: Fontana.

5

EDUCATION FOR CITIZENSHIP

Will Kymlicka

It is widely accepted that a basic task of schooling is to prepare each new generation for their responsibilities as citizens. Indeed, the need to create a knowledgeable and responsible citizenry was one of the major reasons for establishing a public school system, and for making education mandatory. Education for citizenship includes, but also goes far beyond, classes in 'civics'. Citizenship education is not just a matter of learning the basic facts about the institutions and procedures of political life; it also involves acquiring a range of dispositions, virtues and loyalties that are intimately bound up with the practice of democratic citizenship. Children acquire these virtues and loyalties not just (or even primarily) in civics classes. Rather, they are inculcated throughout the educational system. The aim of educating citizens affects what subjects are taught, how they are taught, and in what sorts of classrooms. In this sense, education for citizenship is not an isolated subset of the curriculum but, rather, one of the ordering goals or principles that shape the entire curriculum.

In this chapter, I will discuss some of the issues raised by citizenship education. I will begin by considering what citizenship means in modern democratic societies, and what sorts of capacities and dispositions it requires (first section). I hope to show that liberal democratic citizenship is more complicated than is often realised, and that even 'minimal' conceptions of citizenship impose significant obligations and constraints on individual and group behaviour. I will then discuss why schools must play a role in educating children for citizenship (second section). It would be unrealistic to expect schools by themselves to develop the skills and virtues needed for democratic citizenship. People learn to be responsible citizens not only in schools, but also in the family, neighbourhood, churches, and manifold other groups and forums in civil society. Schools are not the only, or perhaps even the primary, forum for learning citizenship, but they are, I believe, indispensable. These other institutions supplement, but cannot replace, the provision of citizenship education in schools.

The rest of the chapter will then consider three inter-related areas of controversy: whether citizenship education requires common schooling (third section); whether promoting responsible citizenship requires promoting personal autonomy (fourth section); and whether promoting a shared civic identity requires teaching not only shared political values or principles but also promoting particular national or cultural identities (fifth section). These three issues are by no means exhaustive of the range of controversies that arise, but they suggest the centrality of education for citizenship to both political theory and educational philosophy.

The nature and importance of citizenship

There has been an explosion of interest in the concept of citizenship amongst political theorists. In 1978, it could be confidently stated that 'the concept of citizenship has gone out of fashion among political thinkers' (van Gunsteren 1978: 9). Fifteen years later, citizenship had become the 'buzz word' amongst thinkers on all points of the political spectrum (Heater 1990: 293).

Interest in citizenship has been sparked by a number of recent political events and trends throughout the world: increasing voter apathy and long-term welfare dependency in the United States, the resurgence of nationalist movements in Eastern Europe, the stresses created by an increasingly multicultural and multiracial population in Western Europe, the backlash against the welfare state in Thatcher's England, the failure of environmental policies that rely on voluntary citizen cooperation, and so on.

These events have made clear that the health and stability of a modern democracy depends, not only on the justice of its 'basic structure',[1] but also on the qualities and attitudes of its citizens: for example, their sense of identity, and how they view potentially competing forms of national, regional, ethnic or religious identities; their ability to tolerate and work together with others who are different from themselves; their desire to participate in the political process in order to promote the public good and hold political authorities accountable; their willingness to show self-restraint and exercise personal responsibility in their economic demands, and in personal choices that affect their health and the environment. Without citizens who possess these qualities, democracies become difficult to govern, even unstable.[2]

Many classical liberals believed that a liberal democracy could function effectively even in the absence of an especially virtuous citizenry, by creating checks and balances. Institutional and procedural devices such as the separation of powers, a bicameral legislature and federalism would all serve to block would-be oppressors. Even if each person pursued her own self-interest, without regard for the common good, one set of private interests would check another set of private interests. Kant, for example, thought that the problem of good government 'can be solved even for a race of devils' (quoted in Galston 1991: 215). However, it has become clear that procedural-institutional mechanisms to balance self-interest are not enough, and that some level of civic virtue and public-spiritedness is required.

Consider the many ways that public policy relies on responsible personal lifestyle decisions: the state will be unable to provide adequate health care if citizens do not act responsibly with respect to their own health, in terms of maintaining a healthy diet, exercising regularly, and limiting their consumption of liquor and tobacco; the state will be unable to meet the needs of children, the elderly or the disabled if citizens do not agree to share this responsibility by providing some care for their relatives; the state cannot protect the environment if citizens are unwilling to reduce, reuse and recycle in their own consumer choices; the ability of the government to regulate the economy can be undermined if citizens borrow immoderate amounts or demand excessive wage or salary increases; attempts to create a fairer society will flounder if citizens are chronically intolerant of difference and generally lacking in a sense of justice. Without cooperation and self-restraint in these areas, 'the ability of liberal societies to function successfully progressively diminishes' (Galston 1991: 220).[3]

In short, we need 'a fuller, richer and yet more subtle understanding and practice of citizenship', because 'what the state needs from the citizenry cannot be secured by coercion, but only co-operation and self-restraint in the exercise of private power' (Cairns and Williams 1985: 43). Yet there is growing fear that the civility and public-spiritedness of citizens of liberal democracies may be in serious decline (Walzer 1992: 90).[4]

Certain virtues are needed in virtually any political order, whether it is liberal and democratic or not. These would include general virtues, such as courage and law-abidingness, as well as economic virtues, such as the capacity to delay self-gratification or to adapt to economic and technological change.[5] But there are also certain virtues that are distinctive to a liberal democracy, relating to the basic principles of a liberal regime, and to the political role citizens occupy within it, and it is these I wish to focus on. I will consider four such virtues:

1 public-spiritedness, including the ability to evaluate the performance of those in office, and the willingness to engage in public discourse;
2 a sense of justice, and the capacity to discern and respect the rights of others, and to moderate one's own claims accordingly;
3 civility and tolerance;
4 a shared sense of solidarity or loyalty.

Many commentators argue that the fourth virtue is inapplicable to liberal democracies, or perhaps more accurately, is redundant, since it supervenes on the first three. On this view, whatever sense of shared loyalty is required in a liberal democracy simply involves loyalty to principles of tolerance, justice and democracy. Shared commitment to these basic political principles is a sufficient foundation for a shared political identity or loyalty. I think that is mistaken, and will return to this point in sections below.

For the moment, however, I want to focus on the first three, starting with 'public-spiritedness'. This includes the ability and willingness to engage in public discourse about matters of public policy, and to question authority. These are perhaps the most distinctive aspects of citizenship in a liberal democracy, since they are precisely what distinguish 'citizens' within a democracy from the 'subjects' of an authoritarian regime.

The need to question authority arises in part because citizens in a representative democracy elect representatives who govern in their name. Hence an important responsibility of citizens is to monitor those officials, and judge their conduct. The need to engage in public discourse arises from the fact that the decisions of government in a democracy should be made publicly, through free and open discussion. But the virtue of public discourse is not just the willingness to participate in politics, or to make one's views known. Rather, as William Galston notes, it

> includes the willingness to listen seriously to a range of views which, given the diversity of liberal societies, will include ideas the listener is bound to find strange and even obnoxious. The virtue of political discourse also includes the willingness to set forth one's own views intelligibly and candidly as the basis for a politics of persuasion rather than manipulation or coercion.
>
> (Galston 1991: 227)

Stephen Macedo calls this the virtue of 'public reasonableness'. Liberal citizens must give reasons for their political demands, not just state preferences or make threats. Moreover, these reasons must be 'public' reasons, in the sense that they are capable of persuading people of different faiths and nationalities. Hence it is not enough to invoke Scripture or tradition.[6] Liberal citizens must justify their political demands in terms that fellow citizens can understand and accept as consistent with their status as free and equal citizens. It requires a conscientious effort to distinguish those beliefs that are matters of private faith from those capable of public defence, and to see how issues look from the point of view of those with differing religious commitments and cultural backgrounds. As I discuss below, this is a stringent requirement that many religious groups find difficult to accept.

The virtue of public reasonableness is less relevant for citizens who do not wish to participate in political affairs, and there will always be a portion of the population who have little or no desire to be politically active. Some people will find their greatest joys and projects in other areas of life, including the family, or the arts, or religion. A liberal democracy must respect such diverse conceptions of the good life, and should not compel people to adopt a conception of the good life which privileges political participation as the source of meaning or satisfaction.[7] For these more or less apolitical people, the virtue of public reasonableness may be less important.

Some commentators would argue that most people in contemporary democracies will fall into this apolitical camp, that meaningful political participation is almost inevitably confined to elites. According to T. H. McLaughlin, this is one of the important points of division between 'minimal' and 'maximal' conceptions of citizenship. On the minimal view, citizenship for most people primarily involves passive respect for laws, not the active exercise of political rights. By contrast, maximal conceptions of democracy insist that a true democracy, or that political justice, must aim for more widespread participation (McLaughlin 1992a).

Justice clearly requires that everyone should have the opportunity to become active citizens, if they so choose, which means eliminating any economic or social barriers to the participation of disadvantaged groups, such as women, the poor, or racial and ethnic minorities. But whether we should encourage all individuals to choose to be active political participants is another matter. Whether active citizenship should be encouraged depends, I think, on the second virtue listed above – namely, a sense of justice. To have a sense of justice does not simply mean that we do not actively harm or exploit others. It also involves the duty to prevent injustice, by creating and upholding just institutions. So if there are serious injustices in our society which can only be rectified by political action, then citizens should recognise an obligation to protest against that injustice. So if our political institutions are no longer functioning, perhaps due to excessive levels of apathy, or to the abuse of power, then citizens have an obligation to protect these institutions from being undermined. To sit passively by while injustices are committed, or democratic institutions collapse, in the hope that others will step in, is to be a free rider. Everyone should do their fair share to create and uphold just institutions.

The extent of injustice, and the health of political institutions, will vary from society to society. In some times and places, though perhaps only in rare and fortunate circumstances, our natural duty of justice will not require us to participate actively. Where a society is basically well ordered, and its institutions healthy, then individuals should be free to follow their own conceptions of the good, even if these give little or no weight to political participation.

So there will be times and places where minimal citizenship is all that we can or should require. And for minimal citizens, the stringent demands of 'public reasonableness' will be less significant. But even here, the requirements of liberal citizenship are by no means trivial. The obligations of minimal citizenship are often described in purely negative terms, i.e. the obligation not to break the law, and not to harm others, or restrict their rights and liberties. Minimal citizenship, in short, is often seen as simply requiring non-interference with others.

But that ignores one of the most basic requirements of liberal citizenship, albeit one that is often neglected in theoretical discussions. This is the virtue of 'civility' or 'decency', and it is a virtue that even the most minimal citizen must learn, since it applies not only to political activity, but also – indeed, primarily – to our actions in everyday life, on the street, in neighbourhood shops, and in the diverse institutions and forums of civil society.

'Civility' refers to the way we treat non-intimates with whom we come into face-to-face contact. To understand civility, it is helpful to compare it with the related requirement of non-discrimination. The legal prohibition on discrimination initially only applied to government actions. Government laws and policies discriminating against people on the basis of race or gender have gradually been struck down in Western democracies, since they violate the basic liberal commitment to equality of opportunity. But it has become clear that whether individuals have genuinely equal opportunity depends not only on government actions, but also on the actions of institutions within civil society: corporations, schools, shops, landlords, and so on. If people are discriminated against by prejudiced shop-owners or real estate agents, they will be denied equal citizenship, even if the state itself does not discriminate. Hence legal requirements of non-discrimination have increasingly been applied to 'private' firms and associations.

This extension of non-discrimination from government to civil society is not just a shift in the scale of liberal norms, it also involves a radical extension in the obligations of liberal citizenship. For the obligation to treat people as equal citizens now applies to the most common everyday decisions of individuals. It is no longer permissible for businesses to refuse to hire black employees, or to serve black customers, or to segregate their black employees or customers. But not just that. The norms of non-discrimination entail that it is not permissible for businesses to ignore their black customers, or treat them rudely, although it is not always possible to enforce this in law. Businesses must in effect make blacks feel welcome, just as if they were whites. Blacks must, in short, be treated with *civility*. The same applies to the way citizens treat each other in schools or recreational associations, even in private clubs.

This sort of civility is the logical extension of non-discrimination, since it is needed to ensure that all citizens have the same opportunity to participate within civil society. But it now extends into the very hearts and minds of citizens. Liberal citizens must learn to interact in everyday settings on an equal basis with people for whom they might harbour prejudice.

The extent to which this requirement of civility can (or should) be legally enforced is limited. It is easier to compel businesses to be non-discriminatory in hiring than to compel them to treat black customers with civility. But the recent spread of laws and regulations against sexual and racial harassment, both in society generally and within schools and businesses, can be seen as an attempt to ensure a level of civility, since they include forms of offensive speech as well as physical intimidation, And while it is obviously impossible to compel civility between citizens in less formal settings – for example whether whites smile or scowl at an Asian family in the neighbourhood park – liberal citizenship nonetheless requires this sort of civility.

It is easy to trivialise this requirement of civility as being simply 'good manners'. Philip Rieff, for example, dismisses the insistence on civility as a superficial facade that simply hides a deeper indifference to the needs of others. As he puts it, 'We have long known what "equality" means in American culture: it means . . . a smile fixed to the face, demanding you return a smile' (quoted in Cuddihy 1978: 6). John Murray Cuddihy views civility as the imposition of a Protestant (and bourgeois) sense of 'good taste' on other religious groups. He argues that Catholics and Jews (and now Muslims) have had to abandon their conception of true faith, which required the public expression of contempt for other religions, to conform to this 'religion of civility'.

It is true that liberal societies have reinforced, and thereby partially conflated, the moral obligation of civility with an aesthetic conception of 'good manners'. For example, the expectation of civility is sometimes used to discourage the sort of forceful protest that may be needed for an oppressed group to be heard. For a disadvantaged group to 'make a scene' is often seen as 'in bad taste'. This sort of exaggerated emphasis on good manners can be used to promote servility. True civility does not mean smiling at others no matter how badly they treat you, as if oppressed groups should be nice to their oppressors. Rather, it means treating others as equals on the condition that they extend the same recognition to you. While there is some overlap between civility and a more general politeness, they are nonetheless distinct: civility involves upholding norms of equality within the public life of a society, including civil society, and thereby upholding essential liberal values.[8]

The need for citizenship education in schools

Even the most minimal conception of liberal citizenship, therefore, requires a significant range of civic virtues. But are schools the appropriate arena to teach these virtues, given that this would involve inculcating substantive (and controversial) moral beliefs? I believe the schools have an unavoidable role, in part because no other social institution can take their place.

To be sure, other institutions can play a supplementary role in promoting civic virtue. For example, theorists of the 'New Right' often praise the market as a school of virtue. Many Thatcher/Reagan reforms of the 1980s aimed to extend the scope of markets in people's lives – through freer trade, deregulation, tax cuts, the weakening of trade unions, and reducing welfare benefits – in part in order to teach people the virtues of initiative and self-reliance. Moreover, markets are said to encourage civility, since companies that refuse to hire black employees, or serve black customers, will be at a competitive disadvantage.

However, the limits of the market as a school of civic virtue are clear. Many market deregulations arguably made possible an era of unprecedented greed and economic irresponsibility, as evidenced by the savings-and-loan and junk bond scandals in America. Markets teach initiative, but not a sense of justice or social responsibility (Mulgan 1991: 39). And so long as a sizeable portion of the population harbours prejudices towards certain groups, then businesses will have an economic incentive to serve that market, by creating goods and services that exclude these groups.[9] In any event, the market cannot teach those civic virtues specific to political participation and dialogue, such as the virtue of public reasonableness.

Following Rousseau and J. S. Mill, many 'participatory democrats' assume that political participation itself will teach people responsibility and toleration. As Adrian Oldfield notes, they place their faith in the activity of participation

> as the means whereby individuals may become accustomed to perform the duties of citizenship. Political participation enlarges the minds of individuals, familiarises them with interests which lie beyond the immediacy of personal circumstance and environment, and encourages them to acknowledge that public concerns are the proper ones to which they should pay attention.
>
> (Oldfield 1990a: 184)

Unfortunately, this faith in the educative function of participation seems overly optimistic. Emphasizing participation does not yet explain how to ensure that citizens participate responsibly – namely, in a public-spirited, rather than self-interested or prejudiced, way (Mulgan 1991: 40–1). Empowered citizens may use their power irresponsibly by pushing for benefits and entitlements they cannot ultimately afford; or by voting themselves tax breaks and slashing assistance to the needy; or by 'seeking scapegoats in the indolence of the poor, the strangeness of ethnic minorities, or the insolence and irresponsibility of modern women' (Fierlbeck 1991: 592). Successful political participation requires the ability to create coalitions, which encourages a partial development of the virtues of justice and public reasonableness. No one can hope to succeed in political life if they make no effort to listen to or accommodate the needs and views of others. But in many cases, a winning coalition can be built while ignoring the claims of marginalised groups. Indeed, if a significant portion of the population is prejudiced, then ignoring or attacking such groups may be the best route to political success.

'Civil-society theorists' emphasise the necessity of civility and self-restraint to a healthy democracy, but deny that either the market or political participation is sufficient to teach these virtues. Instead, it is in the voluntary organisations of civil society – churches, families, unions, ethnic associations, cooperatives, environmental groups, neighbourhood associations, support groups, charities – that we learn the virtues of mutual obligation. As Michael Walzer puts it, 'The civility that makes democratic politics possible can only be learned in the associational networks' of civil society (Walzer 1992: 104).

Because these groups are voluntary, failure to live up to the responsibilities that come with them is usually met simply with disapproval, rather than legal punishment. Yet because the disapproval comes from family, friends, colleagues or comrades, it is in many ways a more powerful incentive to act responsibly than punishment by an impersonal state. It is here that 'human character, competence, and capacity for citizenship are formed', for it is here that we internalise the idea of personal responsibility and mutual obligation, and learn the voluntary self-restraint that is essential to truly responsible citizenship.

The claim that civil society is the 'seedbed of civic virtue' (Glendon 1991: 109) is essentially an empirical claim, for which there is little hard evidence one way or the other.[10] It is an old and venerable view, but it is not obviously true. It may be in the neighbourhood that we learn to be good neighbours, but neighbourhood associations also teach people to operate on the 'NIMBY' (not in my backyard) principle when it comes to the location of group homes or public works. Similarly, the family is often 'a school of despotism' that teaches male dominance over women (Okin 1992: 65); churches often teach deference to authority and intolerance of other faiths; ethnic groups often teach prejudice against other races, and so on.

Walzer recognises that most people are 'trapped in one or another subordinate relationship, where the "civility" they learned was deferential rather than independent and active'. In these circumstances, he says, we have to 'reconstruct' the associational network 'under new conditions of freedom and equality'. Similarly, when the activities of some associations 'are narrowly conceived, partial and particularist', then 'they need political correction'. Walzer calls his view 'critical associationalism' to signify that the associations of civil society may need to be reformed in the light of principles of citizenship (Walzer 1992: 106–7).

But this may go too far in the other direction. Rather than supporting voluntary associations, this approach may unintentionally license wholesale intervention in them. Governments must of course intervene to protect the rights of people inside and outside the group, if these rights are threatened. But do we want governments to reconstruct churches, for example, to make them more internally democratic, or to make sure that their members learn to be critical rather than deferential? And, in any event, wouldn't reconstructing churches, families or unions to make them more internally democratic start to undermine their essentially uncoerced and voluntary character, which is what supposedly made them the seedbeds of civic virtue?

Indeed, it would be unreasonable to expect churches to teach the virtue of public reasonableness. Public reasonableness is essential in political debate, but is unnecessary and sometimes undesirable in the private sphere. It would be absurd to ask church-goers to abstain from appealing to Scripture in deciding how to run their church.

Civil-society theorists demand too much of voluntary associations in expecting them to be the main school for, or a small-scale replica of, democratic citizenship. While these associations may teach civic virtue, that is not their *raison d'être*. The reason why people join churches, families or ethnic organisations is not to learn civic virtue. It is, rather, to honour certain values, and enjoy certain human goods, and these motives may have little to do with the promotion of citizenship. To expect parents or priests to organise the internal life of their groups so as maximally to promote citizenship is to ignore why these groups exist in the first place. (Some associations, like the Boy Scouts, are designed to promote citizenship, but they are the exception not the rule.)

It seems, then, that we cannot rely on the market, the family or the associations of civil society to teach civic virtue. People will not automatically learn to engage in public discourse, or to question authority, in any of these spheres, since these spheres are often held together by private discourse and respect for authority.

This suggests that schools must teach children how to engage in the kind of critical reasoning and moral perspective that defines public reasonableness. And indeed, as I noted earlier, promoting these sorts of virtues was one of the fundamental justifications for mandatory education. But using schools to promote civic virtue raises many controversies, of which I will briefly examine three: the role of separate schools, the teaching of autonomy, and the relationship between civic and cultural identities.

Citizenship and separate schools

The need for citizenship education raises questions about the role of separate schools in a liberal democracy, particularly religious schools. Various religious groups have sought to establish separate schools, partly in order to teach their religious doctrine, but also to reduce the exposure of their children to the members of other religious groups. Most liberal states have accepted this demand, as a way of respecting parental rights and religious freedom, but have insisted that such schools teach a core curriculum, including citizenship education.

It is not clear, however, that this compromise position – separate schools with a common curriculum – provides the appropriate sort of citizenship education. Such schools are obviously capable of teaching basic facts about government. But as I noted earlier, citizenship education is not simply a matter of knowledge of political institutions and constitutional principles. It is also a matter of how we think about and behave towards others, particularly those who differ from us in their race, religion, class, and so on. Liberal citizenship requires cultivating the habit of civility, and the capacity for public reasonableness, in our interaction with others. Indeed, it is precisely these habits and capacities that most need to be learned in schools, for they are unlikely to be learned in smaller groups or associations, like the family, neighbourhood or church, which tend to be homogeneous in their ethnocultural backgrounds and religious beliefs.

It is not clear that separate religious schools can provide an adequate education in either civility or public reasonableness. For these virtues are not only

88

or even primarily learned through the explicit curriculum. For example, common schools teach civility not just by telling students to be nice, but also by insisting that students sit beside students of different races and religions, cooperating with them on school projects or sports teams (Gutmann 1987: 53).

Similarly, common schools teach public reasonableness not only by telling students that there are a plurality of religious views in the world, and that reasonable people disagree on the merits of these views. They also create the social circumstances whereby students can see the reasonableness of these disagreements. It is not enough simply to tell students that the majority of the people in the world do not share their religion. So long as one is surrounded by people who share one's faith, one may still succumb to the temptation to think that everyone who rejects one's religion is somehow illogical or depraved. To learn public reasonableness, students must come to know and understand people who are reasonable and decent and humane, but who do not share their religion. Only in this way can students learn how personal faith differs from public reasonableness, and where to draw that line. This sort of learning requires the presence within a classroom of people with varying ethnocultural and religious backgrounds (Callan 1995).

In these ways, religious schools are limited in their capacity to provide an adequate citizenship education. Of course, it is important not to idealise common schools, which suffer their own deficiencies. For example, while common schools in North America typically contain a diversity of religions, they are more segregated than religious schools by class, race and academic talent (Gutmann 1987: 115–17). Yet divisions of class and race are equally important obstacles to civility and public reasonableness as are religious divisions. Indeed, one could argue that the greatest failure of liberal citizenship in the United States is not the division between religious groups, but the increasing desire of middle-class whites to distance themselves (both physically and emotionally) from inner-city blacks, or the poor more generally. In terms of teaching students how to have a public dialogue with the disadvantaged, religious schools may well do better than a common school in the suburbs full of well-off (but religiously diverse) whites.

Moreover, it is important to distinguish temporary or transitional separate schooling from permanent separation. The requirements of liberal citizenship suggest that common schooling is necessary – or at least highly desirable – at some point in the educational process. But there is no reason why the entire process should be integrated. Indeed, there are good reasons for thinking that some children may do best by having their early schooling in separate schools, alongside others who share their background, before moving into a common school later in the process. For example, this may be true of historically disadvantaged groups (girls, blacks) who can best develop their self-esteem in an environment free of prejudice (McLaughlin 1992b: 122). More generally, schooling within a particular ethnocultural or religious setting may provide virtues unavailable within the common schools. If common schools do a better job promoting a shared sense of justice, separate schools may do better at providing children with a clear sense of what it is to have a stable sense of the good. They may provide a better environment for developing the capacity for in-depth engagement with a particular cultural tradition, and for loyalty and commitment to particular projects and relationships (McLaughlin 1992b: 123–4; Callan 1995: 22–3). There is more than one starting point from which children can learn liberal citizenship.[11]

The requirement of common schools – even if limited to the later stages of children's education – will be rejected by some religious groups, who insist on keeping their children separate and apart from the rest of society. Should a liberal state impose integrated common schools, in the name of citizenship education? In answering this, it is worth distinguishing two kinds of religious groups that might seek exemption from common schooling. Some groups, like the Amish, voluntarily isolate themselves from the larger society, and avoid participating in either politics or the mainstream institutions of civil society. They do not vote, or hire employees, or attempt to influence public policy (except where a proposed policy would jeopardise their isolation), and seek only to be left alone. Since they do not participate in either politics or civil society, it is less urgent that they learn the virtues of civility and public reasonableness. Jeff Spinner calls the Amish 'partial citizens', and he argues that because they have relinquished the right to participate, they can also be absolved of the responsibilities that accompany that right, including the responsibility to learn and practise civility and public reasonableness (Spinner 1994: 98). Hence he supports their right to withdraw their children from school at the age of fourteen, before they would have to learn about the larger society, or interact with non-Amish children. Assuming that such groups are small, and sincerely committed to their self-imposed isolation, they pose no threat to the practice of liberal citizenship in society generally. Such groups should not be encouraged, since they accept no responsibility to work together with other citizens to solve the country's injustices and problems. They are free riders, in a sense, benefiting from a stable liberal order that they do nothing to help maintain.[12] But a liberal state can afford a few such free riders.[13]

By contrast, other religious groups seeking exemption from integrated schools are active participants in both civil society and politics, and seek to influence public policy generally. This would include fundamentalist Christians in the United States, or Muslims in Britain. In these cases, one could argue that, having chosen to exercise their rights as full citizens, they must accept the sort of education needed to promote responsible citizenship, including the obligation to attend common schools at some point in the educational process.

Citizenship and personal autonomy

A related question is whether schools, be they separate or common, should promote the capacity for individual autonomy. 'Autonomy' means different things to different people. I am using the term to refer to the capacity to reflect rationally on, and potentially revise, our conceptions of the good life. An autonomous person is capable of reflecting on her current ends, and assessing whether they are worthy of her continued allegiance. Autonomy, on this view, is consistent with people endorsing their inherited way of life, if they reflectively prefer it to the alternatives. But it is inconsistent with an uncritical attitude towards inherited traditions, or with an unquestioning acceptance of the pronouncements of parents, priests or community leaders regarding the worth of different ways of life.[14]

I did not include autonomy in my list of the basic virtues of liberal citizenship in the first section, and I do not think that autonomy, in and of itself, is necessary for the practice of democratic citizenship. However, there are good reasons to think that autonomy will be indirectly promoted by citizenship education, since it is closely associated, both conceptually and developmentally, to various civic virtues.

For example, responsible citizenship involves the willingness to hold political authorities accountable. Hence schools should teach children to be sceptical of the political authorities who govern in our name, and to be cognisant of the dangers of the abuse of power. As Amy Gutmann puts it, children at school 'must learn not just to behave in accordance with authority but to think critically about authority if they are to live up to the democratic ideal of sharing political sovereignty as citizens'. People who 'are ruled only by habit and authority . . . are incapable of constituting a society of sovereign citizens' (Gutmann 1987: 51).

This democratic virtue is exercised in public life, and promoting it does not entail or require encouraging children to question parental or religious authority in private life. As Galston puts it, the need to teach children how to evaluate political leaders 'does not warrant the conclusion that the state must (or may) structure public education to foster in children sceptical reflection on ways of life inherited from parents or local communities' (Galston 1991: 253). But there will likely be some spillover effect. Indeed, there is strong evidence that adolescents' attitudes towards authority tend 'to be uniform across all the authority figures they encounter', so that encouraging scepticism of political authority will likely encourage questioning of familial or religious authority (Emler and Reicher 1987). Galston himself admits that it is not easy for schools to promote a child's willingness to question political authority without undermining her 'unswerving belief in the correctness' of her parents' way of life.

Citizenship education not only involves promoting a certain sort of critical attitude towards authority, it also involves developing habits of civility and the capacity for public reasonableness. Both of these indirectly promote autonomy, since they encourage children to interact with the members of other groups, to understand the reasonableness of other ways of life, and to distance themselves from their own cultural traditions.

Consider civility. In the first section, I emphasised that norms of civility and non-discrimination protect ethnic and religious groups from prejudice and discrimination; groups wishing to maintain their group identity and cultural practices will face fewer legal barriers or social stigmas. But civility also increases the interaction between the members of different groups, and hence the likelihood that individuals will learn and adopt new ways of life. Historically, cultural boundaries have often been maintained by the visible expression of prejudice towards outsiders; people stayed within their group because they were not welcome elsewhere. The spread of civility in social institutions (including schools) means that these boundaries tend to break down. Members of one group are more likely to cooperate with and befriend children of other groups, and so learn about other ways of life, and possibly adopt new identities and practices.

Simply by teaching and practising civility, schools make this sort of mingling and fraternising between the members of different groups more likely, and hence make the breakdown of cultural barriers more likely. In some cases, adopting other ways of life may be done in an unreflective way, by simply imitating one's peers, and hence does not count as the exercise of autonomy. But schools also promote a more reflective process, by teaching the virtue of public reasonableness. Because reasonable people disagree about the merits of different religions and conceptions of the good life, children must learn to distinguish reasons based on private faith from reasons that can be publicly accepted in a diverse society. To develop this capacity, children must not only learn how to distance themselves from beliefs that are taken for granted in their private life, but they must also learn to put themselves in other people's shoes, in order to see what sorts of reasons might be acceptable to people from other backgrounds. The virtue of public reasonableness does not require that children come to admire or cherish other ways of life. But it does require that children be exposed to competing ways of life, and be encouraged to view them as the expressions of coherent conceptions of value which have been sincerely affirmed by other reasonable people. Learning to view other ways of life in this way does not inevitably lead to the questioning of one's own way of life, but it surely makes it more likely, since it requires a sort of broad-mindedness that is hard to combine with an unreflective deference to traditional practices or authorities.

For all these reasons, education for democratic citizenship will almost unavoidably, albeit indirectly, promote autonomy. Through citizenship education, children both become aware of alternative ways of life and are given the intellectual skills needed to understand and appreciate them. As Gutmann puts it, citizenship education involves 'equipping children with the intellectual skills necessary to evaluate ways of life different from that of their parents', because 'many if not all of the capacities necessary for choice among good lives are also necessary for choice among good societies' (Gutmann 1987:

30, 40). Democratic citizenship and personal autonomy, while distinct, are interconnected at various levels.

As a result, those groups that rely heavily on an uncritical acceptance of tradition and authority, while not strictly ruled out, are bound to be discouraged by the critical and tolerant attitudes that civic education encourages (Macedo 1990: 53–4). This indeed is why religious groups often seek to establish separate schools, even when they have to teach a common curriculum. They fear that if their children attend common schools, they will be more likely to question traditional practices, even if the school curriculum does not directly promote this sort of autonomous attitude. To preserve an uncritical deference to communal traditions, children can only be exposed to a minimal level of citizenship education, one that teaches facts about government, but not civility, public reasonableness, or critical attitudes to political authority.

I should note two qualifications here. First, citizenship education historically has often discouraged, rather than encouraged, autonomy. The aim of citizenship education, in the past, was to promote an unreflective patriotism, one that glorifies the past history and current political system of the country, and which vilifies opponents of that political system, whether they are internal dissidents or external enemies (Nelson 1980). This sort of civic education, needless to say, promoted passivity and deference rather than a critical attitude towards political authority or a broad-mindedness towards cultural differences. Today, however, educational theorists and policy-makers increasingly reject this model of civic education, in favour of one that promotes more active and reflective forms of citizenship.[15] The earlier form of civic education can still be found, of course, and some people continue to defend it (see AASA 1987: 26; Galston 1991: 244). However, if our aim is to produce self-governing democratic citizens, rather than passive subjects of an authoritarian government a different sort of civic education is required, one much more likely to promote autonomy.

Second, I have suggested that the promotion of personal autonomy should be seen as the indirect consequence of civic education, not as its direct or explicit purpose. I do not mean to deny, however, that there might be other reasons for directly promoting personal autonomy. Indeed, a strong case could be made that promoting autonomy is an integral part of an adequate education for modern life. While autonomy may not be needed to fulfil the social role of citizen, it may be needed if children are to enjoy life to the greatest extent possible. If so, then children may have a right to an autonomy-promoting education, even where their parents resist it. To pursue this question, however, would raise issues that go far beyond this chapter. While I am myself attracted to the view that schools should promote autonomy, it would be misleading to defend this as a precondition of democratic citizenship. Autonomy, I think, is valuable not because it makes people better citizens, but because it enables people to lead more fulfilling lives, quite independently of their role as citizens.[16]

Citizenship and national identity

Finally, I want briefly to address the issue of identity. As I noted earlier, many commentators argue that social unity in a liberal democracy rests not on a shared identity but, rather, on shared allegiance to political principles. As Rawls puts it, 'although a well-ordered society is divided and pluralistic . . . public agreement on questions of political and social justice supports ties of civic friendship and secures the bonds of association' (Rawls 1980: 540; cf. Strike 1994: 8). According to this view, by teaching certain common political principles – like principles of justice, tolerance and civility – citizenship education provides the foundation for national unity as well.

I think this is a mistake. Shared political principles obviously are helpful to maintain social unity; indeed, deep conflict over basic principles can lead to civil war. But shared principles are not sufficient. Consider the case of Canada. As a result of the rapid liberalisation of Quebecois society since the 1960s, there has been a pronounced convergence of political principles between English-speaking and French-speaking Canadians over the last 30 years, so that it would now be 'difficult to identify consistent differences in attitudes on issues such as moral values, prestige ranking of professions, role of the government, workers' rights, aboriginal rights, equality between the sexes and races, and conception of authority' (Dion 1991: 301). If the 'shared principles' approach were correct, we should have witnessed a decline in support for Quebec secession over this period, yet nationalist sentiment has in fact grown consistently.

The fact that anglophones and francophones in Canada share the same principles of justice is not a strong reason to remain together, since the Quebecois rightly assume that their own national state could respect the same principles. Deciding to secede would not require them to abandon their political principles, since they could implement the same principles in their own state.

The fact that increased Quebec nationalism has gone hand in hand with increased convergence on political principles is often seen as a 'paradox'. But it reflects a very general trend. Consider the Flemish in Belgium, or the Basques in Spain. Throughout the West, an increasing convergence on liberal values has gone hand in hand with continued, even increasing, demands for self-government by ethnonational minorities.

This suggests that shared political principles are not sufficient for social unity. The fact that two groups share the same principles of justice does not necessarily give them a strong reason to remain together, rather than splitting into two separate countries.[17] If two groups want to live together under a single state, then sharing political principles makes it easier to do so. But shared political principles is not, in and of itself, a reason why two groups should want to live together.

Social unity, then, requires not only shared principles, but also a sense of shared membership. Citizens must have a sense of belonging to the same community, and a shared desire to continue to live together. Social unity, in short, requires that citizens identify their fellow citizens as one of 'us'. This sense of shared identity helps sustain the relationships of trust and solidarity needed for citizens to accept the results of democratic decisions, and the obligations of liberal justice (Miller 1995).

What underlies this shared national identity? In non-liberal states, shared identity is typically based on a common ethnic descent, religious faith, or conception of the good. However, these cannot provide the basis for social unity in a liberal state, since none of them is shared in modern pluralist states.

What then makes citizens in a liberal state feel that they belong together, that they are members of the same nation? The answer typically involves a sense of shared history, and a common language. Citizens share a sense of belonging to a particular historical society because they share a language and history; they participate in common social and political institutions based on this shared language and which manifest and perpetuate this shared history; and they see their life-choices as bound up with the survival of this society and its institutions into the indefinite future. Citizens can share a national identity in this sense, and yet share very little in terms of ethnicity, religion, or conceptions of the good.[18]

The need for this sort of common national identity raises many questions for citizenship education. I will focus on two, regarding the teaching of languages and the teaching of history, both of which are fundamental to the construction of a national identity.

First, what should be the language of the school system? This is a remarkably neglected question in liberal theory.[19] The need for a common national identity suggests that states should inculcate a common language. And indeed the definition, standardisation and teaching of an official language has been one of the first tasks of 'nation-building' throughout the world (Gellner 1983).

But whether imposing a common language promotes social unity depends on the circumstances. The historical evidence suggests that voluntary immigrant groups are willing to adopt the language of the mainstream society. They have already uprooted themselves from their original homeland, and know that the success of their decision to emigrate depends on some measure of integration into their host society. Insofar as they demand education in their mother-tongue, it is in addition to, or as a means of facilitating, learning the common language, not as a substitute. Much of the opposition to bilingual education for immigrant groups is, I think, misguided, but liberal states have a legitimate interest in ensuring that these programmes do ultimately lead to competence in the language of the mainstream society.

The case of territorially concentrated language groups, whose homeland has been incorporated into larger states – like the Quebecois, Puerto Ricans, or Flemish, or indigenous peoples around the world – is very different. They have strongly – even violently – resisted the attempt to have the majority language imposed on them. This reflects the fact that they typically view themselves as forming their own 'nation' or 'people', and so have their own sense of national identity, with their own language, history and encompassing social institutions.

States with such groups are not nation states, but multi-nation states, and attempts to impose a single national identity on these 'national minorities' are likely to undermine rather than promote social unity. Multi-nation states are most stable if they are seen as a federation of peoples, each with their own historic territories, language rights and powers of self-government.[20]

In multi-nation states, then, citizenship education typically has a dual function: it promotes a national identity within each constituent national group, defined by a common language and history, but it also seeks to promote some sort of transnational identity that can bind together the various national groups within the state. Unfortunately, recent developments in multi-nation states – for example, the breakdown of Yugoslavia and Czechoslovakia, the constitutional crises in Belgium and Canada – suggest that it is very difficult to construct and maintain this transnational identity. And indeed, schools have little idea how to go about promoting this identity.

This points to an important gap in political and educational theory. Most liberal accounts of civic identity argue that shared political principles are the basis of civic identity. Implicitly, however, they typically assume that citizens share not only principles but also a common language and sense of membership in a national community. The problem is that neither the explicit emphasis on principles, nor the implicit emphasis on shared language and history, can explain social unity in multi-nation states. If schools are to fulfil their responsibilities regarding citizenship education, we need an entirely new account of the basis of shared identity in multi-nation states.

Insofar as a common national identity rests on identifying with a shared history, as well as a common language, this raises important questions about the teaching of history. One way – a particularly effective way – to promote identification with a group's history is deliberately to misrepresent that history. As William Galston puts it, with reference to the United States, 'rigorous historical research will almost certainly vindicate complex "revisionist" accounts of key figures in American history. Civic education, however, requires a nobler, moralising history: a pantheon of heroes who confer legitimacy on central institutions and are worthy of emulation' (Galston 1991: 244). Similarly, Andrew Oldenquist argues that information about the American nation and government

> should be taught so as to provide grounds for developing pride and affection . . . If instead we start nine-year-olds with a litany of evils and injustices, they will be likely to learn cynicism and alienation. A teacher may respond, 'But I teach about problems and injustices because I want to make my country better: if I did not have concern and affection for it I would not care about reforming it.' Precisely.

96

The teacher did not acquire affection for our country by being told that we exterminated Indians, lynched Blacks, and slaughtered Vietnamese. The teacher's concern and affection survived this knowledge because of prior training and experience, and the pupils, like the teacher, need to acquire a basis for good citizenship before they are plunged into what is ugly.

(AASA: 1987: 26)

This raises a number of troubling questions about citizenship education. For one thing, this way of promoting a national identity may undermine another goal of citizenship education: the development of the capacity for independent and critical thought about society and its problems. Moreover, the proper development of civic virtue may require an honest appreciation of how those virtues were lacking in our history. It seems unlikely that children can learn the true meaning of civility and public reasonableness when historical figures who were in fact insensitive to great injustices are held up as exemplars of civic virtue (Callan 1993).

Also, it seems clear that the sanitised version of history that Galston and Oldenquist defend can itself be a cause of disunity. An account of history that focuses on the 'pantheon of heroes', while ignoring the historical mistreatment of women, blacks, Indians, Jews and others, is essentially an account of the history of upper-class white men. And it is precisely this view of history which many minorities find so offensive. They are insulted by the way their struggles are rendered invisible in school books.

For these reasons schools should, I think, teach history truthfully. But that doesn't mean that history should not play a special role in the curriculum. There is, I think, a legitimate role for schools to promote an emotional identification with our history. Students should view the nation's history as their history, and hence take pride in its accomplishments, as well as shame in its injustices. This sense of identification with the nation's history is one of the few means available to maintain social unity in a pluralistic state, and may be needed if citizens are to embrace their responsibilities for upholding just institutions and rectifying historical injustices.[21]

This shows, yet again, that citizenship education is not simply a matter of teaching the basic facts about governmental institutions or constitutional principles. It is also a matter of inculcating particular habits, virtues and identities.

Notes

1 Rawls says that the 'basic structure' of society is the primary subject of a theory of justice (1993: 257–89).
2 This may account for the recent interest in citizenship promotion amongst governments (for example Britain's Commission on Citizenship, *Encouraging Citizenship* 1990, Senate of Australia, *Active Citizenship Revisited* 1991, Senate of Canada, *Canadian Citizenship: Sharing the Responsibility* 1993).

3 Hence recent theories of citizenship emphasise that citizenship requires a balance of rights and responsibilities. For a survey of recent work on citizenship theory, which I am drawing on in this section, see Kymlicka and Norman (1994). For a useful collection of recent articles, see Beiner (1995). For a more historical survey of citizenship theory, see Walzer (1989), and the readings collected in Clarke (1994).

4 According to a recent survey, only 12 per cent of American teenagers said voting was important to being a good citizen. Moreover, this apathy is not just a function of youth: comparisons with similar surveys from the previous fifty years suggest that 'the current cohort knows less, cares less, votes less, and is less critical of its leaders and institutions than young people have been at any time over the past five decades' (Glendon 1991: 129). The evidence from Great Britain is similar (Heater 1990: 215).

5 For a helpful discussion and typology, see Galston (1991: 221–4).

6 See also Audi (1989) and Strike (1994).

7 This is why liberals cannot endorse a strong version of 'civic republicanism'. In one sense, civic republicanism refers to any view that highlights the importance of civic virtues, and the extent to which the functioning of a democracy requires certain virtues and identities amongst its citizens. In this sense, as I have argued, liberals must be republicans. But in another stronger sense, civic republicanism refers to the view that the best life – the most truly human life – is one that privileges political participation over other spheres of human endeavour. This sort of position is defended by Oldfield (1990b), Beiner (1992), Pocock (1992) and Skinner (1992), amongst others. However, it is inconsistent with liberalism's commitment to pluralism, and in any event is implausible as general account of the good life for all persons. See Kymlicka and Norman (1994: 361–2).

8 My discussion here draws extensively on Jeff Spinner's account of civility (1994: ch. 3). It also draws on Patricia White's (1992) account of civility, or what she calls 'decency', although I disagree in part with her emphasis. She seems primarily concerned with improving the overall level of 'decency' in society, rather than with eliminating glaring instances of incivility aimed at identifiable groups. For example, she compares the smiling and cooperative waiters in a Canadian café with the surly and uncooperative waiters in a Polish café (1992: 208), and argues that we should educate children to be friendly with strangers rather than surly. While I agree that it is a good thing for people to display this sort of decency, and that a minimal level of it is a precondition of a functioning democracy, I do not think this is the fundamental problem for citizenship education. From my point of view, waiters who are only minimally cheerful to all their customers are morally preferable to waiters who are generally very cheerful but who are surly to black customers. The latter may display more decency overall, but their behaviour towards an identifiable group threaten the most basic norms of liberal citizenship. However, I agree with White that it is important to be sensitive to the cultural variations in norms of civility (White 1992: 215); Iris Young makes a similar point about cultural variations in norms of public reasonableness (Young 1993).

9 For example, real-estate agents have an economic incentive to maintain segregated housing. In any event, New Right reforms arguably violated the requirements of liberal justice, since cutting welfare benefits, far from getting the disadvantaged back on their feet, has expanded the underclass. Class inequalities have been exacerbated, and the working poor and unemployed have been effectively disenfranchised, unable to participate in the social and political life of the country (Fierlbeck 1991: 579). So even if the market taught civic virtue,

laissez-faire capitalism violates the principle that all members of society have an equal opportunity to be active citizens.

10 See Putnam (1993) for a ground-breaking (and highly disputed) effort to establish the link between government functioning and the number and vitality of civic associations.

11 For more detailed explorations of this theme, see Callan (1995) and McLaughlin (1992b).

12 I am here disagreeing with those who defend the exemption for the Amish by arguing that their separate schools provide adequate citizenship education. This was the view of the American Supreme Court, which said that the Amish education system prepared Amish children to be good citizens, since they became productive and peaceful members of the Amish community (Wisconin v Yoder 406 US 205 (1972)). However, as I noted earlier, liberal citizenship requires more than being law-abiding and economically self-sufficient. For a critique of Yoder's account of civic responsibilities, see Arneson and Shapiro (1996).

13 As Spinner notes, there are unlikely to be many such groups, since the price of 'partial citizenship' is to cut oneself off from the opportunities and resources of the mainstream society (Spinner 1994: ch. 5).

14 I mean to distinguish this account of autonomy from two other interpretations. On one (Kantian) view, the exercise of choice is intrinsically valuable, since it is the most distinctly human attribute. On another (Millian) view, the exercise of choice is valuable insofar as it leads to greater 'individuality' – that is, insofar as it leads individuals to reject traditional ways of life, and construct their own unique way of life. People who reject these views may nonetheless accept the more modest idea that informed choice is valuable because our current beliefs about the good may be mistaken, and so it is important for people to be able to assess the value of alternative ways of life. On this, see Kymlicka (1989: ch. 2).

15 We can mark this shift by comparing two accounts of the relationship between civic education and moral reasoning. Writing in 1980, Jack Nelson objected that contemporary accounts of civic education promoted passive deference, and so conflicted with the sort of autonomy he felt was required by true moral agents. By 1991, however, William Galston was arguing that contemporary accounts of civic education excessively promote critical reflectiveness, and so undermined the sort of moral identity and moral commitment underlying many religious groups.

16 I am skipping lightly over a very deep division within liberal political philosophy. There is an important debate between 'political' or 'pragmatic' liberals and 'comprehensive' or 'ethical' liberals over the role of autonomy within liberal theory. Political liberals, like John Rawls and Charles Larmore, argue that because many groups within society do not value autonomy, liberals must look for a way of justifying liberal institutions which does not appeal to such a 'sectarian' value (Larmore 1987; Rawls 1993). Comprehensive liberals, like Joseph Raz, argue that liberal institutions can only be defended by appealing to the value of autonomy (Raz 1986). I discuss this debate, and defend the comprehensive liberal option, in Kymlicka (1995: ch. 8). See also Callan (1996), who argues that the distinction between political and comprehensive liberalism cannot be sustained in the educational context. However, for a critique of the emphasis on autonomy, and a defence of Muslim demands for a separate school system that restricts the development of autonomy, see Halstead (1990, 1991).

17 For a more detailed development of this argument, see Norman (1995). For a related critique of the idea that shared principles underlie social unity, see Paris (1991).

18 This is a thumbnail sketch of the nature of national identity in a liberal state, and its role in promoting political stability and relationships of trust and solidarity. For accounts of liberal nationalism, see Tamir (1993), Spinner (1994: ch. 7), Kymlicka (1995) and Miller (1995).

19 As Brian Weinstein put it, political theorists have had a lot to say about 'the language of politics' – that is, the symbols, metaphors and rhetorical devices of political discourse – but have had virtually nothing to say about 'the politics of language' – that is, the decisions about which languages to use in political, legal and educational forums (Weinstein 1983: 7–13).

20 For evidence of this, see Hannum (1990) and Gurr (1993).

21 For a sensitive exploration of this issue, see Callan (1993).

References

American Association of School Administrators (1987) *Citizenship: Goal of Education*, Arlington: AASA Publications.

Arneson, R. J. and Shapiro, I. (1996) 'Democratic autonomy and religious freedom', in I. Shapiro and R. Hardin (eds) *Political Order* (Nomos Series 38), New York: New York University Press.

Audi, R. (1989) 'The separation of church and state and the obligations of citizenship', *Philosophy & Public Affairs* 18(3): 259–96.

Beiner, R. (1992) 'Citizenship', in *What's the Matter with Liberalism?* Berkeley: University of California Press.

—— (ed.) (1995) *Theorising Citizenship*, Albany: State University of New York Press.

Cairns, A. and Williams, C. (eds) (1985) *Constitutionalism. Citizenship and Society in Canada*, Toronto: University of Toronto Press.

Callan, E. (1993) 'Beyond sentimental civic education', *American Journal of Education* 102: 190–221.

—— (1995) 'Common schools for common education', *Canadian Journal of Education* 20: 251–71.

—— (1996) 'Political liberalism and political education', *Review of Politics* 58: 5–33.

Clarke, P. B. (ed.) (1994) *Citizenship*, London: Pluto Press.

Cuddihy, J. M. (1978) *No Offence: Civil Religion and Protestant Taste*, New York: Seabury Press.

Dion, S. (1991) 'Le nationalisme dans la convergence culturelle', in R. Hudon and R. Pelletier (eds) *L'Engagement Intellectuel: Melanges en l'honneur de Leon Dion*, Sainte-Foy: Les Presses de l'Université Laval.

Emler, N. and Reicher, S. (1987) 'Orientations to institutional authority in adolescents', *Journal of Moral Education* 16(2): 108–16.

Fierlbeck, K. (1991) 'Redefining responsibilities: the politics of citizenship in the United Kingdom', *Canadian Journal of Political Science* 24(3): 575–83.

Galston, W. (1991) *Liberal Purposes: Goods, Virtues, and Duties in the Liberal State*, Cambridge: Cambridge University Press.

Gellner, E. (1983) *Nations and Nationalism*, Oxford: Blackwell.

Glendon, M. A. (1991) *Rights Take: The Impoverishment of Political Discourse*, New York: Free Press.

Gurr, T. (1993) *Minorities at Risk: A Global View of Ethnopolitical Conflict*, Washington: Institute of Peace Press.

Gutmann, A. (1987) *Democratic Education*, Princeton, NJ: Princeton University Press.

Halstead, J. M. (1990) 'Muslim schools and the ideal of autonomy', *Ethics in Education* 9(4): 4–6.

—— (1991) 'Radical feminism, Islam and the single-sex school debate', *Gender and Education* 3(1): 263–78.

Hannum, H. (1990) *Autonomy, Sovereignty, and Self-Determination: The Adjudication of Conflicting Rights*, Philadelphia: University of Pennsylvania Press.

Heater, D. (1990) *Citizenship: The Civic Ideal in World History Politics and Education*, London: Longman.

Kymlicka, W. (1989) *Liberalism, Community and Culture*, Oxford: Oxford University Press.

—— (1995) *Multicultural Citizenship: A Liberal Theory of Minority Rights*, Oxford: Oxford University Press.

Kymlicka, W. and Norman, W. (1994) 'Return of the citizen: a survey of recent work on citizenship theory', *Ethics* 104(2): 352–81. (Reprinted in Beiner 1995.)

Larmore, C. (1987) *Patterns of Moral Complexity*, Cambridge: Cambridge University Press.

Macedo, S. (1990) *Liberal Virtues: Citizenship, Virtue and Community*, Oxford: Oxford University Press.

McLaughlin, T. H. (1992a) 'Citizenship, diversity and education', *Journal of Moral Education* 21(3): 235–50.

—— (1992b) 'The ethics of separate schools', in M. Leicester and M. J. Taylor (eds) *Ethics, Ethnicity and Education*, London: Kogan Page.

Miller, D. (1995) *On Nationality*, Oxford: Oxford University Press.

Mulgan, G. (1991) 'Citizens and responsibilities', in G. Andrews (ed.) *Citizenship*, London: Lawrence and Wishart.

Nelson, J. (1980) 'The uncomfortable relationship between moral education and citizenship instruction', in R. Wilson and G. Schochet (eds) *Moral Development and Politics*, New York: Praeger.

Norman, W. (1995) 'The ideology of shared values', in J. Carens (ed.) *Is Quebec Nationalism Just?* Montreal: McGill-Queen's University Press.

Okin, S. (1992) 'Women, equality and citizenship', *Queen's Quarterly* 99(1): 56–71.

Oldfield, A. (1990a) 'Citizenship: an unnatural practice?' *Political Quarterly* 61: 177–87.

—— (1990b) *Citizenship and Community: Civic Republicanism and the Modern World*, London: Routledge.

Paris, D. (1991) 'Moral education and the "tie that binds" in liberal political theory', *American Political Science Review* 85(3): 875–901.

Pocock, J. G. A. (1992) 'The ideal of citizenship since classical times', *Queen's Quarterly* 99(1): 33–55.

Putnam, R. (1993) *Making Democracy Work: Civic Traditions in Modern Italy*, Princeton, NJ: Princeton University Press.

Rawls, John (1980) 'Kantian constructivism in moral theory', *Journal of Philosophy* 77(9): 515–72.

—— (1993) *Political Liberalism*, New York: Columbia University Press.

Raz, J. (1986) *The Morality of Freedom*, Oxford: Oxford University Press.

Skinner, Q. (1992) 'On justice, the common good and the priority of liberty', in C. Mouffe (ed.) *Dimensions of Radical Democracy: Pluralism, Citizenship and Community*, London: Routledge.

Spinner, J. (1994) *The Boundaries of Citizenship: Race, Ethnicity and Nationality in the Liberal State*, Baltimore, MD: Johns Hopkins University Press.

Strike, K. (1994) 'On the construction of public speech: pluralism and public reason', *Educational Theory* 44(1): 1–26.

Tamir, Y. (1993) *Liberal Nationalism*, Princeton, NJ: Princeton University Press.

van Gunsteren, H. (1978) 'Notes towards a theory of citizenship', in F. Dallmayr (ed.) *From Contract to Community*, New York: Marcel Decker.

Walzer, M. (1989) 'Citizenship', in T. Ball and J. Farr (eds) *Political Innovation and Conceptual Change*, Cambridge: Cambridge University Press.

—— (1992) 'The civil society argument', in C. Mouffe (ed.) *Dimensions of Radical Democracy: Pluralism, Citizenship and Community*, London: Routledge.

Weinstein, B. (1983) *The Civic Tongue: Political Consequences of Language Choice*, New York: Longman.

White, P. (1992) 'Decency and education for citizenship', *Journal of Moral Education* 21(3): 207–16.

Young, I. M. (1993) 'Justice and communicative democracy', in R. Gottlieb (ed.) *Radical Philosophy: Tradition, Counter-Tradition, Politics*, Philadelphia, PA: Temple University Press.

Part III

VIRTUES, PRACTICES AND THE EDUCATION OF CHARACTER

6

THE DEMANDS OF MORAL EDUCATION

Reason, virtues, practices

Paul H. Hirst

In this chapter I wish to tackle what seem to me to be the most fundamental matters that must determine our approach to moral education. I am doing this because relatively recent social and political changes (as well as philosophical and other intellectual developments) have, I think, now fatally undermined those forms of consensus on which liberal-minded educators have sought to base their understanding of the moral life and moral education. In a context of increasingly conflicting social pressures and even stronger religious, ethnic, national and political fundamentalisms, current intellectual critique of the liberalism that was widely espoused in the 1960s and 1970s has, I think, left many not only confused but deeply uncertain about how best to conceive the very notion of moral education. I shall not here concern myself with the complex social and ideological changes that face us. But I shall try to get behind these to the intellectual changes affecting our basic understanding of morality and moral education. My concerns are primarily philosophical.

I shall begin by looking at the position many of us have defended for a long time, convinced as we were that, the moral life being essentially the rational life, the development of moral reason must be seen as the key to everything in moral education. From that I shall move on to the contrasting approach, which has insisted that the moral life and moral education must be grounded in personal fulfilment, which can be achieved most fully by personal choice within a framework of firmly developed personal and social moral virtues. That the central concerns of these approaches are crucial in moral education I do not doubt. But, I shall argue, they both rest on serious mistakes about the nature and significance of moral reason and moral virtues. What I wish to maintain is that in the moral life, reason and virtue must be rooted in, anchored in, the mastery of and commitment to complex sets of social practices without which they become empty, impotent concerns. The moral life is essentially a matter of socially developed and socially conducted practices. If we unstick moral reasoning and moral virtues from the very practices in which they are necessarily embedded, we put our personal and social lives in peril. If we insist on seeing moral reason and moral virtues as simply personal achievements that alone or together are adequate to the independent autonomous creation of individual moral lives, we will inevitably see the failure of our aspirations for ourselves and our society. I think it is precisely this detachment of reason and virtue from the specific complex realities of the social practices of daily life that has disastrously undermined our approaches to moral education and sapped them of their force. Our efforts have thereby become irrelevant to the young. What we need to do, I will suggest, is to re-characterise the moral life and moral education in terms of developing the successful pursuit of quite specific existing and rationally evolving social practices within which personal fulfilment is to be found. But enough of what I am here trying to do. Let me set about the task.

The development of moral reason

In the 1960s and 1970s much powerful argument was deployed in support of a sophisticated account of the moral life and moral education based largely, though not exclusively, on certain Kantian-style rationalist doctrines. In these terms the moral life is seen as a life exemplifying adherence to a set of objective, universal, rational principles that can be justified by a form of Kantian 'transcendental deduction'. Such principles as those of promoting individual freedom and equality of treatment, the consideration of personal interests and truth-telling are held to be constitutively definitional of the moral life. The moral life is then a matter of rationally applying these principles in the natural, personal and social circumstances in which we find ourselves so as to maximise adherence to them. In different circumstances these principles might lead to different social practices and arrangements, though common features within human nature and our environment will lead to at least a limited number of well-nigh universal practical rules concerning physical well-being, personal relationships and political arrangements. But there is no reason to suppose that beyond these there is in close detail only one particular pattern of morally acceptable social life or only one form of the morally good life for any given individual.

This view – according to which, reason and reason alone can determine first the fundamental principles of morality and then, on that basis, the details of moral living both individually and socially – is anchored in certain assumptions about human nature. Above all, it assumes that our cognitive capacities are at least in principle able to operate in isolation from all else in our nature – especially our desires, feelings, inclinations – in determining what we ought to do. It then sees us as able to follow the dictates of reason, by harnessing all our other capacities to act according to its conclusions. In affect and feeling, in disposition and will, we are thus able at least in principle to conform with reason, to live rationally autonomous moral lives, lives rooted in rationally determined principles.

Moral education, according to this view, is at its heart concerned with cognitive development, which leads to a grasp of the fundamental moral principles that are constitutive of rational living, for that is the very nature of the moral life. It requires an education in understanding the natural, personal and social world we inhabit so that the implications of these principles can be worked out and that rational choices can be made as to what we ought to do in practice. As disciplined alignment of the individual's affective and conative capacities is needed alongside this rational cognitive development, the demands of reason must come to structure the individual's feelings and motivations in the development of rationally based virtues. The moral life is thus achieved as a life marked throughout by rational thought and judgement, rational actions and rational character. If it is assumed that at birth human beings are cognitively, affectively and conatively unformed, then there is at least the hope that we can educate them into the rational moral life in these terms, provided we do not confuse or block the process. At any rate, what is centrally required of moral education is here set out with some clarity, and from this we can hope to progressively discern its practical demands.

Limitations of the rational approach

But there are serious difficulties with this approach, impressive though it is in many ways. First, is it in fact the case that we can determine on abstract theoretical grounds a valid set of powerful universal moral principles? Is there a valid form of 'transcendental argument' that shows these principles to be necessary to all rational consideration of human action? And even if this is in some sense the case, can these principles lead us to clear rational judgements on what to do in particular circumstances? The more this view has been explored in critical debate, the more these very general formal principles have been seen to be dealing not at all with the freedoms and equalities of practical living but with abstracted ideal notions that have little real bite on what we actually do in practice. The detached theoretical perspective they relate to is in fact found to be one emptied of the intricate details of contemporary practical life, which are precisely what morality is all about. The more sharply the principles are set out, so that they can be theoretically justified, the more empty they become for all practical purposes.

Equally untenable in this approach is the belief on which it rests: that the activities of reason can be separated off from all other aspects of human nature, especially from our feelings and interests, so that moral principles can be purely cognitively determined. This detached, spectatorial, objective understanding of all we survey, including ourselves, is surely an idealised myth rather than an accurate account of the operation of reason. And even if all such objective understanding necessary for moral judgements were possible, can we really believe that our rational conclusions could then be systematically and coherently built into our affective and conative functioning so as to produce a rationally virtuous moral life? What we have in fact here is a picture of a life concerned simply with the satisfaction of reason, with all other wants and desires being made to conform to its demands. This model of human nature, its capacities and their relationship to each other is, I suggest, a philosophical fantasy. Human beings are not of their nature just bundles of operationally distinct capacities, with cognitive capacities such that all else in human nature can be made subject to their achievements. We are indeed beings with wide-ranging cognitive, affective and conative capacities, but these can only be partially and artificially isolated in analytical and abstract theoretical terms. In practice these elements are inextricably inter-related, mutually influencing each other in complex ways within human experience which cannot be understood by the piecing together of such analytically separated elements. But in addition to these capacities we have wide-ranging given natural wants and desires – physical, psychological and social – whose satisfactions, using our capacities, constitute human living. If we accept all of this as given, to see the moral life as fulfilled simply in the satisfactions of bringing all under a set of abstract idealised theoretical principles is indeed to pursue a rationalist myth. The moral life, the good life, is about the achievement of human fulfilment individually and socially. In this, reason must play a major role but nevertheless its pursuits and satisfactions are neither the beginning nor the end of matters.

To see moral education as above all else a form of cognitive development is thus to mistake the fundamental rationale of the enterprise by misconstruing its very *raison d'être*. This is not to deny the place in moral education of developing capacities for moral reasoning, but such a view demands a reconsideration of the character and goals of that reasoning within the very different and very wide-ranging pursuit that is most surely characteristic of moral education as a whole.

Moral education as personal fulfilment

In contrast to the narrow and distorted rationalist view of moral education that I have all-too briefly outlined, a more promising view has in recent years tried to do full justice to naturally given human wants and desires. Here the moral life is seen as the maximisation of human satisfactions, their diverse physical, psychological and social character being readily assumed. In these terms our cognitive capacities are to be understood as essentially part of the means we have for pursuing these satisfactions in ways that constitute human fulfilment. In coming to understand more fully our wants and desires and the diverse forms these and their satisfactions can take in the modern world, we are able to take more effective means to the ends we seek and we can develop more satifying and more coherently coordinated patterns of life. Reason, knowledge and understanding are understood as essentially instrumental in our constructing – personally and socially – relationships and structures of living that constitute our greatest good. But individual wants and capacities vary in many details, and the ever more sophisticated differentiation of wants and satisfactions that is open to us means that the good life for each of us must be personally determined and generated. At the heart of the good life, then, there must be self-knowledge, personal choice and self-direction. But the personal and social reconciliation of the decisions and activities thus generated is clearly crucial if the good life for any of us is to be achieved. Certain minimal social rules and principles will need to be empirically determined. But even these will require something more fundamental: a framework of certain common, overarching personal and social virtues necessary to all good lives in our society. Such virtues, or dispositions of character, such as liberality, fairness and truthfulness, are seen as providing the structure within which each of us can build our personal good life. Such a framework, it is maintained, is neutral as to choice between the patterns of life in which we can individually find our greatest good.

In these terms moral education (as education for the good life) demands wide-ranging knowledge and understanding of oneself, the natural and social environment, of available activities and practices for the satisfaction of wants and desires, and of coordinated ways of life. It demands, too, the skills that are necessary to making informed rational judgements in relation to one's considered wants and the practical means for actually achieving their satisfaction. But above all else, moral education demands the development of the virtues that are vital to personal fulfilment. It is an education of character that makes good lives possible.

The development of rational practice

This second view certainly does much to redress a number of what are surely fundamental deficiencies in the rationalist approach. But it seems to me it is still inadequate in its account of human nature and thus in its basic mapping of this whole enterprise. In pursuing these weaknesses I therefore wish to suggest a third approach that nevertheless takes on board the strengths of the first two.

To begin with, in rejecting the rationalist idea that reason alone has the power to determine (and indeed in the end also to motivate) the moral life, the second view seems to me to go too far in another direction. It is, I think, a mistake to see reason merely as an instrument in promoting the satisfaction of quite other desires and wants when a rationally ordered life is in itself one of the powerful satisfactions we naturally pursue. Morality is surely in part driven by a desire to be rational in what we think and do as well as by many other desires for personal and social satisfaction. The exercise of reason is therefore in part constitutive of the moral life, and hence a necessary and not just an instrumental element that is one of the goals of moral education. And being a natural desire, the exercise of reason is a vital motivating force in the moral life and, indeed, in moral education itself.

But further, this second approach seems to persist with the rationalist view of reason as a disengaged, spectatorial, theoretical enterprise whose achievements are then simply available to serve our independently given wants and desires. In fact, as I have suggested earlier, our naturally given cognitive capacities are from the very start locked into our wide-ranging pursuit of the satisfaction of wants and desires and are inextricably tied up with our exercising of our other given capacities of feeling and acting. We must, I think, begin by recognising that reason is part and parcel of our pursuit of our interests and is therefore, of its nature, primarily a practical affair. That being so, it is not surprising that the first concepts we form are concerned with distinctions marking out objects and events that give us pleasure, pain or other states of satisfaction and dissatisfaction. Amongst activities likewise, we first discriminate those leading to such states and learn how to take simple means to desired ends. But the understanding thus developed is not primarily theoretical or 'know that'. It is, rather, a matter of 'know how', of skill and judgement in action, that is only in part consciously articulated conceptually. It is because of their practical significance in relation to our wants, not because of their merely observable qualities, that objects are first conceptually distinguished. When it comes to propositions, the primary propositions of reason are, I suggest, generalisations concerning practical situations producing satisfaction or dissatisfaction, not disinterested truths about objective states of affairs. What is more, we must surely accept that such rational articulation within practice is necessarily achieved by concepts that abstract from all the implicit, tacit elements that vary in different practical situations. It can at best capture limited general aspects of such situations, its concepts stripping away unique and particular considerations. According to this view, reason is primarily practical in character, and it is in relation to successful practice that acceptable propositional knowledge is first formulated in general rules for practice, though they are limited and partial in their significance.

This exercise of practical reason is not, however, some early immature activity needing to be replaced by theoretical reason in due course. The development of rational practice is of its nature a matter of progressively making practice itself more successful, and that can only be achieved in the doing, individually and collectively. No amount of abstract conceptualisation can of itself give us the sufficient basis for rational practice. It is in practical experiment that we individually discover new forms and patterns of satisfaction and more effective means to ends. Yet the sustained development of ever more successful practices requires the generation and use of conceptual schemes within practice, and such development of practice can be systematic and ordered only to the degree that adequate concepts are achieved. It is in social cooperation and the generation of shared conceptual schemes in the shared, public language of practical reason that ever more successful forms of fulfilment are individually and collectively achievable. We must recognise, then, that the morally good, the fulfilling life personally and socially, requires the development of rational practice in the exercise of practice itself in a reflective manner. It is solely by so living in and through such socially developed practices that the good life is attainable.

But what, then, of the whole world of theoretical reason and knowledge that we have come to value so much in, say, the natural and social sciences, in mathematics and philosophy? Against the first, the rationalist approach, I was maintaining that such theoretical knowledge cannot alone provide the basis of the moral life. Against the second approach, I am now arguing that theoretical reason cannot hope to provide a grasp of either the ends or even the most effective means for such a life, for the good life must be practically developed as informed by a mode of reasoning generated in practice itself. What, then, is the significance in such a life of theoretical knowledge? The answer, I have already suggested, lies in seeing such knowledge as arising when reason comes to abstract from the satisfaction of all our other wants and desires and to seek its own peculiar satisfaction. It is of the nature of reason to form concepts, to propositionalise and so to distinguish what is and is not the case. In practical reason we seek to distinguish what is and is not the case in producing satisfactions. In theoretical reason we seek to distinguish what simply is and is not the case for the satisfaction that such understanding brings of itself. In this sense it is the achievement of propositional truths for their own sake that theoretical reason pursues. To achieve that, concepts must be formed that seek to abstract beyond all other interests. In doing so, however, what we can come to understand under any set of concepts is now doubly abstracted from practice. It is abstracted from practice first in seeking only cognitive satisfactions, and then – second – in seeking within those the specific satisfaction of achieving propositional truths. Theoretical reason is therefore only concerned with some very limited and partial aspect of what lies behind our practices. But by its means alone we can become clearer about certain of the presuppositions of the development of rational practice and thus be in a position coherently and systematically to pursue successful practice. Theoretical knowledge is therefore not the basis from which the moral life can be constructed but, rather, a means for constantly seeking to make explicit and to validate assumptions about ourselves and our context that are otherwise implicit in our understanding of our wants and their satisfactions. The concepts of any form of theoretical knowledge are not themselves properly those of any area of practical activity or of the principles on which practice can rationally operate. Rational practice develops in experience itself, engendering its own practical concepts in the process. Theoretical knowledge can but provoke a realignment in that process in ways that can make the pursuit of satisfaction more successful.

Insofar as moral education requires the development of moral reason, it requires this third view, understood as the development of the capacity to reflect critically on current personal and social practice, primarily in the light of experience, so as above all to promote our adequate and coherent satisfactions. Rational choice is not a matter of applying the results of detached, neutral, theoretical judgement but of following or appropriately modifying, for our own good, existing generally successful practices, according to our own particular circumstances. It is a question of exercising rationally informed practical know-how in the continuous making of our own good lives.

The social dimension of moral learning

There is a further fundamental weakness in both the approaches I have outlined in that they both accept a basically atomic view of the moral individual. In this we are believed to associate together in personal relationships and social systems simply to carry out what we decide we ought to do either on purely rational grounds or in pursuit of our satisfactions. Social relations are regarded as merely contingent arrangements designed for us to achieve as best we can our individually determined ends. But certain fundamental wants and desires are of their nature social and cannot be satisfied purely individually. What is more, in social relationships the satisfaction of wants and desires of all kinds, personal and social, can be pursued in ever more sophisticated and adequate ways. Practices can be constructed in association with others which individually are inconceivable. As I have already asserted, at the heart of these possibilities lies the creation of that shared public language through which alone rational practices can be systematically developed. But it is by coming to share in existing social practices in all their many complex features that our naturally given wants and desires become differentiated, structured and transformed, even from the moment of birth, in socially determined ways. In a most fundamental sense, persons as we know them are social constructions. We are what we are as individuals only by virtue of the web of socially constructed relationships and practices that together constitute the ways we think, feel and act. To be a human person is to inherit and come to dwell in some set of specific, socially created traditions within which diverse forms of human satisfaction are pursued. In these terms the moral life must be understood as the pursuit of a rational life developed personally from the possibilities available in the social groupings to which we belong. But this does not simply mean conformity to existing traditions as if these permitted no choice and are not themselves open to modification. What is more, the very notion of the good, the moral, the rational life, is itself a social construction and individuals can attain it only if they are initiated into it by way of the mastery of the practices of critically reflective personal response. We have in human societies created an enormous variety of specific practices and ways for satisfying human wants and desires. It is within these that we are formed. But these are rational for us individually – that is, fulfilling for us in an overall and considered sense – to varying degrees. It is insofar as we take on board rationally developed practices in the exercise of practical reason itself that we can individually hope to live a moral life and to contribute to the development of yet more rational personal and social practices in our society.

In moral education based on my first two models, detached individual rational choice is the foundation of the moral life, and it is only if we are confident that certain existing social practices can be justified in these terms for all those concerned that we can directly teach such practices. Indeed, according to the second view, confidently handing on directly any existing social practices is altogether too restricting on any individual choice. It is far better, some claim, to pursue less specific ends, a set of personal virtues rather than firm commitment to particular activities. Let us seek to develop honest, courageous, altruistic, fair-minded individuals, for such values are compatible with personally choosing from widely different actual practices and, indeed, spontaneously creating new practices oneself. But, I have argued, individuals are from the very start necessarily initiated into social practices for the satisfaction of their wants, and the idea of educating them to make detached rational choice is a nonsense. From the very start education can only get off the ground by initiating individuals into what are considered the most rational practices for them that are currently available in the society. What is more, the idea of pursuing a set of practice-neutral moral virtues is an equal nonsense. Virtues can only be developed by engaging in actual activities and, whatever practices are chosen, their successful pursuit requires the exercise of personal qualities or virtues distinctive of those practices. Initiation into any social practice thereby necessarily develops certain virtues that it embodies. Moral virtues like moral reason are the product of educating pupils in moral practices. Moral education is not achieved by pursuing moral reason and applying its dictates, nor by pursuing or seeking to replace it with a set of independently formulated moral virtues. Moral practices are rational social practices which of their nature require for their conduct the exercise of moral reason and moral virtues. If moral education is to be coherently conducted it must consist of initiation into such rational practices, and it will thereby develop moral – that is, practical – reason and rational moral virtues.

Features of the moral life

The view of the moral life for which I have argued has the following central features:

1   It takes as given that human beings have of their nature a wide range of wants and desires: physical, psychological and social.

2   It also takes as given that they have of their nature a wide range of capacities: physical, cognitive, affective and conative.

3   It sees morality as arising in the search for patterns of living that most fully satisfy human wants and desires. That search is understood to be primarily a practical matter, success being assessed in terms of the maximisation of satisfactions.

4   Forms of successful moral living are seen as emerging in social experimentation in which patterns of thinking, feeling and acting are established as social practices. It is in the practices of daily life, in personal and social relationships, the pursuits of industry, commerce, education, law, politics, religion, the arts, the sciences and so on that human satisfaction and fulfilment are to be found.

5   Central to the conduct and development of successful practices is the exercise of our cognitive capacities in practical and theoretical reason. Using practical reason, shared conceptual structures have led to the systematic creation and development of successful practices. Using theoretical reason, the character of such practices is more adequately understood and their development can be more purposefully directed. The moral life is thus a life of rational practices: that is, of practices developed by reason so as to maximise the satisfaction of human wants and desires.

6   In participating in social practices, naturally given capacities for thinking, feeling and acting become structured in particular ways, as do the wants and desires the practices seek to satisfy. To develop as a human person is thus for an individual's capacities, wants and desires to become structured and ordered by a set of practices. It is by responding to socially constructed rational practices that an individual comes personally to live a moral life, to exercise moral reason and to be marked by moral virtues.

7   The moral life for any individual is thus that form of life which most successfully satisfies their personal wants and desires. It must be lived within a network of existing but developing social practices. It can by definition be the most successful form of life only insofar as it is itself the overall rational practice of responding to specific rational practices. To that end, the overall pattern of life and its consistent practices are constantly subject to rational reflection and modification as circumstances change.

8   The moral life as so conceived is not to be understood as essentially individualistic and egocentric, as if the wants and satisfactions on which it is based are of their nature purely personal. Rather, these wants and satisfactions are to be seen as of their nature socially patterned from their very first articulation within us individually. Their fulfilment in the moral life is thus to be found in a network of practices that have been developed to maximise socially interlocking satisfactions. Properly understood, the rational practices of the moral life are of their nature developed for the pursuit of personal fulfilment in socially structured terms.

Moral education as initiation into social practices

But what now of moral education if such a moral life is to be achieved? What can be said on the basis of the philosophical considerations I have been discussing? In the interests of consistency one thing must be kept clear. Moral education has got to be recognised as itself a form of social practice, and therefore its most successful form can only be achieved in rationally developing that practice itself. Yet philosophical clarification, as a theoretical pursuit, can cause us to revise the presuppositions underlying that practice, and the notion of the moral life for which I have argued certainly seeks to set out some of the terms within which successful practice must be developed. Let me therefore try to be explicit about these.

We must conceive of the enterprise of moral education as from the start concerned with the rational development and satisfaction of physical, psychological and social wants, and with developing the exercise of given capacities to that end. But equally we must recognise that the substantive content of that education must necessarily be certain quite specific social practices that will structure individual wants and satisfactions. When individuals are initiated into such practices, their thinking, feeling and acting will progressively take on the characteristics embedded in those practices, for practices are simply complex inter-related packages of such elements as knowledge, beliefs, criteria of success, judgements, values, activities, skills, dispositions, virtues, sensations and emotions.

At each stage the practices that moral education seeks to develop must be selected by those best able to judge how each individual's existing wants and satisfactions can be progressively more rationally developed. This demands close attention to emerging wants and desires and to particular capacities. At the earliest stage practices must be selected by others. But as wants, capacities and achievements are rationally developed, each individual becomes more able to judge personally those practices that can constitute for them the moral life. In the process each individual becomes progressively more able personally to modify the practices into which they have been initiated, to contribute to their social development and rationally to choose other forms of practice.

But to what existing social practices for the content of education do these considerations point? I suggest they fall into three distinguishable if interlocking domains. First, there are those very varied basic practices of everyday life which are necessary for anyone to achieve the rational satisfaction of wants and desires in their given physical, personal and social circumstances. Second, there are those many optional practices from which an individual rational life can be constructed according to developing personal wants, desires and capacities. Both these kinds of practices would seem to have their place in education right from the start. Progressively, however, if an individual's life is to develop its rational character, there must be included practices of a third kind. These are of a higher order, being practices of critical rational reflection on practices of the first two kinds. By these further practices, already acquired practices can be modified in personal judgement and new practices pursued in the rational self-direction of life. These are the practices that can be seen as the exercise of rational autonomy, though not the free, detached autonomy that marks the rationalist model I outlined. Though always pre-supposing some mastery of lower-order practices, critical reflection is not to be seen as possible or necessary for only a limited few. Without its pursuit, rational self-determination is not possible in any meaningful sense, and that distinctive form of human desire and the capacities for its satisfaction remain unfulfilled.

Amongst the rich diversity of practices available to most of us are those concerned with the systematic pursuit of theoretical or academic knowledge. These I see as falling within the second of my categories, and they are likely to figure as major elements in the life of relatively few. As I have argued, however, their development in society is crucially important because their specialist achievements contribute substantively, if only indirectly, to the rational development of the practices in all three domains. Theoretical or academic knowledge is important in the social development of the practices of critical reflection the moral life requires. Mastery of theoretical practices themselves is, however, in general not necessary for the individual's conduct of the moral life. The critical reflection the moral life requires is in itself a matter of prac-tical reason in the light of the results of theoretical reason. Theoretical prac-tices themselves are quite another matter.

From this point of view, moral education is essentially education in the conduct of a rationally fulfilling life by initiation into an ever developing web of social practices. Its whole point is that it is at every stage personally fulfilling in a rationally developing sense. A person's education as a whole is or is not to a greater or lesser degree a moral education. Its parts are significant insofar as they do or do not contribute to that whole. But within that whole, moral education can be and often is more narrowly defined as concerned directly with certain particular questions to do with personal, family, community and wider social relationships. But what matters about those rela-tionships is the web of practices in which they exist and solely within which they can be properly understood. Such are the practices and activities that matter as pursuits in which the participants and others prosper and are thereby personally fulfilled. Moral education in this narrower sense must be initia-tion into those personal and social practices we consider will constitute for pupils a progressively fulfilling life. To reduce that to initiation into reasoning about practice in the light of a set of general principles is to empty out its truly practical character, to shift its focus from personal fulfilment to rational achievement and thereby to drain the whole enterprise of its funda-mental significance and motivation. To set about initiation into practices but then to set our eyes directly on developing a set of virtues, rather than to pursue personally fulfilling practices themselves, is again to misconstrue the enterprise.

Moral education *is* concerned with reason, practical reason. It is also concerned with virtues. But in no way will those be properly achieved other than by educating youngsters at home, in school and in the wider contexts in which they live, in a developing web of practices they find to be personally and socially fulfilling, and that across the fullest possible range of their evolving needs, wants, interests and the satisfactions of the exercise of their capacities. Until we get down to the detail of the practices of daily life into which we are initiating youngsters, we are just playing inadequately at the task. For good or ill, we get out of moral education what we put into it: lives formed by the practices – that is, the beliefs, actions, dispositions, emotions, reasoning, skills and so on – that we initiate them into. But only insofar as they can individually find in these pursuits the satisfaction of their socially evolving desires. When youngsters find nothing for them in what we offer, they reject it – rightly so – and turn to other things. We have simply got to learn that if the next generation is to be meaningfully morally educated they must find in what we offer rational practices of living that bring them personal satisfaction and fulfilment. If we offer them simply independently derived principles, virtues or both, simply asking them to live these out, they will have none of it. For these so presented will not adequately 'speak to their condition', as the Quakers say, in the modern world. What they need is help and guidance in how best to live in the specific practices they are faced with here and now. We need to stop preaching and get down to the business of initiating them into finding the good life in the practices of home, school, church, community, peer group, and wherever else in our contemporary world they must fashion their form of life. They cannot escape that context or significantly change it except from within, and we must help them work things out from where they really are.

7

HOW TO SEEM VIRTUOUS
WITHOUT ACTUALLY BEING SO

Alasdair MacIntyre

The issues it is my chief purpose to raise in this chapter are political and educational. My aim is to provide support for two conclusions. The first is that the adherents of any tolerably systematic and coherent account of the virtues, which they believe to be rationally defensible, will be committed to drawing a distinction between what they take to be genuine virtues and what they take to be, to some significant extent at least, mere counterfeits of those virtues, qualities that have the appearance of, but are not in fact, genuine virtues. The second is that because there are in our present society a number of rival and incompatible accounts of the virtues – each taken by its adherents to be warranted by rational argument and each unable so far to refute the claims of its rivals by appeal to generally shared and agreed criteria – and because more than one of these accounts claims the allegiance of significant groups within our society, there can be no rationally defensible shared programme for moral education for our society as such, but only a number of rival and conflicting programmes, each from the standpoint of one specific contending view.

The arguments I am going to advance concern the virtues. But there are parallel arguments available concerning rules. And since what these arguments on both topics lead to is the conclusion that ours is a society lacking a shared morality, it is scarcely surprising that they support the further conclusion that the possibilities of shared moral education are not what they are sometimes taken to be. Of course the proponents of shared public moral education – and they are enormously influential – insist to the contrary that we do in fact share a morality, and therefore my first task in this chapter is to suggest why it is that they are able successfully to deceive both themselves and others on this and kindred topics. I shall suggest that they are able to do so because although the society at large does not share a morality, the spokespersons for our political culture do share with a significant audience a moral rhetoric. How that rhetoric differs in its treatment of the virtues

118

from *any* rationally defensible systematic account of the virtues, is then my opening question.

Behind the facade of moral consensus

Let me begin by contrasting what I shall call the commonplace rhetorical usage of the virtue-words – 'commonplace', that is, in the contemporary public metropolitan cultures of the so-called advanced societies, such as our own – with the kind of meaning the virtue-words must be understood to have, if they are used to give expression to any tolerably systematic and coherent understanding of the virtues. Both those who judge some particular person to be courageous or generous or just or whatever (using those words in accordance with commonplace usage) and those who apparently judge similarly (using those very same words, but doing so in order to give expression to their own particular systematic and coherent understanding of the virtues) will of course do so on the basis of some set of actions by that person. And it may well be the case, indeed it often enough is the case, that it is on the basis of the very same set of actions, performed in some limited set of situations, that both parties judge that particular person courageous or generous or just. Because he or she on a limited, but sufficiently numerous, range of occasions has done particular brave or generous or just actions and has not performed any clearly cowardly or niggardly or unjust actions, a settled disposition so to act is ascribed. But what it is crucial to notice is that although both parties are ascribing a disposition, using the same words to do so, it is not the same disposition that is being ascribed. The same sentences are being employed, but the judgements to which they give expression are in fact different. Wherein does the difference lie?

When someone utters what he or she takes to be a well-founded and thought-out judgement on the basis of some tolerably systematic and coherent understanding of the virtues, he or she is characteristically committed to giving answers of a certain kind to four different questions. The first of these questions concerns the counterfactual judgements to which he or she is thereby committed: if I judge someone (on the basis of what he or she has hitherto done, or has refrained from doing) to be brave or generous or just, to what set of counterfactual judgements about what he or she would have done – if such and such, which did not in fact occur, had occurred, or if such and such, which has not yet occurred, were to occur – am I committed? In answering this question adequately someone will also be specifying what type of future actions or refrainings from action would provide good reasons for modifying or withdrawing one's previous judgement.

A second question concerns the type of reason for acting as he or she does which is ascribed in judging that someone is brave or generous or just. For it is a contention of every tolerably systematic and coherent understanding of the virtues which has been advanced so far, that to be virtuous it is not sufficient for someone to do what a virtuous person would do. It is also necessary that the relevant actions are performed for what are taken by adherents of that particular standpoint to be the right types of reason. What may be taken to be, by an external observer, examples of one and the same type of action will not necessarily be accounted such from the standpoint of a systematic conception of the virtues; for how actions are to be characterised in order to be judged virtuous or vicious is never entirely independent of considerations concerning the reasons for which the action was performed.

So it will be held from the standpoint of a systematic understanding of the virtues that someone who puts him or herself into a situation in which he or she confronts some danger only because it will be a favourable occasion for exhibiting his or her agility and skill to an admiring audience, does not perform the same action as someone who confronts that same danger because he or she has perceived what kind of danger it is and judges worthwhile the good to be obtained by averting it. Of course there will be levels of characterisation at which a true characterisation of the two actions will be the same: both of my imaginary characters, let us say, picked up an about-to-explode grenade and threw it away, but the one who did so because it was an exploding grenade and a child was standing by it, warrants a set of characterisations of his or her action very different from those warranted by the action of someone who only wanted to exhibit his skills as an outfielder. The latter was inviting admiration, albeit recklessly; the former was saving a life, albeit skilfully. Such characterisations of action unavoidably involve reference both to reasons and to intention; and we may indeed say that the former's action unintentionally invited admiration and the latter's unintentionally saved a life. But how the intention of an agent is to be described depends upon what reasons are to be ascribed to that agent.

So in calling some particular person brave or generous or just, I will always, if I am giving expression to some tolerably systematic and coherent conception of the virtues, be committed to a particular type of answer to the question: for what reasons did he or she act as he or she did? Notice that the answers to this second question will not be logically independent of the answer to the first question: what counterfactual judgements are entailed or implied by this or that judgement that someone is virtuous? For to say what reasons someone had for acting always has implications concerning what that person would have done, had circumstances been different from what they were. The person who picked up the hand grenade and threw it in order to exhibit his or her skill in the outfield, would have had the same reason to pick up the object and throw it had it been not a grenade, but a baseball.

A third question to which an answer is characteristically implied by a judgement giving expression to some tolerably systematic and coherent account of the virtues is: what was it, both in the situation and the action, which pleased or pained the agent? To the question about the virtuous agent's reasons there is added this question about his or her responses of feeling and desire. To be virtuous is, according to this type of view, not only to do what some particular virtue or virtues require for the relevant type of reason, but also to do so in a way that involves taking pleasure in certain features both of actions and of situations, and in being pained by others. The virtuous person takes pleasure in averting danger through courage, in his or her own or another's generosity and so on, and is correspondingly pained by such happenings and states as the exposure of the innocent to danger, gross need, or niggardliness in the face of such need.

A fourth question to which some answer is characteristically presupposed by any ascription of a virtue made from the standpoint of a tolerably systematic and coherent understanding of the virtues is: what range of different types of action performed by some particular individual in different types of situation provides a sufficient warrant for such an ascription of a virtue to that individual? Earlier I suggested that those ascriptions made on the basis of commonplace contemporary usage, and those ascriptions giving expression to some systematic point of view, both required what I called a sufficiently numerous range of instances as a basis for judgement. This deliberately imprecise formulation captures very well the requirements of commonplace moral usage. What it does not capture is the need – not only for a number of instances of action – to justify the ascription of virtues from a systematic standpoint, but the additional requirement that those instances be of sufficiently different types to justify both the relevant set of extrapolations to counterfactual conclusions, and the relevant set of inferences to judgements about the agent's reasoning, and about what it is in which he or she takes pleasure, or by which he or she is pained.

To this fourth question, therefore, the adherents of a variety of systematic standpoints give a more precise, detailed and determinate answer than that presupposed by those who are doing no more in what they say about the virtues than giving expression to present-day commonplace usage. And the same contrast in respect of degree of determinacy is found also in the answers to the other three questions. For where a number of different developed, systematic standpoints concerning the virtues each both supply and require highly determinate and consistent answers to all four questions – even if these answers vary from standpoint to standpoint, for each of these standpoints is after all at odds with the others – the answers supplied by commonplace usage are highly indeterminate. To call someone brave or generous or just according to the mode of present-day commonplace usage is to leave largely open and undecided what answers are to be given to questions concerning the counterfactual commitments, reasoning, and pleasures and pains of virtuous agents, and the range of types of action on the basis of which virtues may be justifiably ascribed. This indeterminacy in respect of what is entailed or implied by judgements that some particular person is virtuous – an indeterminacy of meaning – has two alternating aspects.

On the one hand, insofar as commonplace usage concerning the virtues merely leaves open and unanswered to some large degree these four questions to which systematic conceptions of the virtues return definite and conclusive answers, commonplace usage appears more or less consistent with all and any of those rival systematic conceptions. It seems to say less than any of them do, rather than something other. But on the other hand, insofar as commonplace usage functions so as to embody a silent, but insistent and continuing refusal to supply answers to those same four questions, it appears to be equally inconsistent with any one of them. Why is it that we should not be too surprised that the conception of the virtues embodied in the commonplace usage of contemporary public cultures assumes these alternating and incompatible aspects?

Ours is a political culture deeply fractured by fundamental moral disagreements. It is also a political culture whose public rhetoric is well designed to disguise and to conceal the extent of that disagreement by invoking an idiom of consensus with regard to values. In order to function effectively that rhetoric must be able to make use of sentences that both command widespread assent and yet which are at the same time available for the expression of sets of quite different and incompatible moral judgements. Thereby an illusion is created of agreement in valuing such virtues as courage, generosity and justice, while at the same time disguising the range of alternative and conflicting conceptions of such virtues, and of the nature of virtue in general, which in fact informs the attitudes and actions of different individuals and groups. Thus a large and largely unnoticed gap exists between the nature and grounds of those ascriptions of the virtues figuring so notably in commonplace usage and public political rhetoric, and those verbally similar ascriptions giving expression to some systematic and coherent account of the virtues. And this gap functions so as to protect from scrutiny the presentation of self in contemporary public and political life of those holding and aspiring to public office. For what our contemporary political culture requires from those who claim public and political authority is an appearance of virtue congruent with the rhetoric of shared values. And both that appearance and that rhetoric are well served by the indeterminacy of the virtue-concepts of contemporary commonplace usage.

Moral immaturity and counterfeit virtue

My first contrast, then, was between the virtue-concepts of present-day commonplace usage and the virtue-concepts of *any* tolerably systematic and coherent account of the virtues. But the fact that all such accounts are at odds with such commonplace usage does not diminish the significance or the intractability of the disagreements between them. So my second contrast is between the virtues as they are and the virtues as they are conceived to be in a mode of theory and practice which does not fail by reason of indeterminacy in its answers to the four questions, but rather by reason of giving false or defective answers to those questions, so that once again an appearance of the virtues is contrived which is discrepant with their reality. Notice that this second type of contrast, unlike the first, can be drawn only from some single particular systematic standpoint; and it is from such a standpoint that I now proceed to draw it.

All education into the virtues, especially the education of the young, has to begin by discovering some way of transforming the motivations of those who are to be so educated. Their initial appetites and passions will inevitably be directed towards their own satisfactions and towards pleasing those upon whom they depend to procure those satisfactions for them. Normally, indeed, pleasing such persons – parents, surrogate parents, aunts, first teachers – very early becomes one of the chief, if not *the* chief, of such satisfactions. And it is among such persons that moral educators are generally to be found. Their central problem with their pupils is how to enable those pupils to pass from pursuing certain particular goals internal to certain types of activity in certain highly specific ways, only or largely because those pupils have recognised that their pursuit of those goals in those ways pleases their teachers, so that they themselves are in turn pleased by giving this kind of pleasure, to pursuing those same goals in those same ways because they have come to appreciate those goals and those particular ways of pursuing them as worthwhile in themselves. That is, their problem is how to enable their pupils to come to value goods just as and insofar as they are goods, and virtues just as and insofar as they are virtues. If pupils make this transition successfully, they may continue to take pleasure in pleasing others, when and if they happen to do so, but such pleasure will be incidental to, and accidental in relation to, the good or goods for the sake of which they act and the virtues through which they are able to achieve that good or goods. But what if, for some reason, those pupils fail to make that transition?

They will then continue on some occasions to do what a genuinely virtuous person would do; their actions will perhaps often enough happen to conform to the requirements of courage or generosity or justice or whatever. But because they have misidentified what it is about these actions that would make them genuine examples of some particular virtue, they will extrapolate falsely in making inferences as to what the virtues require in situations other than those with which they were at first familiarised. And these false extrapolations may be of at least two different kinds. For on the one hand their evaluative classifications of action may still be in terms of the propensity of those actions to give pleasure to their parents and teachers, so that they remain permanently immature, their adult judgements being the unacknowledged outcome of the continuing, less-than-adult interactions between id and superego. But they may instead, on the other hand, classify and characterise actions in terms of the propensity of those actions to please those others, whoever they are, who now provide the social environment of their daily lives. So for them the virtues will have come to be understood, or rather misunderstood, as those qualities that when exhibited in action cause others to be pleased, and oneself to be pleased that those others are pleased, and those others to be pleased that one is pleased that they are pleased. And correspondingly the vices will be understood in terms of the propensities of actions to cause oneself and others to be pained.

The sources of such reciprocal pleasures and pains will characteristically be twofold: mutual sympathy and shared conceptions of utility. Reflection upon these sources will provide the basis for the articulation of a type of theory of the virtues in terms of pleasure and pain, sympathy and utility, which will both give expression to and articulate a rationale for the moral experience of this kind of person. Both in such experience and in such a theory the relationship of the virtues to the pleasure taken in them will have been inverted: where the teachers of the virtues took pleasure in certain types of action because they were virtuous, the pupils of those teachers – and doubt-less the pupils of those pupils when they in turn become teachers – will have come to treat certain types of action as virtuous because of their propensity to cause pleasure. This inversion can be spelled out in the answers to three of those four questions identified earlier, in terms of which rival theories of the virtues define their standpoints and consequently their disagreements. So although on many occasions one and the same set of actions will be judged virtuous both from this counterfeit standpoint and from that of the genuine virtues, the counterfactuals entailed by those judgements will be signi-ficantly different. How they differ will vary, partly depending on whatever group or groups of persons' virtues taken as qualities that please – because of their utility or because of sympathy – are the object of reciprocal rela-tionships. And just as there is a difference in the relevant sets of counter-factuals, so there is a corresponding difference in the type of reasons adduced to support judgements about the virtues. From the standpoint of the genuine virtues, true judgements about what virtues are required in some particular situation, and about what those virtues require by way of action, always either presuppose or are explicitly derived from some conception of the human *telos* as being the achievement of a type of life of which the virtues are necessary constitutive parts. So that the structure of supporting argument is one in which, implicitly or explicitly, a premise about that *telos*, supplemented by premises about this particular agent's particular situation, support that prac-tical conclusion that is, if the agent has the requisite virtues, the performance of the action required.

From the alternative and rival standpoint that we have been considering, a virtue is a disposition to respond to an envisaged possibility of procuring pleasure or averting pain; and such responses are not reasoned. They may indeed be responses of appetite or passion to some object proposed by reason; and how that object is to be achieved in order that this particular pleasure may be procured or this particular pain averted will be a matter of means–ends reasoning. But reason, from this point of view, is in practical matters a servant of the appetites and passions; that it is such a servant is itself to be taken to be a conclusion of reason and a keystone of the theory underpinning this standpoint.

The first question concerned counterfactuals; the second, supporting reasons. The third, it will be recalled, concerned what it is in which pleasure and pain are taken. Here the difference between the two positions is perhaps most radical. For there are certain types of disposition which the genuinely virtuous will value as virtues, but which those who give their allegiance to this kind of counterfeit will not perceive as virtues at all, but rather as vices. I refer to those dispositions the exercise of which has the specific purpose of transforming one's appetites and passions, so that what before or at the onset of one's moral education gave one pleasure or pain will no longer do so, and one will instead come to take pleasure in or to be pained by quite other states and qualities. To acquire the virtues, according to this view, requires the cultivation of a certain asceticism about the initial (and in this sense natural) objects of the appetites and passions – a denial of certain pleasures and the voluntary enduring of certain pains, which must appear pointless and even self-deforming to those for whom it is in the cultivation and enjoyment of reciprocally afforded pleasures that the point and purpose of the virtues is to be found. So the sharpest of contrasts emerges here between the virtues as they are and the virtues as presented from this rival standpoint.

Why a shared public system of moral education is impossible

The characterisation of this latter contrast is bound to evoke two immediate responses. First, it is unlikely that anyone has failed to notice that what I have characterised as the genuine virtues are the virtues as understood and practised by the adherents of an Aristotelian point of view, and what I have presented as counterfeit virtues are the virtues as understood and practised by the adherents of a Humean point of view. It will at once be charged that I have thereby begged a, indeed *the*, crucial question at issue, that of whether Aristotle is indeed in the right rather than Hume. To this accusation of question-begging I plead guilty; but it in no way affects the principal point at issue. For suppose that we were now to reverse the terms of the characterisation and to rewrite the chapter from a Humean standpoint, treating as genuine virtues those taken to be such in *A Treatise of Human Nature*, and as mere duplicitous counterfeits the qualities presented as virtues in the *Nicomachean Ethics*, except insofar as they on occasion coincide with the virtues as described and praised by Hume. Two things would be unaffected by this reversal. The first is the extent and nature of the difference between the two standpoints. The second is a matter of how the Humean, quite as much as the Aristotelian, is bound to treat the virtues-as-prescribed-by-rival-views as counterfeits. Hume himself, it is true, was blind to this, supposing (as he did) that agreement about the virtues among mankind is in fact over-whelming, even if disguised by the vagaries of social circumstance. And this is why I call the position I have described Humean rather than Hume's. But nothing of substance in my argument is affected thereby.

A second response to the argument will be to note that in choosing to attend to Aristotelian and to Humean accounts of the virtues, in order to bring out the need for each standpoint to distinguish the genuine from the counterfeit, I have been arbitrarily selective. There are, it may be urged, other rival accounts of the virtues deserving of equal attention, Stoic, utilitarian, whatever. But to concede this, as I willingly do, strengthens rather than weakens the overall argument. For in each case it will turn out that serious and system-atic practice of what each such account takes the virtues to be presupposes and embodies the theory in question; so that each such theory, as with Aristotle's theory and Humean theory, must be understood as a theory articulating and justifying one specific type of moral practice, each such type being in key part incompatible with and antagonistic to other such types. And as exam-ples of such different theories of the virtues are accumulated, so is support for the conclusion that there is no theory-neutral, pre-philosophical, yet adequately determinate account of the virtues to be given. What of course may masquerade as just such a theory-neutral, pre-philosophical account – and the only account likely to be presented in such a masquerade – will be the significantly indeterminate, usually tacit account of the virtues embodied in the rhetoric of contemporary commonplace usage. But it too, as we have already seen, is not neutral, insofar as it is incompatible with the whole range of systematic and coherent accounts of the virtues. So it also becomes clear that there can be no theory-neutral education into the practice of the virtues. For rival and mutually antagonistic accounts of the virtues require as their social counterpart rival and mutually antagonistic institutionalised modes of moral education. Consider, for example, the ways in which Aristotelian and Humean modes of moral education would have to differ if each were to com-municate effectively what it takes to be involved in learning how to live the life of the virtues. This learning must include, in the Aristotelian case, learning how to distinguish genuine virtues from their Humean and other counter-feits; in the Humean case, learning (in a parallel way) must distinguish genuine virtues from their Aristotelian and other counterfeits.

A Humean, like Hume himself, will want to inculcate in his or her pupils a general responsiveness to the pleasures and pains of others, whosoever they may be, and, more especially, a responsiveness to what in the social life of his or her own time and place is such that others are generally pleased by it or generally pained by it. By contrast an Aristotelian will want to distin-guish what it is that pleases or pains the virtuous person from what it is that pleases or pains the vicious or the immature or the akratic. So he or she will encourage in his or her pupils a certain lack of responsiveness to pleasure or pain as such and a denial that, where preferences are concerned, everybody is to count for one. But this will entail two different kinds of habituation of the pupil. The Aristotelian pupil will have to learn not always to respond with pleasure to the approbation of those who value utility and sympathy. Being unsympathetic will often enough be required, especially in certain types of social milieu. And being useful is a positive vice in those whose actions are well designed as means for ends not prescribed by reason.

For the Humean, as I already noted, reason prescribes no ends. And this Humean view issues in two further differences from Aristotelianism with respect to moral education. A first concerns the Aristotelian thesis that training in the exercise of practical judgement requires a particular kind of appropriation of moral experience, something unavailable to the immature, both by reason of their lack of a sufficient range of experiences and by reason of their as yet insufficient training in the disciplining and redirection of the passions. (Where I have spoken of the immature, Aristotle speaks of 'the young'; but, in this sense of being 'young', as our political leaders of every hue provide evidence, one can still be young when one is old.) What one has to learn, according to an Aristotelian view, is how to conceptualise and to classify, so that in practical reasoning one's descriptions of the situations and issues upon which universal moral truths concerning the virtues have to be brought to bear are in the appropriate form. Lacking this capacity, one will know neither which generalisations are appropriately to be brought to bear in particular situations nor how to generalise from particular experiences. And underlying this Aristotelian thesis is, of course, an essentialism governing modes of classification which is not only morally, but metaphysically and epistemologically at odds with any Humean view.

A second further difference is immediately apparent. What kind of theory one must have and what content that theory must have, if theory is to be an effective background to practice (and Hume in the *Treatise* was as insistent as Aristotle in the *Ethics* on the practical benefits to be derived from his theorising), are questions that will receive very different answers in the course of constructing a syllabus for any programme of moral education.

Finally it is worth noticing at least one example of the different conception each view has of particular virtues. Justice provides a striking example. For the Aristotelian, justice is necessarily a matter of desert and merit, desert and merit in respect of contributions to or failures to contribute to the common life of a *polis*, of that type of political community in which only human beings can achieve their good through that cooperative friendship which is itself a central virtue. For a Humean, as much as for a Rawlsian, justice has nothing to do with desert or merit, although for very different reasons. The implications for economic life (in the modern sense of 'economic') are perhaps the most striking. For an Aristotelian, acquisitiveness as such, *pleonexia*, is a vice, indeed the vice that is the principal form of injustice. And justice in exchange requires that conceptions such as those of a fair wage and a just price should have application. But to hold both those theses is to set oneself

127

in radical opposition to any economy dominated by markets and requiring the accumulation of capital, an opposition not only not required from, but quite alien to, either a Humean or a Rawlsian standpoint.

That Aristotelianism is thus at odds with the standpoint of the established economic systems of advanced modernity is of course treated by many as sufficient reason not to take its claims seriously. But that this is so strengthens my claim that there is no non-controversial stance to be taken on the virtues, and that is so in a way and to a degree that makes it impossible for there to be a single shared public system of moral education with determinate and substantive moral content.

Moral education in consequence will have to proceed through two very different stages. The first of these will be one in which the adherents of each viewpoint will have to provide for the education of their own young from their own point of view; and what at this stage is required has been set out in seminal form by Aristotle in the latter books of the *Politics*. What the young are to read will have to be prescribed, and the selectiveness of their reading will necessarily involve a certain form of censorship, admitted or unadmitted. It will only be when they are adequately instructed – or as their opponents will see it, indoctrinated – that they will be ready to embark upon a second stage of their moral education, that in which they are initiated, each from his or her own standpoint, into the key systematic controversies between the various competing rival standpoints and into the ethics and politics of such controversy. The first stage of such education will be one in which, for Aristotelians, the acknowledgement of the teacher's authority on moral questions will be crucial. For the young have to embark upon learning how to be just and courageous and temperate and above all prudent (in the medieval sense of *prudentia*, not the modern sense of 'prudence') before they are able to understand, except in highly inadequate ways, what these virtues are and what their embodiment in their lives will involve. So the beginner in such education must initially entrust him or herself to another. But that trust will only be justified if the teacher has been chosen for his or her role, not only on the grounds of his or her training in theory, but also because of outstanding moral character. And what is accounted outstanding moral character by Aristotelians will be notably different from what is so accounted by, for example, Humeans.

To appoint teachers on the grounds of their moral character is something so much at odds with the general beliefs of the dominant liberal culture about education that there will be a good deal of reluctance even to entertain this possibility. But the argument as I have developed it up to this point may have made one thing clear that has so far gone largely unrecognised, namely that the issues raised by moral education are very much the same as those raised by religious education; and that just as an education that purports to be neutral between rival controversial religious standpoints always ends up in teaching no religion at all, and thereby irreligion, so an education that purports to teach a morality neutral between rival controversial standpoints concerning the virtues will end up in teaching a largely indeterminate morality. This morality, that of the rhetoric of commonplace usage, lacks determinate answers to those questions in terms of which any substantive and determinate account of the virtues has to state its positions. But would this matter? And, if so, why?

The inadequacy of a 'shared public morality'

Let me approach these questions by first considering a type of defence of the moral rhetoric of commonplace usage that might be offered in the face of these considerations. Of course, it might be said, the morality of the virtues presupposed by and advanced in such rhetoric is not determinate in the way and to the degree that the Aristotelian or the Humean or other rival and controversial standpoints are. How could it be? For it represents, so far as possible, what is generally acceptable, what the adherents of every standpoint and none are able to agree in asserting. And this shared minimum is just what the political order as such should uphold and require: no less, but also no more. It is this minimum that allows the political order to be neutral between rival standpoints, tolerating all, so far as their adherents comply with the requirements of public order, but endorsing none. What can be wrong with that?

The problem is that this shared morality necessarily, by reason of its indeterminateness, fails us at just those points at which the political, social and cultural order most needs what only the virtues can supply. The success or failure of any system of the virtues – by its own standards, that is – is largely a matter of how successful or otherwise those educated by it and in it are in extrapolating, in their practice as well as in their theory, from those situations in which they first learned not only what justice, courage, generosity and the rest require, but actually to act as justice, courage, generosity and the rest require – in the right way, at the right time, to the right degree, and so on – to other new and relatively unfamiliar types of situation. The weaknesses of the shared morality of commonplace usage arise from the conjunction of the fact that its indeterminateness in respect of extrapolation leaves its adherents without adequate instruction at just this point, and of the fact that it is just in those new and relatively unfamiliar situations – new and unfamiliar, that is, from the standpoint of the maxims that embody commonplace usage concerning the virtues – that a crucial need for the virtues is most evident. Consider some different examples of this type of situation, each concerned with a specific cluster of virtues.

A first concerns courage and honesty. Imagine the case of, let us say, a marine officer who has learned how to act in accordance with what these two virtues do in fact require in certain highly specific types of situation. He or she has learned, that is, to be courageous to the point of self-sacrifice in the face of harms and dangers posed to the security of his or her country by some external enemy. And he or she has learned to be honest, both in his or her dealings with his or her fellow officers and in reporting to his or her superiors. Suppose now that at some later time he or she is ordered by those superiors, for the sake of some cause inseparable from the security of his or her country, to organise and undertake some clandestine scheme, clandestine because it must remain unknown to that country's enemies. But suppose now that he or she, in order to achieve the ends of what he or she judges to be a highly necessary clandestine scheme, has to deceive not only those enemies, but also the political authorities to whom in the last resort he or she and his or her superiors are accountable, and the public to whom in turn those authorities are accountable. What will be crucial will be the capacity of that officer to extrapolate from the paradigm cases of courage and honesty through which he or she first learned to find systematic application for these concepts, to this later complex situation. What it is in fact right for him or her to do there is little need for me to discuss, for the only point that matters for my argument is that too indeterminate a conception of the virtues of courage and honesty will necessarily leave such an officer morally resourceless; and too indeterminate a conception is just what the morality of commonplace usage will supply.

A second example concerns temperateness and justice. Imagine in this instance someone engaged in commercial activity who has learned the maxims of commonplace usage in respect of restraining intemperate desires in everyday life and of giving to each what is properly his or hers. Now suppose that this person has to extend what he or she has thus learned beyond the domestic, commercial and other contexts in which they were originally learned to situations in which the criteria for judging what temperateness and justice require are not in significant respects the same as those appropriate to the initial contexts. Such a person may discover that by taking a quite new kind of risk with legitimately borrowed money, he or she has a reasonable expectation of making sums of money in extraordinary excess of what has hitherto been possible; *but* the lenders never envisaged this kind of risk and the consequences for the economy in general are incalculable. Once again it is scarcely necessary to spell out the right answer; what is clear is that in the face of such a question, the person with too indeterminate a conception of temperateness and justice will be morally resourceless. And once again, too indeterminate a conception is just what the morality of commonplace usage will supply.

A third example is that of the scientific researcher who knows that he or she can only hope to obtain further funding for a very important research project, if he or she can produce some positive findings *now*. But it is in fact a good deal too soon for it to be possible to produce such findings. The researcher thus faces the following dilemma: *either* to falsify his or her reports of the data so far, *or* to imperil the entire project. The researcher has learned to value two kinds of good: those to be achieved in and through the exercise of the intellectual virtues in scientific enquiry, and those of the virtues of integrity and honesty both in the contexts of enquiry and elsewhere. How, in such a situation, the researcher extrapolates from the examples and from the teaching by which he or she was originally instructed, will of course depend upon his or her understanding the relevant virtues in terms of a detailed and determinate hierarchical ordering of human goods. But the indeterminateness of the conceptions of the virtues as understood in terms of commonplace usage precludes the possession of such a capacity in those whose moral education was limited to those conceptions.

These three examples have been presented in a way that is designed to avoid so far as possible the accusation that I have used them to advance partisan solutions. For in each case I have focused not upon the question of what ought to be done or left undone in each situation, but upon the lack of resources afforded in that type of situation by the shared public morality of commonplace usage. And it matters a good deal that what I have described are of course not imaginary, but real cases, and that each of them is just the type of case that evokes in the public forums of our society a demand for improved moral education as a remedy against their recurrence. Yet what these examples reveal is that the only type of moral education consistent with the shared moral rhetoric of our contemporary political order, so far from providing a remedy, actually engenders the type of character that is bound to fail when put to this sort of test. What the morality of the virtues articulated in and defended by the moral rhetoric of our political culture provides is, it turns out, not an education in the virtues but, rather, an education in how to seem virtuous, without actually being so.

8

EDUCATION IN CHARACTER AND VIRTUE

Terence H. McLaughlin and J. Mark Halstead

Education has for its object the formation of character. To curb restive propensities, to awaken dormant sentiments, to strengthen the perceptions, and cultivate the tastes, to encourage this feeling and repress that, so as finally to develop the child into a man of well proportioned and harmonious nature – this is alike the aim of parent and teacher.

(Herbert Spencer)

Of the major strategies for moral education which have been developed in the last forty years, 'character education' is probably the one having the biggest impact at present in schools in the USA. This impact may be judged not only in terms of the number of recently published key texts devoted to character education[1] and the number of recently opened independent or university-based centres devoted to this strategy,[2] but, more significantly, in terms of the number of schools seeking to adopt its techniques. This impact has not so far been felt so strongly in quite the same way in England and Wales, although some concerns typically expressed in terms of 'character education' can be detected (sometimes implicitly) in recent initiatives relating to values and moral education.[3]

It would be wrong, however, to see an interest in 'character education' as a merely contemporary phenomenon. A realisation that moral development and moral education requires not only the achievement of certain cognitive or rational capacities on the part of the person but also the development of qualities of character and virtue, is an insight that has its roots in Plato and Aristotle and which has preoccupied and puzzled philosophers ever since. Philosophical discussions of moral education during the last twenty-five years, for example, have acknowledged at least to some extent the place that the wider development of the person must have in any adequate account of moral education,[4] and a number of philosophers have laid particular emphasis upon this wider dimension of the task.[5] Contemporary developments in moral and ethical theory such as those associated with 'virtue ethics'[6] and with the

132

assertion of the centrality to ethical life of dispositions[7] are likely to reinforce and deepen this acknowledgement and these emphases.

'Character education' is, however, ripe for careful critical attention at present because of its salience in some areas of current educational policy and practice in various parts of the world, and because of the controversial issues to which it gives rise. Certain conceptions of 'character education' seem to embody an attractive commonsense message. But the apparent attractiveness and simplicity of this message is deceptive, and the controversial issues to which the message gives rise are inescapable and deep-seated, as can be readily seen from the following sorts of questions: what is meant by the notion of a 'character'? What sort of character, and range of virtues more generally, should we be seeking to develop in students, and with what justification? Is it possible, particularly in the context of the pluralism and diversity of a liberal democratic society, to articulate a conception of character formation and education which can be defended against accusations of illicit value influence (and even indoctrination) regarding the way it is conducted and the conceptualisations and values it embodies? Does an emphasis on 'character' involve a unjustifiable neglect of the development of critical reasoning in students and the need to attend to the possible inadequacy of social and political conditions and policies? To what extent is it possible to teach virtue at all, and what strategies and contexts are required for this? How, if at all, can success in these matters be identified and evaluated?

Adequate attention to the full range of these questions is clearly beyond the scope of this chapter. However, it will address a number of these issues with the aim of illuminating those respects in which the formation of character is a defensible goal, exploring how far certain widely advocated strategies of character education are acceptable from an educational perspective, and identifying the considerations that require sustained investigation if the task of educating in character and virtue is to be brought into sharper focus.

The chapter has four sections. In the first we draw a distinction between two broad conceptions of 'character education', which we label the 'non-expansive' and the 'expansive' conceptions respectively. In the second we offer an exposition of the 'non-expansive' conception and its distinctive claims, together with the contemporary movement in support of it. A critique of this 'non-expansive' conception is offered in the third section. In the fourth, an outline is given of 'expansive' conceptions of character education, together with an indication of the difficulties and concerns to which they give rise.

Conceptions of 'character education'

'Character education' is clearly no single thing, and is capable of being interpreted in a number of different ways. It is closely related to the broader notion of education in the virtues, not least because of the strong link between the notions of 'character' and 'virtue'. As Steutel has rightly insisted, it is important to achieve clarity about the different senses in which terms like 'the virtue approach' to moral education can be understood (Steutel 1997).

An education in character and virtue is concerned with the formation and shaping of persons in a wide-ranging way, and is based on the realisation that what is important in education (and specifically moral education) is the sort of person one is or becomes, and not merely the nature of the thinking one engages in. Such an education gives rise to matters both of complexity and controversiality.

Matters of complexity arise because of the multifaceted nature of the notions of both 'character' and 'virtue'. This complexity can be illustrated by a preliminary outline of a number of familiar general features of both notions, beginning with the notion of a virtue.

A virtue is a trait or state of character of a person which is relatively entrenched and which specifies an excellence of some kind acquired and developed over time which is exhibited non-sporadically and non-arbitrarily. Virtues have a 'success' component in that possession of a virtue implies reliability in achievement of the excellence at stake. What can count as a virtue is wide ranging and extends beyond the realm of the moral to include (for example) social graces and intellectual virtues. What has been regarded as a virtue has changed over the years, and there are many lists and classifications of virtues and accounts of the proper overall relationship of virtues to each other, as in doctrines relating to their unity. Virtues differ in kind from each other. Some are virtues of self-control, whilst others are virtues of attachment, or of right direction of attitude, value and feeling. Virtues are composite in that they are related to (though not reducible to) feeling, desire, emotion, perception, reason, judgement, self-determination, will, action and motivation. Whether there is a core or unifying concept of a virtue has been a matter of much discussion, as has the question of whether some virtues are universal and fundamental with respect to their significance for human life or whether virtues in general are inherently relativistic and particularistic. Virtues have corresponding vices. Most virtues have an end specified through motivation. The notion of the identification and ordering of virtues in the light of their contribution to the fulfilment of a substantial conception of human well-being or flourishing (involving in some cases the notion of an overall end, or *telos*, of human life as a whole) is prominent in virtue theory. Virtues are therefore often associated with an 'ethics of aspiration'.

The connection between 'virtue' and 'character' is strong in that a virtue is a state or disposition of character. A person's virtues and vices are partly constitutive of a person. 'Character' refers to a person's enduring traits, and therefore plays an important role in explaining not only how a person acts now, but how he or she can be counted upon to act. Peters notes that character traits are centrally related to what can be an object of decision for a person. Thus, a person's character can be distinguished from his or her temperament, personality, inclinations, desires or nature. A person's character is seen, rather, in the way in which these features of the person are exercised or regulated (Peters 1974: 245–6). Peters notes that there are at least three ways in which we can speak of 'character': a 'non-committal' sense as referring to the sum total of a person's character traits; a sense that refers to 'types' of character in specifying a distinctive pattern of traits or style in which they are exhibited; and a sense in which a person may be described as 'having character' in that he or she possesses qualities such as consistency, integrity, steadfastness of purpose, incorruptibility and the like, regardless of the specific traits of character possessed and in contrast to a person who is dominated by passing inclinations or by other people (*ibid.*: 247–51).

An enduringly complex question relating to virtue and character concerns their relationship to cognition, judgement and reasoning. The notion of a form of practical rather than theoretical reasoning is central here, as captured in the Aristotelian notion of *phronesis*, which unites virtue and character to appropriate forms of reasoning in an intimate way. This is clearly seen in Aristotle's insistence that 'it is not possible to be fully good without having practical wisdom, nor practically wise without having excellence of character' (Aristotle 1962: 1144b31–2). The nature of the judgement involved in *phronesis* requires practical knowledge of the good, together with intelligent and personally engaged sensitivity to situations and individuals, including oneself, in making judgements about what constitutes an appropriate expression of the good in a given circumstance. Practical judgement of this kind is inherently supple and non-formulable, although the extent to which principles of some kind are involved has been the subject of much debate. Aristotle's invocation of the 'mean' as illuminative of what should properly guide judgement is well known: 'Virtue is a character state concerned with choice, lying in the mean relative to us, being determined by reason and the way the person of practical wisdom would determine it' (Aristotle 1962: 1107a1).[8]

Central to the development of character and virtue is imitation, habituation, training in feeling, attention and perception, and the development of moral insight, sympathy, sensitivity and sensibility through relevant forms of guidance and experience. The presence of forms of cognition and reasoning in these processes should be recognised. As Burnyeat puts it, 'practice has cognitive powers, in that it is the way we learn what is noble or just' (Burnyeat 1980: 73).

This outline of central features of the notions of 'character' and 'virtue' brings readily into focus the complexities involved in gaining a perspicuous understanding of the notions, let alone of the educational conditions needed for their development.

The controversiality that can arise in relation to any account of education in character and virtue is also manifest. It can be seen in some warnings Peters gives about 'character training'. Peters points out that people might agree on the desirability of developing character traits like consistency, integrity and persistence, but disagree about which substantive traits were desirable, which 'type' of character was to be encouraged and which overall conception of the ideal person was to be favoured (Peters 1974: 250–1). After all, education in character and virtue involves the development of some sorts of persons rather than others. Flanagan identifies a central difficulty for the moral development of persons in his observation that 'we no longer think that there is one single and unitary ideal of successful moral personhood, no set of necessary and sufficient conditions definitive of moral goodness' (Flanagan 1991: 329). All accounts of education in character and virtue, especially those that relate to the common schools of a liberal democratic society, must take a stand in relation to this kind of observation, either by claiming the observation is wrong headed or overstated, or by showing how it justifies or falsifies the ensuing programme of development. Nor does controversiality arise simply because we disagree about fundamental questions about the nature of goodness. Again, as Flanagan notes, 'even where we agree on what counts as good, many different modes of psychological organization can bring about the desired class of results. There is a vast array of morally good personalities' (*ibid.*: 332).

Any articulation of a conception of education in character and virtue therefore inevitably gives rise to matters of complexity and controversiality. In gaining a clearer understanding of the differing kinds of conception we distinguish between 'non-expansive' and 'expansive' conceptions.[9] Before proceeding, it is helpful to make two points. First, it is important to note that we are using the terms 'non-expansive' and 'expansive' in a specific way for our own purposes, and the specific sense we give to these terms needs to be borne in mind throughout. Our distinction should also not be seen in too stark a way. It is best expressed in terms of a continuum on which conceptions of character education can be located. The notion of a continuum better captures the inherently imprecise nature of the differences at stake, and underscores the point that no rigidly separable conceptions of 'character education' are intended. Second, we have been using the terms 'character education' and 'education in character and virtue' somewhat interchangeably. 'Character education' tends, however, to be particularly associated with conceptions we label 'non-expansive'. Although 'expansive' interpretations do involve the education of character, they less commonly use the specific designation 'character education', preferring broader labels such as 'education in character and virtue' or avoiding a label separate from the broader educational domain in which they are located (for example 'moral education' or 'education for citizenship'). Whilst we shall continue to use the terms 'character education' and 'education in character and virtue' interchangeably, this tendency of usage should be noted.

All conceptions of 'character education' have in common the belief that adults, in particular teachers, have a duty not merely to teach children *about* character (and virtue more generally) but also to *develop* qualities of character and virtue in the children themselves. 'Character education' is therefore critical of views of moral development and moral education such as those

136

developed by Kohlberg, which are seen as giving undue pride of place to the development of (abstract) reasoning about moral principles (Kohlberg 1981).[10] Further, 'character education' is hostile to the 'values clarification' view of moral education (Raths *et al.* 1966), where the additional vice of relativism is detected.[11]

The expansiveness or otherwise of conceptions of 'character education' on our view relate principally to three features:

1 the nature and extent of the rationale offered for the conception;
2 the nature and extent of the qualities of character and virtue proposed for development; and
3 the nature and extent of the role given to appropriate forms of reasoning on the part of the student.

Before proceeding, it is necessary to re-emphasise that we are using the terms 'expansive' and 'non-expansive' in specific senses. Some conceptions of character education we describe as 'non-expansive' may seem to warrant the label 'expansive' because the virtues and qualities of character proposed for development are seen as general and widely applicable to the whole of a person's life. Similarly, some conceptions we describe as 'expansive' may seem better described as 'non-expansive' because they conceive of the virtues and qualities of character with which they are concerned as intentionally restricted to only part of the life of a person (as, for example, in the case of the 'civic virtues'). However, as mentioned earlier, the precise sense we give to the terms 'non-expansive' and 'expansive' needs to be borne in mind.

'Non-expansive' conceptions of 'character education' are discernible in claims that, with respect to their students, teachers should 'shape and determine their behaviour' or 'form their character' (Wynne 1991: 143), where what is envisaged in this 'shaping', 'determining' and 'forming' is limited in at least the three ways just indicated. First, the rationale typically offered for the conceptions is significantly limited. A common rationale involves a diagnosis of the current moral condition of society and a claim about what is needed in educational terms as a remedy for failures and shortcomings. Second, the sorts of qualities of character and virtue seen as apt for development are regarded as in some sense fundamental and basic. Thus, 'character education' on this interpretation is seen as involving 'a deliberate effort by schools, families and communities to help young people understand, care about and act upon core ethical values' (Character Education Partnership, quoted in Lickona 1996). Third, there is a restricted emphasis upon reasoning on the part of the student. Kilpatrick (1992: 15), for example, rejects the development of moral reasoning and the strategy of values clarification as misguided approaches to moral education and stresses instead the need for direct teaching of character traits and for children to practise these traits until they become second nature. In accounts of 'character education' such as these, the development of sound moral habits rather than abstract moral reasoning is given emphasis and priority. It is true, of course, that, as indicated earlier, the proper form of reasoning in relation to the qualities of character and virtue in the moral life is widely acknowledged to be of a practical and not an abstract kind, insightfully characterised in the Aristotelian notion of *phronesis* or practical wisdom, and in relation to which the formation and development of habits has an important role to play. What is characteristic of non-expansive accounts of 'character education', however, is their neglect of moral reasoning, however conceived.

In spite of Lickona's attempts (1991) to depict character education as an overarching framework of moral education which draws the best from other strategies, including those emphasising moral reasoning and values clarification, approaches to character education of this 'non-expansive' kind are often seen as part of the neo-conservative social and cultural agenda and linked to the call to return to traditional values and teaching methods. For this reason, Molnar describes such approaches as 'traditionalist' (Molnar 1997: x). In this respect, these approaches can be seen as typically involving what Gutmann describes as 'Conservative Moralism' because they take for granted, for example, the importance of a respect for authority (Gutmann 1987: 56). Gutmann contrasts 'Conservative Moralism' with the 'Liberal Moralism' of Rawls and Kohlberg, which emphasises moral reasoning, autonomy and the morality of principle (*ibid.*: 59–64) and the 'Liberal Neutrality' of values clarification, which leaves children free to choose and develop their own values so long as they respect those of others (*ibid.*: 54–6). 'Non-expansive' conceptions typically figure in the current preoccupation with 'character education' which has been described.

Views of 'character education' of a more 'expansive' kind involve an easing of the three sorts of restriction which have been noted. First, the rationale offered by these conceptions is more elaborated and broader. A number of conceptions, for example, offer a sophisticated and nuanced account of the nature and requirements of a liberal democratic society as a context for their argument. Second, the qualities of character and virtue regarded as apt for development go beyond the fundamental and basic, narrowly conceived. An 'expansive' view of these qualities can be seen in certain views of moral education which lay particular emphasis upon the virtues (see, for example, Carr 1991) in accounts of the complex qualities of character and virtue which are seen as requiring development as part of education for citizenship in a liberal democratic society (see, for example, Gutmann 1987; White, P. 1996; Callan 1997), in views of education seen from a communitarian and from a liberationist perspective (see Nash 1997: chs 4 and 6 respectively) and in views of the formation of the person involved in specific conceptions of education such as those linked with a particular religious faith (see, for example, Hauerwas 1975; Dykstra 1981; Isaacs 1984).[12] Third, there is a fuller characterisation of, and emphasis upon, the nature and scope of reasoning seen as appropriate and necessary for development in students.

'Non-expansive' conceptions of education in character and virtue

As already indicated, the contemporary movement for 'character education' is largely concerned with the notion in its non-expansive sense. It has been observed that this movement is somewhat heterogeneous, lacking a common theoretical perspective and core of practice, and adopting an eclectic approach to many matters (Leming 1997: 41; see also Lockwood 1997: 178–9). Further, its arguments are not always developed in a philosophically sophisticated and rigorous way.[13] Notwithstanding all this, however, it is possible to offer some sound generalisations about this general movement.

The movement can be profitably viewed in a historical perspective.[14] It is often described as calling for a return to the educational principles and teaching methods of the nineteenth and early twentieth centuries. Certainly William Bennett's highly successful volume, *The Book of Virtues* (1993), has much in common with McGuffey's *Eclectic Readers*, which sold a phenomenal 100 million copies between 1850 and 1890 (Leming 1994). Both contain poems, Bible and other stories, extracts from philosophers, famous sayings and folktales, all designed to promote moral conduct and build character while at the same time developing cultural literacy. But whereas the moral messages of McGuffey's *Readers* were grounded in a generalised form of Protestantism, character education since the start of the twentieth century came to promote a set of virtues based on a secular morality. These virtues were considered to be universally applicable (and therefore compatible with religion), and they were promoted by teachers, clubs, parents, national organisations like Uncle Sam's Boys and Girls, and professional organisations like the Character Education Institution, founded in 1911. The latter organisation published the 'Children's Morality Code', a four-page leaflet that set out ten desirable character traits: self-control, kindness, self-reliance, reliability, truth, good workmanship, teamwork, duty, sportsmanship and good health (Hutchins 1917). By 1931, in Chicago alone there were over 200 competing character education plans that schools could adopt (Wooster 1990: 52). However, by the mid-1930s character education went into decline, largely because of an adverse report from a major research project at the Columbia University's Teachers College (Hartshorne and May 1928–30), which concluded that the exercise of character was 'situationally specific', that character education programmes were generally ineffective and that the development of virtues such as self-control and honesty was largely a matter of chance.[15] With the decline of character education, citizenship became the major focus of values education in American schools until the advent of values clarification in the 1960s.

The revival of character education since the early 1980s has drawn heavily on these earlier approaches to the notion both for its underlying philosophy and its methodology. The main elements involved in the articulation of contemporary character education of a 'non-expansive' kind can be outlined as follows:

(a) A diagnosis of the sorts of individual and social ills for which 'character education' is seen as a remedy, which is frequently presented in terms of moral and social deterioration and crisis. There is widespread agreement among proponents of the contemporary character education movement about the nature of the ills at stake, and the perception that (a certain form of) education is an appropriate remedy for them.[16] The movement is therefore driven by a distinctive moral, political and social agenda.

(b) A claim that certain 'basic' or 'core' values can be identified and justifiably developed in students in the form of qualities of character and virtue. Thus, it is typically claimed that there are certain fundamental ethical values that are recognised and admired by adults throughout the civilised world, such as caring, honesty, fairness, responsibility and respect for self and others, and that these values form the basis of good character (Lickona 1996: 95). In *The Book of Virtues* (1993), Bennett lists what he considers desirable qualities of character: self-discipline, compassion, responsibility, friendship, work, courage, perseverance, honesty, loyalty and faith. It is, however, typically acknowledged: (i) that no two persons' lists of virtues will be identical – others, for example, may wish to include integrity, generosity, politeness, tolerance and sensitivity to others; (ii) that these qualities may be defined and prioritised in different ways; (iii) that there may be other qualities of character such as patience, patriotism, humility, selflessness (Lasley and Biddle 1996) or the capacity to defer gratification (Goldman 1996) which are more controversial, and (iv) that the qualities need not be seen in exclusively moral terms. They extend to the prudential, the cultural, the social and the civic (Heslop 1995: 196ff). Overall, it is claimed that 'there is fairly general agreement as to what elements constitute good character in an individual' (Bennett 1991: 131)[17] and that these elements are importantly non-relative. Several authors make an explicit link of some kind between such values and those of democracy and citizenship.

(c) A claim that it is necessary not only to bring about an *understanding* of these 'basic' or 'core' qualities of character and virtue on the part of students, but to shape the students so that the qualities are developed in them. Thus Bennett argues that we want not merely to teach students about the traits of character we most admire, but also to ensure that our children possess the traits (*ibid.*: 133). Therefore, there is a strong emphasis on the behaviour and actions of the child as evidence for the success of the approach.

(d) A claim that the task of developing the desired and desirable qualities of character and virtue in students should be approached systematically and explicitly and not left to, say, chance or the processes of the 'hidden curriculum'.

(e) A claim that, although a range of pedagogical strategies are needed to achieve the aims of character education, three sets of influences are particularly significant: (i) the example set by the teacher, (ii) the organisation and 'ethos' of the school and (iii) direct instruction.

With regard to (i), it is argued that character formation clearly begins in the home, and it is here that the powerful influence on the developing character of the young of the example set by morally mature adults is first seen. It is by the example they set that adults show to children how the virtues 'work for the good in human life' and this has particular significance for the work of the teacher. Proponents of character education refer approvingly to Buber (1965), who emphasises the significance of the example teachers set in their dialogical relationships with students, and who maintains that teachers are different from all other influences in that their part in the development of character is a conscious choice, implicit in their vocation (see Bennett 1991: 134). Teachers may consciously model good moral conduct by working diligently, displaying goodwill towards colleagues, taking pride in the school, and so on (Wynne 1991: 147).

With regard to (ii), it is insisted that the organisation and 'ethos' of the school is central to its moral influence. The moral climate of the school, it is urged, should be consistent with the values promulgated through direct instruction, so that character development is integrated into every aspect of the daily life and relationships of the school (Lickona 1991: ch. 17). The values may be reinforced in assemblies, school ceremonies, school policy documents and through awards and other ways of publicly recognising good conduct (Wynne 1991: 147–8). Further, students need repeated opportunities to practise good behaviour until it becomes a habit and part of their 'personal narrative'. It is by grappling with real-life challenges, says Lickona, that 'students develop practical understanding of the requirements of fairness, co-operation and respect' (Lickona 1996: 95).

With regard to (iii), it is widely claimed that teaching by example and the moral influence of the organisation and ethos of the school needs to be supplemented by direct instruction in which teachers spell out the difference between right and wrong and reinforce the importance of good character. Such instruction need not involve separate courses, but can be integrated into the existing curriculum. In particular, stories drawn from history and literature are seen to be an effective way of teaching the virtues because they expand the moral imagination and develop the emotional side of a child's character (Lickona 1991: 79ff). Kilpatrick (1992: ch. 15) offers a guide to 120 books that may contribute to children's character development.[18] The instructional process may also include the study of heroes and of people who have demonstrated a particular virtue, as well as discussion, problem-solving, cooperative learning, experience-based projects, integrated thematic learning, and so on. The importance of sustained and demanding academic study in general for the development of character is also stressed.

(f) A claim that the consideration and discussion of difficult and controversial moral issues (seen as central in Kohlberg's approach to moral education) should not be attempted in schools until children have been taught the importance of, and have been shaped by, moral values and personal qualities of character. The processes involved in this shaping, such as exemplification, imitation, habituation, practice, exhortation and instruction, should come first. As Bennett insists, 'the formation of character and the teaching of moral literacy come first, the tough issues later, in high school or college' (Bennett 1991: 137).

'Non-expansiveness' in its different aspects can be seen in relation to a number of features of the approach which have been identified. The rather limited rationale is apparent in (a), the narrowly conceived qualities of character and virtue in (b) and the restricted emphasis given to reasoning in (c), (e) and (f).

Proponents of character education in 'non-expansive' terms point to four main benefits of this approach for moral education. First, it is seen as a direct response to the perceived crisis in the values and conduct of young people (Leming 1994: 123) and as crucial to the task of making individuals 'fully human' (Lickona 1997: 45) and morally literate (Bennett 1991: 133), as well as being central to the reversal of the tide of antisocial behaviour and the amelioration of other social ills and helping to rebuild a moral society (Lickona 1996). Second, it is claimed that the direct teaching of standards of right and wrong enjoys much more widespread public support than those approaches to moral education (such as that favoured by Kohlberg and by advocates of values clarification) which fail to 'give unqualified support to the content of any particular set of moral standards' (Pritchard 1988: 470). Third, it is argued that there is research evidence to suggest that character education not only influences students' moral development but may also improve their academic performance (*ibid.*: 471) and enhances the conduciveness of schools to the tasks of teaching and learning. Finally, it is urged that there is an egalitarian dimension to character development, since it is non-competitive and not dependent on academic ability, and therefore makes success open to any student. In turn this may result in less student alienation from school (Wynne and Walberg 1985–6).

Critique of 'non-expansive' conceptions

'Non-expansive' conceptions of character education are open to a number of interrelated lines of significant criticism:

1   The diagnosis of the individual and social ills for which these conceptions of character education are seen as a remedy is open to criticism on
the grounds that they seem to assume that 'the independent value-based
behavior of individuals is the best explanation for social virtue or moral
decay' (Molnar 1997: 164). The significance of context and circumstance
is neglected. More specifically, Purpel argues that 'character education'
seeks to divert attention from societal, economic and political factors to
the attitudes and behaviour of individuals, and to the alleged failures of
schools in relation to them (Purpel 1997; see also Kohn 1997: 155–6).
There is thus an emphasis upon psychological explanations and on interventions focused on individuals. However, for Purpel, 'to talk of personal
character and a moral community is inevitably to speak of political, social,
cultural and economic structures' (Purpel 1997: 151; see also Purpel 1989
and Jonathan in this volume). Other objections to the diagnosis of the
ills for which character education is seen as a remedy include the claim
that the diagnosis is based on a pessimistic view of human nature (Kohn
1997: 156), and that it neglects alternative explanations of the matters
at issue (Nash 1997: 33–8).

2   There is a failure to elaborate a 'comprehensive framework' of value of
a moral, religious, social, political, cultural and economic kind, in the
light of which the rationale and programmes of proponents of character
education can be understood and assessed. Such proponents fail to offer
either 'ideological analysis' or 'ideological affirmation', and their ideological assumptions of various kinds are left unacknowledged and unex-
plored (Purpel 1997: 146). Purpel points to the need for proponents of
character education to have 'some reasonably comprehensive framework
that gives order and meaning to their critique and program' (*ibid.*: 147).
Too often, he complains, we are offered a framework that is 'skimpy' and
'thin', and which gives rise to an inadequate debate about the matters
at stake and the possibility of misunderstanding.[19]

3   Under the guise of an emphasis upon 'basic' or 'core' values, a set of moral
and ethical values that are both substantial and significantly controversial are being transmitted. This 'particular moral point of view and cultural
vision' (Purpel 1997: 144) typically contains a number of elements that
identify it as at least harmonious with the agenda of neo-conservatism
and the political Right, including an emphasis upon the work ethic, obedience to authority, civility, orderliness and the like, all of which serve to
preserve the *status quo* and inhibit legitimate and necessary critique (Purpel
1997: esp 145–52; see also Nash 1997: 48–50). Examples of such controversial elements in character education proposals can be readily identified. In his account of what is needed in the development of loyalty in
students, for example, Wynne points to the need to keep 'revisionism'
under control, requiring vigilance in relation to 'historical materials with
an undue interest in deprecating the contributions of previous traditional

leaders and notable past achievements' (Wynne 1997: 69), whilst Benninga criticises what he sees as the anti-American bias of some schools (Benninga 1997: 84–6).[20] Because the message of such proponents of character education is seen by some as a form of preaching, these proponents have been described as 'ministers of moral character' and as 'virtuecrats' (Nash 1997: 5–6).[21] In contrast to such approaches, Purpel insists that 'schools are important public arenas for ideological debate and struggle' (Purpel 1997: 146). In sum, therefore, the approach stands accused of neglecting the force of the point that 'there will always be competing conceptions of what is true and good in a secular pluralist democracy, and the best way to resolve philosophical, religious, and political differences in a diverse world is through . . . open-minded, mutually respectful conversations in the classroom about what actually constitutes truth and morality' (Nash 1997: 39).[22] At a deeper level, the whole adequacy of the 'neo-classical' virtues for life in a liberal democratic society is called into question (Nash 1997: chs 2, 3).[23] As Nel Noddings observes, the replacement of 'character education' by cognitive developmentalism of the sort articulated by Kohlberg was caused by an increasing realisation of the hetereogenity of contemporary American society (Noddings 1997: 3).

4   There is a failure adequately to specify as a context for the task of 'character education' the notion of a liberal democratic society, with its distinctive features, values, principles and requirements. Thus, for example, Purpel claims that, in contrast to earlier writing on character education and initiatives in relation to it, there is only a token mention by its contemporary proponents of the need to sustain a democratic consciousness and the vitality of democratic institutions, and to resist forces and realities inimical to them.[24] One consequence of this failure to specify the democratic context of the discussion is a lack of emphasis upon the need to educate students for democratic citizenship and for personal autonomy, properly understood (see McLaughlin 1992). Another consequence of this failure is inattention to several concepts and distinctions (most notably the notions of the 'public' and 'non-public') which could enable the difficulty of justifying potentially controversial value influence upon students to be met or at least eased (see McLaughlin 1996a). Some proponents of character education of a non-expansive kind seek to make their proposals more widely acceptable to all groups in society, including those with considerable reservations about aspects of liberal democratic theory and practice. It is necessary, however, for such proposals to be fully articulated in relation to democratic principles if they are to be fully assessable.

5   Whilst not wholly ignored, there is relative neglect of the development of reasoning and critical independence in students (see (iii) and (iv) above), and of an appropriately rich form of practical judgement.[25]

Wynne explicitly insists that his approach involves indoctrination (Kohn 1997: 158). Such emphases underplay the role of forms of reasoning in the habituation of character (for Aristotle's view of this see, for example, Sherman 1989: ch. 5). Further, in seeming to downgrade the element of voluntariness on the part of students, such accounts remove a vital ingredient of morality (see Carr in this volume). Proponents of conceptions of character education of this kind are criticised for being predominantly concerned with 'moral compliance', which, at its worst, encourages 'submission, conformity, and docility' (Nash 1997: 31). Apart from the objections to this aim arising from its infringement of the moral autonomy and dignity of pupils, objections of a more practical kind arise, relating to the inadequacy of such a moral formation for the inevitable demands made on moral judgement and decision by a modern society.[26] What is needed by all students, it is urged, is 'deep, critical reflection about certain ways of being' (Kohn 1997: 161).

6   The 'basic' or 'core' values selected for development are frequently underdetermined with respect both to their meaning and 'content'. In part this is an implication of the failure to provide a fuller elaboration of the sort of 'comprehensive framework' of rationale and value alluded to in (ii). In the absence of such a framework, it is often difficult to discern how a virtue of (say) 'loyalty' is to be understood. Often, in the literature relating to conceptions of character education of this kind, such virtues and qualities of character are presented as mere names or labels. This neglects a number of important questions regarding the nature of these qualities which are rich in educational implication. These questions include considerations relating to the extent to which the qualities at stake are unitary in nature, discrete from each other, situation-sensitive and the like (see, for example, Flanagan 1991: ch. 13). The structural and other relationships between the virtues are often relatively neglected. Often the virtues are presented as if they were distinct items on a list which can be tackled systematically and separately by educators. This has been described as the 'If it's Tuesday, this must be Honesty' approach (Kohn 1997: 154). Further, the impression is sometimes given that the virtues are merely separable and isolatable pieces of behaviour.[27] In the absence of an overall and adequately sophisticated characterisation of the nature and structure of the virtues, and a specification of the ingredients of the sort of practical reasoning with which they must be inseparably connected, proponents of 'character education' are in danger of being left with a mere 'bag of virtues' for transmission. This makes it difficult to address, let alone resolve, questions of meaning, priority and coherence with respect to the virtues. For example, it is difficult to attend to important considerations relating to the overall structure of a person's qualities of character and virtue.[28] In addition, questions of justification tend to become obscured, and a misleading degree of consensus can be

invoked which is based merely on a positive reaction to certain virtue labels.[29] A further difficulty is that teachers and students may verbally assent to the names or labels of certain virtues, whilst not actually really being committed to the virtues at stake, properly understood. All these points have considerable implication for the coherence and effectiveness of pedagogical strategies, as well as for the fair illumination of value diversity.

7   The approach is too narrow and limited to facilitate the sort of adequate public debate that is needed about the task of moral education and value education more generally. Purpel insists that the contemporary movement for character education is really only a *part* of the discourse of moral and value education as a whole, and that it must not be allowed to monopolise and control that discourse, since it offers a 'truncated' dialogue (Purpel 1997: 147, 151).

8   The approach has failed to work out a well-grounded and systematic pedagogy. Thus Nash, for example, argues that the approach is 'strong on prescription and exhortation' but has yet to develop 'an effective praxis' (Nash 1997: 10).[30] The relative neglect of methods relating to the development of appropriate forms of critical reasoning is a source of particular concern (see Kohn 1997: 157–62).

It is important to ensure that the critique of the contemporary movement for education in character and virtue in its 'non-expansive' form is not overstated. First, it is necessary in developing a fuller critical appraisal of this general tradition to attend to the detailed features of the arguments of particular thinkers. These thinkers should not be lumped together too uncritically, nor should the nuance and sophistication of some of their views be overlooked. Second, in assessing this movement it is necessary to avoid exaggeration and to guard against other forms of unbalanced judgement, such as prejudice against the individual writers or their general perspective (see Nash 1997: 32–3). Third, critics of this movement often concede that, despite its shortcomings, the perspective contains a good deal of truth. After all, few would deny that the development of character and virtue is an important aspect of education.[31] The location of the truth in this general perspective is therefore an important aspect in its overall appraisal.

Expansive conceptions of education in character and virtue

Many of the criticisms of 'non-expansive' conceptions of character education seem to invite in response the development of more 'expansive' conceptions, where a fuller and more substantial account is offered of matters such as the nature and extent of its rationale, the qualities of character and virtue aimed at, and the role given to appropriate forms of reasoning on the part of students. Calls for a more 'expanded' conception, or at least application, of 'character education' are regularly heard. For example, it has been argued that the 'core' or 'basic' values that 'non-expansive' conceptions promote cannot ignore issues of multiculturalism. As Gay insists, one can always ask: 'Honesty, truth, and responsibility about what, when and for whom?' (Gay 1997: 98).

Some 'expansive' conceptions of 'character education' are intended to apply to particular schooling contexts, such as religious schools, where a mandate exists for the exercise of (at least certain sorts of) value influence extending beyond that acceptable to society as a whole. However, a difficulty exists for 'expansive' views of 'character education' which are intended to apply to a common conception of education, and to common schools, in a liberal democratic society.[32] This difficulty, which was indicated earlier, has been put by Gutmann in this way: 'No set of virtues remains undisputed . . . in any modern society that allows its members to dispute its dominant understandings' (Gutmann 1987: 36). Gutmann is drawing attention here to the suspicion from a liberal democratic philosophical and educational perspective of substantiality and particularity, especially when these involve the shaping of individuals in ways presupposing values and commitments that are, from a democratic point of view, potentially significantly controversial. In such matters, Gutmann contends, educators stand in danger of being accused not so much of pretending to moral superiority, but of illicitly asserting 'political authority over other citizens who reject their conception of virtue' (*ibid.*). In Purpel's words, we lack a 'communal notion of propriety' (Purpel 1997: 146). In the common school, from a liberal democratic perspective, there is a lack of a mandate for the exercise of substantial and wide-ranging moral influence upon the person. Whilst we speak of 'education of the whole child' quite freely in common schools, it is not clear that this can in fact be attempted in any unqualified or unproblematic way in this context (see McLaughlin 1996a).

'Expansiveness' in relation to the specification of qualities of character and virtue is apt to result in substantiality and particularity, and therefore to run the danger of infringing the concerns about undue value influence which have been noted. Onora O'Neill notes how virtue ethics is especially associated with particularism,[33] although it is an association she is keen to call into question (O'Neill 1996). A number of 'expansive' conceptions of 'character education' have been criticised on precisely the ground of exerting undue value influence in this way. Conceptions based on communitarianism in its various forms[34] have been found wanting because of the vulnerability to criticism of their communitarian assumptions (see, for example, Nash 1997: ch. 5).[35] Similarly, the 'liberationist' perspective associated with thinkers such as Freire and McLaren (see Nash 1997: chs 6, 7) have been accused of failing to justify the substantial influence on character and virtue it requires. Specific religious conceptions are seen as unacceptable in the common school. Nash, for example, makes the point that virtues like humility, faith, self-denial and charity are only acceptable for development in the common school if they are purged of their specifically religious associations (Nash 1997: 165–7).

'Non-expansive' conceptions of 'character education' have attempted to meet the difficulty of accusations of undue value influence by appealing to putatively 'basic' or 'core' values acceptable to all members of society. The difficulties arising in relation to this approach have already been noted. However, perhaps the general instinct of this approach in this matter is correct. Without common values, ideals and procedures, a liberal democratic society would lack not only coherence and stability, but also freedom, equality, tolerance and many other features of a moral and civilised life. We should not underestimate the extent of consensus about many virtues and other qualities of character which exists among people of wise practical judgement. The challenge for 'expansive' conceptions of 'character education' is to outline commonly acceptable forms of value influence in the development of character and virtue which extend beyond the minimalist accounts of these matters offered by 'non-expansive' conceptions whilst avoiding accusations of illicit value imposition and shaping.

One kind of 'expansive' character formation that might be thought to be relatively unproblematic from the point of view of liberal democratic values and principles relates to the development of qualities of character and virtue associated with the requirements of learning. Hugh Sockett, for example, discusses a range of personal qualities of will related to these requirements that are manifest as character traits or virtues: determination, carefulness, concentration, self-restraint and forbearance, patience, conscientiousness and endurance, which he categorises under the headings of endeavour, heed and control (Sockett 1988, 1997). All of these virtues, it is claimed, properly conceived and sensitively attuned to cultural difference (Sockett 1988: 208–9), can be confidently developed in any school. If this were not so, indeed, it would be hard to see how the school could invite its students to engage in any kind of sustained learning. Some personal qualities such as these (for example, dispositions to attend and to concentrate) have been described by Charles Bailey as 'serving competences' of a liberal education, whilst the development in students of the disposition to care is given an important place in this conception of education (Bailey 1984: 110–14, see also 152–60). These qualities of virtue and character, whilst not directly moral in nature, clearly have moral aspects and implications, and remind us that different sorts of virtue and character cannot easily be compartmentalised from each other.

What, however, of more directly moral qualities of virtue and character? David Carr's 'expansive' account of education in character and virtue addresses the question of illicit value influence and relativism head-on, and suggests that it can be eased by, for example, distinguishing between questions of ends and means in moral deliberation (Carr 1991: 238–42) and between attitudes and dispositions on the one hand and particular beliefs, codes and practices on the other (*ibid.*: 263–5). For Carr, relativism or doubt in relation to the ends of moral deliberation and to moral attitudes and dispositions (qualities of character and virtue) is misplaced. He writes: 'We cannot reasonably doubt whether it is right . . . to be just or courageous, but we may well wonder whether in doing this or that (evading the draft or going to fight in Vietnam) we are being *really* just or courageous' (*ibid.*: 255). Children need to receive initial training in the virtues and it is incoherent to object to such training as involving illicit influence. Carr argues that 'in training a child to be honest, self-controlled or considerate it is absurd to speak of indoctrination when there exist no *alternative* dispositions to truthfulness and self-discipline into which we might sensibly be said to be initiating children in the name of proper socialisation or education' (*ibid.*: 254–5, see also ch. 12).

Carr holds that whilst open discussion and argument about matters of moral controversy should feature in the later stages of education, 'it cannot occur prior to and actually presupposes some initiation of children into moral attitudes and dispositions of a more fundamental kind' (*ibid.*: 264). Further, Carr insists, 'only when children know something in practice of what courage, self-control, fairness and honesty are, are they in a position to understand or to cast a critical eye over particular or specific human social or moral codes and practices' (*ibid.*). Two questions arise here. The first is whether, given that moral attitudes and dispositions cannot be introduced to children in a wholly abstract way, the introduction that Carr envisages can avoid or minimise significant controversy. In this connection, queries arise about any specific conception of human perfection or flourishing which Carr is building-in to his account (Carr 1997: 346). The issues here are likely to require for their resolution a consideration of detailed teaching materials and strategies. The second question concerns how precisely Carr's position can be distinguished from that of proponents of 'non-expansive' conceptions of 'character education'. Carr's account has an 'expansive' rationale for his conception, a sophisticated account of the nature of the qualities of character and virtue being aimed at in education and a significant role for appropriate forms of reasoning on the part of the student. But how, given his remarks about the postponement of critical reasoning, does the practice he recommends differ from that of his 'non-expansive' counterparts? This matter will be returned to shortly.

One prominent way in which an attempt is made to develop an 'expansive' conception of qualities of character and virtue in students without incurring the criticism of undue value influence is through the notion of 'civic virtue'. Here an attempt is made to link substantive qualities of character and virtue not directly with the moral life as a whole but with the general features and requirements of democracy and citizenship.[36] It is important to note that different forms of liberal democratic education vary with respect to their requirements for 'civic virtue' and for the educational conditions and processes needed to develop it (see Callan 1997: 44). An 'expansive' approach to these matters is associated with such thinkers as Amy Gutmann (1987), Patricia White (1996) and Eamonn Callan (1997).

The need for the development of 'civic virtue' of an 'expansive' kind is out-lined by these thinkers in a number of ways. Amy Gutmann, for example, notes that 'it is at least as crucial to cultivate virtue in a free society as it is in one where citizens are constrained to act virtuously' (Gutmann 1987: 38), and that 'moral character' 'conducive to democratic sovereignty' (*ibid.*: 41), along with laws and institutions, forms the basis of democratic government (*ibid.*: 49). Gutmann sees the formation of such a character as a key part of political education, which she regards as having moral priority over other purposes of public education in a democratic society (*ibid.*: 287). Similarly, Eamonn Callan insists that 'free and equal citizenship is . . . about the kind of people we become, and the kind of people we encourage or allow our chil-dren to become' (Callan 1997: 2). Therefore, for Callan, as for Gutmann, 'creating virtuous citizens is as necessary an undertaking in a liberal demo-cracy as it is under any other constitution' (*ibid.*: 3). (For similar points see White, P. 1996: ch. 1; Kymlicka in this volume, section 1.)[37]

What are the ingredients of this form of 'civic virtue'? Whilst such ideals are 'open-ended' and 'protean' (Callan 1997: 5), they do have a number of determinate features. As a starting point for our exploration of these features it is useful to note Amy Gutmann's reminder of the reciprocal connection between character and reasoning. She writes:

> People adept at logical reasoning who lack moral character are sophists of the worst sort: they use moral arguments to serve what-ever ends they happen to choose for themselves. They do not take morality seriously nor are they able to distinguish between the obvious moral demands and the agonizing dilemmas of life.
>
> (Gutmann 1987: 51)

But, she goes on to insist, 'people who possess sturdy moral character with-out a developed capacity for reasoning are ruled only by habit and authority, and are incapable of constituting a society of sovereign citizens' (*ibid.*). In the case of civic virtue, both the virtues at stake and the forms of reasoning involved are imbued with democratic value and principle.

Gutmann specifies a form of 'deliberative' or 'democratic' character that is central to participation by citizens in the democratic life, and therefore to their ability to participate in 'conscious social reproduction' (*ibid.*: 46). She writes: 'Democratic citizens are committed, at least partly through the inculcation of habit, to living up to the routine demands of democratic life, at the same time as they are committed to questioning those demands whenever they appear to threaten the foundational ideals of democratic sovereignty, such as respect for persons' (*ibid.*: 46). The capacity to give 'careful consideration with a view to decision' (*ibid.*: 52) about matters that demo-cracy demands is central here. The scope of the matters considered as apt for deliberation and decision are illustrated in Gutmann's claim that students should be taught 'how to defend democracy and to reason about our political disagreements' (*ibid.*: 58) and to be encouraged to develop the capacity 'to understand and to evaluate competing conceptions of the good life and the good society' (*ibid.*: 44). For Gutmann, the possession of the capacity for such critical deliberation is vital for attributing democratic virtue to a person; no amount of political trust, efficacy or knowledge can replace it (*ibid.*: 107).

The respects in which civic virtue of this kind is expansive, and yet is potentially compatible with the concerns about undue substantiality and particularity of influence which were raised earlier, comes readily into focus. The conception is expansive in that a complex set of virtues, sensitivities and capacities is involved, based upon and supporting democratic values and principles, which is far from the underdetermined capacities characteristic of the 'non-expansive' approaches considered earlier. On the other hand, the underlying theory of liberalism presupposed on a view of this kind requires that no unduly specific conception of human well-being or flourishing is incorporated into the account. In fact, the account is precisely articulated in terms of making as much room as possible for the reflective consideration and adoption of differing reasonable alternative conceptions of human good.

The complexities involved in a conception of civic virtue of this kind is well illustrated in a recent articulation of such a conception by Eamonn Callan (Callan 1997). Writing of the educational implications of the notion of 'justice as reasonableness', in terms of which he articulates his view of education for citizenship, Callan notes that it 'devolves into a cluster of mutually supportive habits, desires, emotional propensities, and intellectual capacities whose co-ordinated activity requires contextually sensitive judgement' (Callan 1997: 8). For Callan, education for liberal democracy, properly understood, 'shapes the self in profound and often disturbing ways' (*ibid.*: 13). This is in part because of Callan's rejection of Rawls's claim that the implications of acceptance of 'the burdens of judgement' (the sources of ineliminable rational disagreement) can be confined to the 'political' sphere of the person's judgement and life (*ibid.*: ch. 2). On the contrary, claims Callan, acknowledgement of the need for such an acceptance requires for students a kind of education that will 'transform the character of the self in ways that have large consequences for how they will live beyond the realm of civic responsibility' (*ibid.*: 51).[38] Thus, for Callan, acceptance of 'the burdens of judgement' is 'an active and taxing psychological disposition, pervasively colouring the beliefs we form and the choices we make' (*ibid.*: 34). Students must first be brought to accept, and progressively to understand, the notions of 'moral reciprocity' and 'the burdens of judgement' (*ibid.*: 24–8). Part of this acceptance involves the gradual development of the capacity to distinguish between sources of disagreement explained by 'the burdens of judgment' and those arising from some less worthy source (*ibid.*: 217), and therefore come to an understanding of the notion of 'reasonable pluralism' and its role in indicating the nature and scope of appropriate forms of respect for difference. Students must become morally discriminating in their acceptance of diversity (*ibid.*: 19; see esp. 21–4). Crucial for students is 'serious imaginative engagement with rival views about good and evil, right and wrong' (*ibid.*: 40)[39] and engagement in appropriate forms of liberal dialogue.[40] Callan notes that the conditions of fruitful ethical confrontation are not easily achieved: 'they require much of participants in the way of emotional sophistication and cognitive ability, and when the relevant conditions are not met, dialogue may be worse than useless; it may be morally debilitating' (*ibid.*: 213). This would be so, for example, if participants were influenced by a wide-ranging relativism. Central here is the development of judgement, which clearly cannot involve any 'tidy moral calculus' or 'simple master-rule for moral choice' (*ibid.*: 8). Related to the sort of dialogue and judgement Callan envisages are a range of appropriate virtues and qualities of character, such as sympathy, moderation, compromise, responsibility, and an ability and inclination to subject ideas to critical examination. Interestingly, Callan includes among these virtues and qualities of character a 'critical [but] generous . . . susceptibility to those public emotions that bind us to the body politic' (*ibid.*: 121), amounting to a kind of 'liberal patriotism', together with the virtues required to deal with the 'moral distress' Callan sees as an inevitable consequence of living in a liberal democratic society (*ibid.*: ch. 8).[41]

There are a number of critical questions to be raised in relation to 'expansive' conceptions of education in character and virtue of this 'civic' kind. One issue arising is whether the 'virtues' involved in conceptions of this kind are to be properly seen as virtues at all, since they lack several features arguably part of a virtue, properly understood. David Carr, for example, holds that concepts of character are essentially functional or teleological in nature and that therefore they are liable to be 'unsusceptible of complete identification and explication short of reference to specific conceptions of human perfection and flourishing' (Carr 1997: 346). However, he argues, the sort of civic virtues discussed by Patricia White, given her commitment to liberal-democratic principles allergic to substantive conceptions of the good life, are better seen as 'all-purpose dispositions . . . which aspire both to reinforce commitment to some generally morally non-aligned conception of [democratic] public interest and to oil the wheels of social harmony and co-operation' (*ibid.*: 347).

A further issue relates to a potential instability that results from the intricate balance involved in civic virtue between seeking to bring about affiliation and commitment on the one hand and seeking to encourage criticism on the other.

Another issue arising concerns the justification of the underlying conception of civic virtue, and the possibility of achieving consensus on the perspective on civic virtue adopted. It will be recalled that competing conceptions of education for citizenship in a liberal democratic society offer more modest versions of 'civic virtue'. Nash draws attention to the possibility that, at least in the case of US public schools, there may be a lack of genuine consensus about a public good and public morality beyond individual and group interests. This, together with a preoccupation with diversity and relativism, make it difficult for the development of civic virtue of the kind outlined by Callan to get off the ground. Further, a postmodern awareness of the lack of grounding of even 'core beliefs' of democracy adds greater difficulty here (Nash 1997: 42–4). Examples of such core beliefs include Gutmann's principles of 'non-repression and 'non-discrimination' which 'preserve the intellectual and social foundations of democratic deliberations' (Gutmann 1987: 1, see also 44–7). In his remark that 'critical reason in the shape of an implacable scepticism is politically sterile' (Callan 1997: 113), Callan shows his awareness of these difficulties. Nash argues for a postmodern 'conversation' in the classroom which uses a public language that is 'non-foundational', 'multifunctional' and 'non-exclusionary' (Nash 1997: chs 8, 9). To the democratic dispositions, Nash would add the 'postmodern virtues': 'a sensitivity to the realities of incommensurability, indeterminacy and nonfoundationalism; dialectical awareness; and hermeneutical awareness' (Nash 1997: 163, see also 174–80). The precise meaning and implications of such an approach requires careful analysis.

A final difficulty concerns the educational conditions needed for the development of 'civic virtue', and here we return to the point made earlier about how Carr's position in practice can be distinguished from 'non-expansive' alternatives. The differing achievements of character and virtue aimed at by proponents of civic virtue and by Carr must start off from lower-level achievements of the sort that feature in 'non-expansive' conceptions. Peters's discussion of the paradox of reason and habit in moral education bears this out (Peters 1974: ch. 13). As is well known, Kohlberg acknowledged in his later work that his earlier criticisms of 'the bag of virtues' approach to moral education were to some extent misplaced. Writing in 1978, Kohlberg acknowledges: 'I realize now that the psychologists' abstraction of moral cognition . . . is not a sufficient guide to the moral educator . . . the educator must be a socializer' (quoted in Leming 1997: 40), a realisation that led him to acknowledgement of the centrality of the school and its life to moral education and the need for a 'just community' approach (Power et al. 1989: esp. chs 1, 2). This has resonances with some of Lickona's views on the significance of the 'total moral life of the school' in developing character (Lickona 1997). Gutmann notes that the Rawlsian 'morality of association' (where students accept rules because they are appropriate to the fulfilling of certain roles) is superior to the 'morality of authority' (where students follow rules simply because they are issued by authority figures), yet is inferior to the 'morality of principle' (where students are directly attached to moral principles themselves). But, she continues, whilst the 'morality of association' is philosophically a subordinate ideal to the 'morality of principle', it may be a primary political ideal for democratic education in schools, because of the difficulty of achieving the higher aim in schools and also because 'the morality of association' includes the development of the 'cooperative moral sentiments' such as empathy, trust, benevolence and the like. In Gutmann's view these contribute a great deal to democratic education (Gutmann 1987: 59–62). Further, she notes, many of the virtues prized by conservatives (such as honesty, respect for law and self-discipline) are necessary 'for students to appreciate the advantages of democratic politics' (*ibid.*: 58) and should therefore be taught in schools; as should other character traits such as honesty, which 'serve as foundations for rational deliberation of different ways of life' (*ibid.*: 44). Nash is correct in saying that it is only *at its worst* that a 'morality of compliance' encourages submission, conformity and docility (Nash 1997: 31). Whether it does or not depends on the broader aims with which it is associated.

These observations lead to the important point that there may in some ways be a significant overlap between 'non-expansive' and 'expansive' conceptions of education in character and virtue in terms of apparent teaching practices and strategies at certain stages of the educative process. The inculcation of fairly basic dispositions of character and virtue are important as the bedrock for the later sorts of achievement which are valued in 'expansive' accounts. John White is right to point out that our efforts at moral education cannot wait upon a determinate answer to the question of which theoretical account of the nature of morality is the correct one (White, J. 1990: 39–40). There are a range of qualities of character and virtue that we can rightly develop in students (on these see White, J. 1990: 45–9, see also 70; O'Hear and White 1991: section 4; see also Halstead 1996: 1–3).

These observations do not lead to the conclusion that the distinction between 'non-expansive' and 'expansive' conceptions is, after all, an illusory one. The central point here is brought out by Gutmann. 'Moral education begins by winning the battle against amoralism and egoism. And ends – if it ends at all – by struggling against uncritical acceptance of the moral habits and opinions that were the spoils of the first victory' (Gutmann 1987: 62).

The ingredients that 'expansive' conceptions add to education in character and virtue are important. However, it is necessary to acknowledge the strengths as well as the weaknesses of 'non-expansive' conceptions. These conceptions need to be enriched and extended, not abandoned. It is also necessary to acknowledge the considerable imprecision about what the 'added ingredients' of 'expansive' conceptions mean in pedagogic terms. The logic of the practical reasoning involved for the student is inherently non-systematic and non-formulable, and our understanding of ways in which the relevant qualities of character and virtue are developed is patchy,[42] not least because of difficulties in researching the matters at issue (see Leming 1997). Nor should wider issues of a societal kind be neglected.[43]

This brings us back to the question of how, given the overlap at least in the early stages of education between 'non-expansive' and 'expansive' conceptions of 'character education', the two conceptions can really be distinguished from each other in practice. The practical distinction between the two conceptions may not be illusory but it is elusive. The answer to the question of practical distinguishability surely lies in the understanding, practical reasoning, judgement, pedagogic skill, personhood and example of the teacher. In terms of understanding, the teacher must have a grasp of the rationale of the 'expansive' conception at issue, of the nature of the qualities of character and virtue being aimed at and of the sorts of practical reasoning on the part of students that are desired. Judgement is needed to discern precisely what the demands of a particular aim amount to in a given situation, and which means are required to bring about the aim. Pedagogic skill is needed to achieve the aims at stake. The personhood and example of the teacher is vital in exerting influence of the requisite kind.[44]

These expectations and requirements of teachers and their role in the education of character and virtue are demanding and extensive. They involve the possession by teachers of a form of pedagogic *phronesis*. Joseph Dunne draws attention to 'the complicity of phronesis with an established way of life' (Dunne 1993: 373). *Phronesis* seems to demand established and relatively stable 'communities of practice' (see Pendlebury 1990). It might be argued that we no longer have the stable communities of educational practice that *phronesis* demands. We no longer, for example, have a stable and rooted sense of the sort of person that a teacher should be and the sort of practice that education is.

Nothwithstanding these difficulties, however, it seems clear that the teacher is at the heart of any attempt to educate in character and virtue in the 'expansive' sense, and that any such attempt cannot ignore the complex kinds of teacher education, development and support which such an attempt requires if it is to offer to students the elusive additional ingredients that distinguish it from its 'non-expansive' alternatives.

Notes

1 See Ryan and McLean (1987), Benninga (1991), Lickona (1991), Kilpatrick (1992), Wynne and Ryan (1992), Bennett (1993), Etzioni (1993: ch. 3), Heath (1994), Huffman (1994) and Molnar (1997).
2 For a list, see Lickona (1995).
3 See, for example, School Curriculum and Assessment Authority (1996), Qualifications and Curriculum Authority (1997) and Talbot and Tate (1997). The influence of 'character education' has also been felt in other parts of the world. Such influence can be seen, for example, in criticisms offered of an Australian 'Charter of Values' for schools (Freakley 1996).
4 See, for example, Ryle (1972), Hirst (1974: esp. 64–9, ch. 6), Peters (1974: Part Two), Tobin (1989a) and Wilson (1990: ch. 8). Steutel has usefully drawn attention to the pervasive presence of the notion of 'virtues' in many approaches to moral education, including cognitive-developmental ones (Steutel 1997).
5 See, for example, O'Hear (1981: ch. 5), Straughan (1982, 1989), Noddings (1984), Tobin (1989b), Carr (1991) and Hansen (1996).

6 On virtue ethics see, for example, Flanagan and Rorty (1990), Flanagan (1991), Pence (1991), Slote (1992: esp. Parts II and IV), Carr (1995, 1996a), Hursthouse, Lawrence and Quinn (1995), Bond (1996: esp. ch. 8), Baron, Pettit and Slote (1997: esp. ch. 3), Crisp and Slote (1997) and Statman (1997). For critical dialogue between virtue ethics and the ethics of both Kantianism and consequentialism, see Baron, Pettit and Slote (1997: esp. chs 4–6).

7 An important point here, rich in educational implication, is that ethical life in general requires the replication of dispositions, including the basic disposition to attach ethical value to anything (see Williams 1987: esp. 63–5). Compare Williams (1981, 1985). On the educational importance of the shaping of dispositions see White, J. (1990: esp. chs 3, 4, 7); also O'Hear and White (1991: esp. section 4).

8 On all these points about character and virtue see the references indicated in note 1 and also, for example, Rorty (1980), Dent (1984), Sherman (1989) and Zagzebski (1996). On practical reasoning and practical wisdom see, for example, Carr (1991: esp. ch. 11), Dunne (1993: Part 2), Almond (1997) and Smith (1997).

9 This distinction is similar to that drawn between 'traditionalist' and 'expansive' views of 'character education' by Molnar (Molnar 1997: x); see Kohn (1997: 154).

10 For critiques of Kohlberg see, for example, Peters (1974: ch. 15), Dykstra (1981: ch. 1), Locke (1987), Carr (1991: ch. 7) and Thomas (1991).

11 For critiques of 'values clarification' see, for example, Strike (1982: 111–22).

12 It is not being denied here that forms of character formation associated with a particular religious faith can take a 'non-expansive' form.

13 It has been observed that proponents of character education in this sense tend to identify certain cardinal virtues, offer certain fundamental ideas about how these virtues fit together into a general perspective, and give an appropriate explanation of why the exercise of those virtues is imperative. They stop well short, however, of a sophisticated elaboration of an entire underlying philosophical view (Pritchard 1988: 474).

14 For more detail on this perspective see, for example, Leming (1997) and Nash (1997: 6–10).

15 For a critical perspective on the Hartshorne and May study and its relationship to the decline of character education, see Leming (1997: esp. 32–5); also Peters (1974: ch. 12).

16 On these ills see, for example, Molnar (1997: 176–7). For Lickona's ten indicators of moral decline (violence and vandalism, stealing, cheating, disrespect for authority, peer cruelty, bigotry, bad language, sexual precocity and abuse, increasing self-centredness and declining civic responsibility, and self-destructive behaviour) see Lickona (1991: 12–19). See also Nash (1997: 17–18, 33–8).

17 On the 'Six Pillars of Character' articulated at the Aspen Summit Conference on Character Education held in 1994, see Benninga (1997: 87).

18 On the significance of literature, and the Western cultural heritage more generally, in relation to these matters, see also Bloom (1987).

19 Writing in a similar vein, Nash bewails the failure of proponents of character education to be more 'politically forthright' (Nash 1997: x).

20 See also Lickona's claim that 'chastity is in truth one of the virtues . . . that serve the individual and common good' (Lickona 1997: 59).

21 Bennett (1991: 133) links his own concept of 'moral literacy' with Hirsch's 'cultural literacy' (1988), and both have been challenged for paying insufficient attention to the diversity of values in Western societies.

22 For arguments against 'sentimental civic education', see Callan (1997: ch. 5).

23 One of the central issues here is whether we can speak of the virtues in a democratic context without also bringing in talk of rights and principles. One of the difficulties concerns the extent to which ancient Greek ideals of character can be rendered compatible with (say) acting on principles relating to equality between human beings (Pence 1991: 254).

24 Purpel mentions as examples of these forces and realities the effects of an unbridled free market economy, growing economic inequality and systemic poverty (Purpel 1997: 149–50).

25 It is important to note that proponents of 'non-expansive' conceptions do not wholly neglect considerations relating to reasoning. Lickona, for example, acknowledges that a person is always faced by the need for judgement about the application of any particular virtue (Lickona 1991: 43–5).

26 Gutmann writes: 'The inadequacy of habitual behaviour is acute in modern societies where people confront new problems for which old habits supply insufficient guidance, and all the more acute in modern *democratic* societies where the ultimate court of appeal in politics is popular sovereignty, not past authority' (Gutmann 1987: 57).

27 Lickona defines these as 'types of behaviours which can be identified in school life' (Lickona 1996: 95).

28 On these matters see, for example, Sherman (1989: ch. 3).

29 Etzioni, for example, is quoted as saying: 'For me these values are independent moral causes, which speak to us in unmistakable terms in their own force – directly to our hearts in a very compelling voice – if you just listen to them' (Cohen 1995: 4). For critical comment on this, see Sockett (1996: 125–6).

30 On difficulties here, especially with the notion that 'inspiring books' can develop virtue, see Nash (1997: 45–52).

31 On the wide-ranging transformations of the person involved in education, see, for example, Passmore (1980: Part II).

32 On the values and principles relating to the common school in a liberal democratic society, see, for example, McLaughlin (1995).

33 O'Neill offers the following account of the views of those who hold a particularist perspective: 'They hope to orient ethical reasoning without appeal to universal principles of inclusive scope, or more generally without claims about what would be good, or right, or obligatory for all human lives, or about ideals that are relevant for all. For the most part they seek to anchor ethical claims by appeal to the actual practices or traditions or patterns of judgement of particular communities or, more radically, without looking beyond the particular sensibilities, attachments or judgements of individuals in particular situations. Some radical particularists doubt whether there are or could be ethical principles either of wide or of narrow scope, hence whether there can be ethical principles of any sort; other historicizing particularists allow that there can be ethical principles, and indeed that these principles can be of universal *form*, but insist that none of them are inclusive, i.e. that none has more-or-less cosmopolitan scope' (O'Neill 1996: 13). See also Luntley in this volume.

34 On three types of communitarianism (sectarian, post-liberal and civic-liberal) and their educational implications, see Nash (1997: ch. 4). See also Tam (1998: esp. ch. 3).

35 For criticism of the positions characteristically associated with MacIntyre, see, for example, Carr (1996b) and Nash (1997: 89–95). See also MacIntyre (1984) and in this volume.

36 Nash refers to this kind of approach as a form of 'civic-liberal communitarianism' (Nash 1997: esp. ch. 4 and 95–100).

37 On the general notion of liberal virtue, see Macedo (1990).
38 Callan writes: 'The essential demand is that schooling properly involves at some stage sympathetic and critical engagement with beliefs and ways of life at odds with the culture of the family or religious or ethnic group into which the child is born. Moreover, the relevant engagement must be such that the beliefs and values by which others live are entertained not merely as sources of meaning in *their* lives; they are instead addressed as potential elements within the conceptions of the good and the right one will create for oneself as an adult' (Callan 1997: 133).
39 Callan illustrates some of the educational requirements of this task in this way: 'the hardness of hard cases must be brought out by investigating specific ethical questions from multiple perspectives once the child or adolescent can learn to understand something of the variety of reasonable views from the inside; the effects of contingencies of social position and experience on disparities among such views must be imaginatively explored; and the various ways in which reasonable ethical doctrines select and give shape to conflicting ways of life' (Callan 1997: 35).
40 On the notion of dialogue, see Callan (1997: ch. 8). On the form of personal autonomy required in Callan's account, see *ibid.*, ch. 6.
41 As examples of the virtues required here, Callan mentions 'to learn to chasten the experience of distress, to forgo the temptations of an implacable belligerence, without at the same time suppressing an emotion that is inseparable from a serious interest in moral truth . . . the affective self-knowledge to differentiate moral from the other varieties of distress that conflict may trigger' (Callan 1997: 212).
42 On the significance of particular subjects in the teaching of these matters see, for example, Wright (1987), Lee (1992), White (1992), Saenger (1993), Arnold (1994), McCulloch and Mathieson (1995) and Sockett (1996).
43 On the claim that virtue-based theories of moral education should take account of 'the structural and material conditions of life', see Jonathan (1993) and in this volume.
44 On the significance in these matters of teaching by example, see Ryle (1972: 446) and Carr (1991: ch. 12). See also Jackson (1992), Hansen (1993a, 1993b, 1995), Jackson *et al.* (1993) and Halstead and Taylor (1999). On more general matters relating to the school as a whole, see McLaughlin (1996b) and Skillen (1997).

References

Almond, B. (1997) 'Seeking wisdom', *Philosophy* 72(281): 417–33.

Aristotle (1962) *Nichomachean Ethics*, tr. M. Ostwald, Indianapolis, IN: Liberal Arts Press.

Arnold, P. J. (1994) 'Sport and moral education', *Journal of Moral Education* 23(1): 75–89.

Bailey, C. (1984) *Beyond the Present and the Particular: A Theory of Liberal Education*, London: Routledge and Kegan Paul.

Baron, M. W., Pettit, P. and Slote, M. (1997) *Three Methods of Ethics: A Debate*, Oxford: Blackwell.

Bennett, W. J. (1991) 'Moral literacy and the formation of character', in J. Benninga (ed.) *Moral Character and Civic Education in the Elementary School*, New York: Teachers College Press.

—— (1993) *The Book of Virtues: A Treasury of Great Moral Stories*, New York: Simon and Schuster.

Benninga, J. (ed.) (1991) *Moral Character and Civic Education in the Elementary School*, New York: Teachers College Press.

—— (1997) 'Schools, character development, and citizenship', in A. Molnar (ed.) *The Construction of Children's Character*, Chicago: National Society for the Study of Education.

Bloom, A. (1987) *The Closing of the American Mind*, New York: Simon and Schuster.

Bond, E. J. (1996) *Ethics and Human Well Being. An Introduction to Moral Philosophy*, Oxford: Blackwell.

Buber, M. (1965) *Between Man and Man*, New York: Macmillan.

Burnyeat, M. F. (1980) 'Aristotle on learning to be good', in A. O. Rorty (ed.) *Essays on Aristotle's Ethics*, Berkeley: University of California Press.

Callan, E. (1997) *Creating Citizens. Political Education and Liberal Democracy*, Oxford: Clarendon Press.

Carr, D. (1991) *Educating the Virtues. An Essay on the Philosophical Psychology of Moral Development and Education*, London: Routledge.

—— (1995) 'The primacy of virtues in ethical theory, part I', *Cogito* 9(3): 238–44.

—— (1996a) 'The primacy of virtues in ethical theory, part II', *Cogito* 10(1): 34–40.

—— (1996b) 'After Kohlberg: some implications of an ethics of virtue for the theory of moral education and development', *Studies in Philosophy and Education* 14(4): 353–70.

—— (1997) 'Review article: Can there be a moral psychology of democratic and civic education?', *Journal of Philosophy of Education* 31(2): 345–54.

Cohen, P. (1995) 'The content of their character: educators find new ways to tackle values and morality', *Curriculum Update* Spring: 1–8.

Crisp, R. and Slote, M. (eds) (1997) *Virtue Ethics*, Oxford: Oxford University Press.

Dent, N. J. H. (1984) *The Moral Psychology of the Virtues*, Cambridge: Cambridge University Press.

Dunne, J. (1993) *Back to the Rough Ground: 'Phronesis' and 'Techne' in Modern Philosophy and in Aristotle*, Notre Dame, IN and London: University of Notre Dame Press.

Dykstra, C. R. (1981) *Vision and Character: A Christian Educator's Alternative to Kohlberg*, New York: Paulist Press.

Etzioni, A (1993) *The Spirit of Community. Rights, Responsibilities, and the Communitarian Agenda*, New York: Crown Publishers.

Flanagan, O. (1991) *Varieties of Moral Personality. Ethics and Psychological Realism*, Cambridge, MA: Harvard University Press.

Flanagan, O. and Rorty, A. O. (eds) (1990) *Identity, Character, and Morality. Essays in Moral Psychology*, Cambridge, MA: The MIT Press.

Freakley, M. (1996) 'The values cop-out and the case for character development in moral education', *Educational Practice and Theory* 18(2): 22–37.

Gay, G. (1997) 'Connections between character education and multicultural education', in A. Molnar (ed.) *The Construction of Children's Character*, Chicago: National Society for the Study of Education.

Goldman, L. (1996) 'Mind, character and the deferral of gratification', *The Educational Forum* 60(2): 135–40.

Gutmann, A. (1987) *Democratic Education*, Princeton, NJ: Princeton University Press.

Halstead, J. M. (1996) 'Values and values education in schools', in J. M. Halstead and M. J. Taylor (eds) *Values in Education and Education in Values*, London: Falmer Press.

Halstead, J. M. and Taylor, M. J. (1999) *The Development of Values, Attitudes and Personal Qualities: A Review of Recent Research*, London: OFSTED.

Hansen, D. T. (1993a) 'From role to person: the moral layeredness of classroom teaching', *American Educational Research Journal* 30(4): 651–74.

—— (1993b) 'The moral importance of the teacher's style', *Journal of Curriculum Studies* 25(5): 397–421.

—— (1995) *The Call to Teach*, New York: Teachers College Press.

—— (1996) 'Finding one's way home: notes on the texture of moral experience', *Studies in Philosophy and Education* 15(3): 221–33.

Hartshorne, H. and May, M. A. (1928–30) *Studies in the Nature of Character, Vols I–III*, New York: Macmillan.

Hauerwas, S. (1975) *Character and the Christian Life: A Study in Theological Ethics*, San Antonio, TX: Trinity University Press.

Heath, D. H. (1994) *Schools of Hope: Developing Mind and Character in Today's Youth*, San Francisco: Jossey-Bass.

Heslop, R. D. (1995) *Moral Education for Americans*, Westport, CT: Praeger.

Hirsch, E. D. (1988) *Cultural Literacy: What Every American Needs to Know*, New York: Vintage Books.

Hirst, P. H. (1974) *Moral Education in a Secular Society*, London: Hodder and Stoughton.

Huffman, H. (1994) *Developing a Character Education Program: One School District's Experience*. Alexandria, VA: Character Education Partnership.

Hursthouse, R., Lawrence, G. and Quinn, W. (eds) (1995) *Virtues and Reasons. Philippa Foot and Moral Theory*, Oxford: Clarendon Press.

Hutchins, W. J. (1917) *Children's Code of Morals for Elementary Schools*, Washington, DC: Character Education Institution.

Isaacs, D. (1984) *Character Building. A Guide for Parents and Teachers*, Blackrock, Ireland: Four Courts Press.

Jackson, P. W. (1992) 'The enactment of the moral in what teachers do', *Curriculum Inquiry* 22(4): 401–7.

Jackson, P. W., Boostrom, R. E. and Hansen, D. T. (1993) *The Moral Life of Schools*, San Francisco: Jossey-Bass.

Jonathan, R. (1993) 'Review essay: Educating the virtues: a problem in the social development of consciousness?', *Journal of Philosophy of Education* 27(1): 115–24.

Kilpatrick, W. (1992) *Why Johnny Can't Tell Right from Wrong: Moral Illiteracy and the Case for Character Education*, New York: Simon and Schuster.

Kohlberg, L. (1981) *Essays on Moral Development Volume 1. The Philosophy of Moral Development: Moral Stages and the Idea of Justice*, San Francisco: Harper and Row.

Kohn, A. (1997) 'The trouble with character education', in A. Molnar (ed.) *The Construction of Children's Character*, Chicago: National Society for the Study of Education.

Lasley, T. J. and Biddle, J. R. (1996) 'Teaching students to see beyond themselves', *The Educational Forum* 60(2): 158–64.

Lee, P. (1992) 'History in schools: aims, purposes and approaches', in P. Lee, J. Slater, P. Walsh and J.White (eds) *The Aims of School History: The National Curriculum and Beyond*, London: Tufnell Press.

Leming, J. (1994) 'Character education and multicultural education: conflicts and prospects', *Educational Horizons* 72(3): 122–30.

—— (1997) 'Research and practice in character education: a historical perspective', in A. Molnar (ed.) *The Construction of Children's Character*, Chicago: National Society for the Study of Education.

Lickona, T. (1991) *Educating for Character: How Our Schools Can Teach Respect and Responsibility*, New York: Bantam Books.

—— (1993) 'Is character education a responsibility of the public schools? Yes', *Momentum* 24(4): 48–52.

—— (1995) 'Promoting character education through the Center for the 4th and 5th Rs (respect and responsibility)', *Moral Education Forum* 20(4): 26–34.

—— (1996) 'Eleven principles of effective character education', *Journal of Moral Education* 25(1): 93–100.

—— (1997) 'Educating for character: a comprehensive approach', in A. Molnar (ed.) *The Construction of Children's Character*, Chicago: National Society for the Study of Education.

Locke, D. (1987) 'Moral development as the goal of moral education', in R. Straughan and J. Wilson (eds) *Philosophers on Education*, London: Macmillan.

Lockwood, A. L. (1997) 'What is character education?', in A. Molnar (ed.) *The Construction of Children's Character*, Chicago: National Society for the Study of Education.

McCulloch, R. and Mathieson, M. (1995) *Moral Education through English 11–16*, London: David Fulton.

McLaughlin, T. H. (1992) 'Citizenship, diversity and education: a philosophical perspective', *Journal of Moral Education* 21(3): 235–50.

—— (1995) 'Liberalism, education and the common school', *Journal of Philosophy of Education* 29(2): 239–55.

—— (1996a) 'Education of the whole child?', in R. Best (ed.) *Education, Spirituality and the Whole Child*, London: Cassell.

—— (1996b) 'Educating responsible citizens', in H. Tam (ed.) *Punishment, Excuses and Moral Development*, Aldershot: Avebury.

MacIntyre, A. (1984) *After Virtue. A Study in Moral Theory*, London: Duckworth.

Macedo, S. (1990) *Liberal Virtues. Citizenship, Virtue, and Community in Liberal Constitutionalism*, Oxford: Clarendon Press.

Molnar, A. (ed.) (1997) *The Construction of Children's Character*, Chicago: National Society for the Study of Education.

Nash, R. J. (1997) *Answering the 'Virtuecrats'. A Moral Conversation on Character Education*, New York and London: Teachers College Press.

Noddings, N. (1984) *Caring. A Feminine Approach to Ethics and Moral Education*, Berkeley: University of California Press.

—— (1997) 'Character education and community', in A. Molnar (ed.) *The Construction of Children's Character*, Chicago: National Society for the Study of Education.

O'Hear, A. (1981) *Education, Society and Human Nature. An Introduction to the Philosophy of Education*, London: Routledge and Kegan Paul.

O'Hear, P. and White, J. (1991) *A National Curriculum for All: Laying the Foundations for Success*, Education and Training Paper No. 6. London: Institute for Public Policy Research.

O'Neill, O. (1996) *Towards Justice and Virtue. A Constructive Account of Practical Reasoning*, Cambridge: Cambridge University Press.

Passmore, J. (1980) *The Philosophy of Teaching*, London: Duckworth.

Pence, G. (1991) 'Virtue theory', in P. Singer (ed.) *A Companion to Ethics*, Oxford: Blackwell.

Pendlebury, S. (1990) 'Practical reasoning and situational appreciation in teaching', *Educational Theory* 40: 171–9.

Peters, R. S. (1974) *Psychology and Ethical Development*, London: George Allen and Unwin.

Power, F. C., Higgins, A. and Kohlberg, L. (1989) *Lawrence Kohlberg's Approach to Moral Education*, New York: Columbia University Press.

Pritchard, I. (1988) 'Character education: research prospects and problems', *American Journal of Education* 96(4): 469–95.

Purpel, D. E. (1989) *The Moral and Spiritual Crisis in Education. A Curriculum for Justice and Compassion in Education*, New York: Bergin and Harvey.

—— (1997) 'The politics of character education', in A. Molnar (ed.) *The Construction of Children's Character*, Chicago: National Society for the Study of Education.

Qualifications and Curriculum Authority (1997) *The Promotion of Pupils' Spiritual, Moral, Social and Cultural Development: Draft Guidance for Pilot Work*, London: QCA.

Raths, L. E., Harmin, M. and Simon, S. B. (1966) *Values and Teaching*, Columbus, OH: Charles E. Merrill.

Rorty, A. O. (ed.) (1980) *Essays on Aristotle's Ethics*, Berkeley: University of California Press.

Ryan, K. and McLean, G. F. (1987) *Character Development in Schools and Beyond*, New York: Praeger.

Ryle, G. (1972) 'Can virtue be taught?', in R. F. Dearden, P. H. Hirst and R. S. Peters (eds) *Education and the Development of Reason*, London: Routledge and Kegan Paul.

Saenger, E. B. (1993) *Exploring Ethics through Children's Literature*, Pacific Grove, CA: Critical Thinking Press.

School Curriculum and Assessment Authority (1996) *National Forum for Education and the Community*, London: SCAA.

Sherman, N. (1989) *The Fabric of Character: Aristotle's Theory of Virtue*, Oxford: Clarendon Press.

Skillen, T. (1997) 'Can virtue be taught – especially these days?', *Journal of Philosophy of Education* 31(3): 375–93.

Slote, M. (1992) *From Morality to Virtue*, Oxford: Oxford University Press.

Smith, R. (1997) 'Judgement day', in R. Smith and P. Standish (eds) *Teaching Right and Wrong: Moral Education in the Balance*, Stoke-on-Trent: Trentham Books.

Sockett, H. (1988) 'Education and will: aspects of personal capability', *American Journal of Education* 96(2): 195–214.

—— (1996) 'Can virtue be taught?', *The Educational Forum* 60(2): 124–9.

—— (1997) 'Chemistry or character?', in A. Molnar (ed.) *The Construction of Children's Character*, Chicago: National Society for the Study of Education.

Statman, D. (ed.) (1997) *Virtue Ethics. A Critical Reader*, Edinburgh: Edinburgh University Press.

Steutel, J. (1997) 'The virtue approach to moral education: some conceptual clarifications', *Journal of Philosophy of Education* 31(3): 395–407.

Straughan, R. (1982) *I Ought to, But . . .: A Philosophical Approach to the Problem of Weakness of Will in Education*, Windsor: NFER-Nelson.

—— (1989) *Beliefs, Behaviour and Education*, London: Cassell.

Strike, K. A. (1982) *Educational Policy and the Just Society*, Urbana: University of Illinois Press.

Talbot, M. and Tate, N. (1997) 'Shared values in a pluralist society?', in R. Smith and P. Standish (eds) *Teaching Right and Wrong: Moral Education in the Balance*, Stoke-on-Trent: Trentham Books.

Tam, H. (1998) *Communitarianism. A New Agenda for Politics and Citizenship*, London: Macmillan.

Thomas, L. (1991) 'Morality and psychological development', in P. Singer (ed.) *A Companion to Ethics*, Oxford: Blackwell.

Tobin, B. M. (1989a) 'Richard Peters's theory of moral development', *Journal of Philosophy of Education* 23(1): 15–27.

—— (1989b) 'An Aristotelian theory of moral development', *Journal of Philosophy of Education* 23(2): 195–211.

White, J. (1990) *Education and the Good Life. Beyond the National Curriculum*, London: Kogan Page.

—— (1992) 'The purpose of school history: has the National Curriculum got it right?', in P. Lee, J. Slater, P. Walsh and J. White (eds) *The Aims of School History: The National Curriculum and Beyond*, London: Tufnell Press.

White, P. (1996) *Civic Virtues and Public Schooling: Educating Citizens for a Democratic Society*, New York and London: Teachers College Press.

Williams, B. (1981) 'Persons, character and morality', in *Moral Luck: Philosophical Papers 1973–1980*, Cambridge: Cambridge University Press.

—— (1985) *Ethics and the Limits of Philosophy*, London: Fontana/Collins.

—— (1987) 'The primacy of dispositions', in G. Haydon (ed.) *Education and Values. The Richard Peters Lectures*, London: Institute of Education University of London.

Wilson, J. (1990) *A New Introduction to Moral Education*, London: Cassell.

Wooster, M. M. (1990) 'Can character be taught?', *The American Enterprise* November/December: 51–5.

Wright, L. (1987) 'Physical education and moral education', *Journal of Philosophy of Education* 21(1): 93–102.

Wynne, E. A. (1991) 'Character and academics in the elementary school', in J. Benninga (ed.) *Moral Character and Civic Education in the Elementary School*, New York: Teachers College Press.

—— (1997) 'For-character education', in A. Molnar (ed.) *The Construction of Children's Character*, Chicago: National Society for the Study of Education.

Wynne, E. A. and Ryan, K. (1992) *Reclaiming our Schools: A Handbook on Teaching Character, Academics and Discipline*, New York: Merrill.

Wynne, E. and Walberg, H. (1985–6) 'The complementary goals of character development and academic excellence', *Educational Leadership* 43(4): 15–18.

Zagzebski, L. T. (1996) *Virtues of the Mind. An Inquiry into the Nature of Virtue and the Ethical Foundations of Knowledge*, Cambridge: Cambridge University Press.

Part IV

PLURALISM, POSTMODERNISM AND MORAL EDUCATION

9

PLURALISM, MORAL IMAGINATION AND MORAL EDUCATION

John Kekes

This chapter is an exploration of how the acceptance of pluralism should influence the aims of moral education. One alternative to pluralism is relativism, according to which all values are conventional and incapable of objective justification beyond the context in which they are held. If this were so, moral education would be the teaching of conformity to the prevailing values of a society. Monism is another alternative to pluralism. According to it, there is a system of objectively justifiable values all rational and sufficiently informed people would accept, regardless of the historical and social variations of the contexts in which they live. Moral education, according to this view, would be the teaching of the one true system of values. Both relativistic and monistic moral education are forms of indoctrination and are anathema to pluralistic societies.

The pluralistic conception of moral education differs from both of these unacceptable alternatives. Pluralists believe that some values are objectively justifiable, yet moral education is not designed to foist these values upon involuntary recipients but to provide some conditions necessary for living a good life, however such a life is conceived.

The argument is presented in four parts. The first provides a general account of pluralism and a brief explanation of how and for what reason it differs from both relativism and monism. The second and third discuss moral imagination, whose cultivation is one central aim of moral education. The fourth makes explicit three central aims of moral education, which follow from the previous discussion of pluralism and moral imagination.

The nature of pluralism[1]

Pluralism is that rare thing: a genuinely new approach to thinking about values. Its novelty, of course, does not preclude historical anticipations: various passages in the writings of Aristotle, Montaigne, Hume, John Stuart Mill, William James and Max Weber readily lend themselves to a pluralistic interpretation. Nevertheless, there exists no authoritative formulation of it, although Isaiah Berlin (1969) and Michael Oakeshott (1991) began the task in the 1940s and 1950s. Due largely to Berlin's influence, pluralism has become by now a recognisable label, which is applied to and often claimed by a variety of contemporary writers.[2]

Pluralism is a theory about values. The point of view from which it approaches values is that of human beings trying to live a good life. Its central thesis is that there are many reasonable conceptions of a good life and many reasonable values upon whose realisation good lives depend. These conceptions and values are often so related, however, that the realisation of one excludes the realisation of another. Conflicts among reasonable conceptions of a good life and among reasonable values consequently must be recognised as unavoidable features of an adequate understanding of morality and politics. Pluralists believe that living a good life must be essentially concerned with coping with these conflicts, but doing so is formidably difficult because the conflicts are often caused by the incompatibility and incommensurability of values whose realisation is regarded as essential.

The incompatibility of values is partly due to qualities intrinsic to the conflicting values. Because of these qualities, the realisation of one value may totally or proportionally exclude the realisation of another. Habitual gourmandising and moderation are totally incompatible, while a lifelong commitment to both political activism and solitude are proportionally so. The incompatibility of values, therefore, derives at least in part from the nature of the values, rather than from the attitude toward them. For having a favourable attitude toward both of two incompatible values does not make them compatible. Their compatibility depends also on whether or not the intrinsic qualities of the values exclude each other. But the intrinsic qualities of some values are only partly responsible for their incompatibility. Another part is contributed by human nature. It is for human beings that the intrinsic qualities of some values are incompatible. If gourmandising did not give human beings pleasure, it would not be incompatible with moderation. If split personalities were normal for human beings, they could combine solitude and political activism.

The basic idea of incommensurability is that there are some things so unalike as to exclude any reasonable comparison between them. Square roots and insults, smells and puns, canasta and telescopes are utterly disparate, and they seem to exclude any common measure by which their respective merits or demerits could be evaluated. That this is so is not usually troublesome because there is scarcely a need to compare them. It is otherwise, however, with values. It often happens that people want to realise incompatible values, and it becomes important then to compare them so that they could choose among them in a reasonable manner. If incompatible values are also incommensurable, however, then reasonable comparisons among them become problematic.

The reasons why pluralists suppose that values are incommensurable are, first, that it does not seem to them that there exists a highest value, such as happiness, to which all other values could always be reasonably subordinated and with reference to which all other values could be authoritatively ranked. Second, they are also dubious about there being some medium, such as money, in terms of which all the different values could be expressed, quantified, or compared in a way that all reasonable people would accept. And third, they are similarly sceptical about claims made on behalf of some single or some few canonical principles, such as the categorical imperative, which could be appealed to in resolving conflicts among values to the satisfaction of all reasonable people.

Incommensurability and incompatibility are logically distinct notions. Patriotism and spelunking are incommensurable, but not incompatible. If values were merely incommensurable, without being incompatible, it would not be hard to reconcile them by developing sufficiently capacious conceptions of a good life to include all the incommensurable values an agent wants to realise. The reason why this strategy cannot work is that many values are also incompatible: they cannot all be fully realised in even the richest conception of a good life. Conflicts are unavoidable because normal and reasonable people often want to realise values that are both incompatible and incommensurable. Nor need incompatible values be incommensurable. Two readily comparable values may yet be mutually exclusive. If I want to be alone for a few days, I could go camping or visit a strange city, but not both at the same time; or, if I want to improve my finances, I could cautiously husband my resources or make risky and possibly lucrative investments, but the more I do of one, the less I can do of the other. Pluralists are committed to the conjunction of two claims: moral conflicts are frequent, and many of them are due to people wanting to realise incompatible and incommensurable values.

The conclusion pluralists draw from this may be expressed either positively: all values are conditional, or negatively: no value is over-riding. The possibility conditionality excludes and on which over-ridingness hinges is that of resolving conflicts among values *always* in favour of one particular value. As it has been succinctly put: 'There is no consideration of any kind that overrides all other considerations in all conceivable circumstances' (Hampshire 1989: 172). Pluralists, of course, do not deny that many conflicts among values can be resolved by appealing to some reasonable ranking of the values in question. Such rankings are acknowledged to be both possible and desirable. The point pluralists insist on is that just as there is a plurality of equally reasonable conceptions of a good life and values, so also there is a plurality of equally reasonable rankings of them. According to pluralists, reason does not require commitment to some single highest value, or to some medium for comparing values, or to some single or few authoritative principles. On the contrary, people may reasonably commit themselves to any one of a plurality of equally reasonable values, ranking schemes, or principles.

Pluralism is intended to occupy the middle ground between two other theories about the nature of values: monism and relativism. Monists are committed to there being some over-riding value, but they need not suppose that it is a single value; their commitment may be to some small number of values, principles, or ranking schemes on the basis of which values could be compared in a way that all reasonable people would find compelling. Some classical versions of monism are the moral theories of Plato, Kant and Bentham. Contemporary versions have been defended by Alan Donagan (1977), Alan Gewirth (1978) and Richard Hare (1952, 1963, 1981), among others.

A value is over-riding, then, if it meets two conditions: in conflicts it always defeats the claims of any other value, and the only justification for violating it on any particular occasion is that by the violation its realisation would be generally served. For instance, if life were an over-riding value, then in conflicts with freedom or justice life would always take precedence; furthermore, the only justification for taking a life would then be to preserve other lives. In contrast with over-riding values, there are conditional values; their claims may be defeated by the conflicting claim of some other value. All non-overriding values are conditional. If, for instance, life were a conditional value, then in conflicts with freedom (for example, is life worth living under tyranny?) or justice (for example, should lives be risked in resisting injustice?), the claims of life could be defeated by the claims of these other values.

Pluralists are opposed to monism because they deny that any value is over-riding. It makes no difference to them whether the over-riding value is thought to be single or a combination of a few values, whether it is a principle or principles, or whether it is a simple or a complex ranking scheme. It is the very idea of there being some evaluative consideration that should *always* take precedence over *all* other evaluative considerations that pluralists oppose. Yet pluralists see, as well as monists do, that if values are incompatible and incommensurable, then they will conflict, and all conceptions of a good life require that there be some reasonable resolution of these conflicts. Pluralists and monists therefore agree about the need for reasonable conflict resolution. Their disagreement concerns the question of whether reasonable conflict resolution can appeal to some over-riding value.

The other theory about values that pluralists reject is relativism. Relativists agree with pluralists that all values are conditional and none is over-riding. But relativists go beyond pluralism and think that all conditional values are conventional. Relativists claim that all values are the products of the customs, practices and beliefs that happened to have developed in a particular tradition, and they deny that any value has moral authority outside of its traditional context. Relativists may concede that reason has a role to play in settling conflicts among values, but, according to them, reason is confined to play that role *within* particular traditions. There is no reasonable way of settling conflicts *between* values belonging to different traditions because what counts as reasonable is itself a product of particular traditions.

Some classical versions of relativism are those of Protagoras, Sextus Empiricus, Montaigne, Vico and Herder. Contemporary versions have been defended by Clifford Geertz (1984), Gilbert Harman (1975), Joseph Margolis (1991), Richard Rorty (1982, 1989) and Michael Walzer (1983), among others.

Pluralists disagree with relativists because they believe that there is a context-independent ground to which it is reasonable to appeal in settling conflicts between incompatible and incommensurable values, even if the values are conditional and the conflicts occur in the context of different traditions. At the same time, pluralists and relativists may join in their opposition to the monistic commitment to an over-riding value. Similarly, pluralists and monists may agree in opposing the relativistic denial of a context-independent ground for resolving conflicts, even as they disagree about basing an over-riding value on that ground.

The central idea that pluralists aim to develop and defend against both monists and relativists is that there is a context-independent ground for settling conflicts among conditional values which would be acceptable to all sufficiently informed and reasonable people. Relativists reject pluralism because they deny that there is such a ground. And monists reject pluralism because, while they agree that there is a context-independent ground, they also think that on its basis some values can be shown to be over-riding, and not merely conditional. One consequence of this dispute is that pluralists must always argue on two fronts: against relativists, to whom they must show the existence of a context-independent ground for resolving conflicts among conditional values; and against monists, to whom they must show that only conditional and not over-riding values can be based on this ground.

The context-independent ground required by pluralism is constituted of the minimum requirements of good lives, regardless of how they are conceived. These requirements are set by universally human, historically constant and socially invariant needs created by human nature. Many of these needs are physiological: for food, shelter, rest, and so forth; others are psychological: for hope, the absence of terror in one's life, companionship, and the like. Yet others are social: for some order and predictability in one's society, for security, for some respect, and so on. The satisfaction of these basic human needs will be called 'primary values', in contrast with 'secondary values'. Secondary values derive from the satisfaction of needs that vary with traditions and conceptions of a good life. It may then be said that the minimum requirements of all good lives are met by the realisation of primary values. The rules, customs and principles protecting people in their pursuit of primary values will be called 'deep conventions'. It follows then that any morally acceptable tradition must protect people belonging to it by means of deep conventions.[3]

The pluralistic claim for the universality, constancy and invariance of primary values concerns only the bare fact that good lives require their enjoyment.

It is readily acknowledged by pluralists that there are vast historical, cultural and individual differences about *how* they are enjoyed. Correspondingly, the pluralistic claim is that any morally acceptable tradition must uphold deep conventions in numerous routine and central cases. Pluralists acknowledge of course that there are also controversial and borderline cases whose treatment may reasonably vary from one tradition to another.

It is now possible to state more clearly why pluralists reject both relativism and monism. The existence of context-independent primary values, and the deep conventions protecting them, does not support the monistic claim that primary values are over-riding, for two reasons. First, primary values may conflict with each other. Even if primary values always over-rode conflicting secondary values, this could not be true of conflicting primary values themselves. Second, primary values are conditional on their contribution to the realisation of the agents' conception of a good life. But agents may reasonably judge in adverse circumstances that they cannot live according to their conceptions, and so they may judge as well that they have no good reason to pursue primary values. If people have no reasonable hope of a good life, then they will have no reason to prize a value that is necessary for a good life.

The reason pluralists have for rejecting relativism is that relativists fail to recognise that there are primary values and that they need to be protected by deep conventions. Primary values and deep conventions will command the assent of all sufficiently informed and reasonable people because they protect the minimum requirements of all good lives regardless of what conceptions of good life and what other values are recognised in any particular tradition. Primary values and deep conventions constitute a context-independent ground for settling some conflicts among some values; they establish an objective ground on which some traditions and conceptions of a good life can be reasonably criticised; and they show that relativists are mistaken in supposing that all values are conventional.

Moral imagination

If pluralists are right, then the everyday moral experience of people who try to make a good life for themselves centrally includes a plurality of often conflicting values. These values appear to them as possibilities that they may incorporate into their lives. As they deliberate about and come to adopt some of these possibilities as their own, so they develop their conception of a good life. Moral imagination is essential to this process because it is through it that people attempt to discover what it would be like to live according to the various possibilities available to them.[4]

Imagination is a general label for a wide variety of human activities, among which the following are particularly important: the formation of images, like the face of an absent friend; resourceful problem solving, exemplified, for instance, by non-linear thinking; the falsification of some aspect of reality, as in fantasising that the facts are other than they are; and the mental exploration of what it would be like to realise particular possibilities, such as being very rich. Moral imagination is a particular instance of the last kind of imaginative activity. It is moral because its central concern is with evaluating the possibilities the agents imaginatively explore as good or evil.

The importance of moral imagination emerges in the context of the ever present need of agents to understand the conduct of both other people and themselves. If people could not do this successfully with much of the conduct of others as it affects them, their civilised interaction would break down. Social order presupposes some degree of predictability, and in most cases involving social life, reliable prediction depends on possessing at least some understanding. The same point holds, although for different reasons, with respect to the need that individual agents should have some understanding of their own conduct. If they did not know what they wanted, what their goals and interests were, and if they could not reasonably predict that their wants, goals and interests will persist for some time, they could not plan for the future, and since such planning is necessary for living a good life, however it is conceived, they would be doomed to frustration.

The first step toward achieving this desirable understanding of themselves and others involves coming to know what the agents actually have been doing. It is possible to reconstruct the lives of individuals by compiling a list of their more important publicly observable actions. But this cannot be more than a first step, for unless the context in which they live, the reasons for their actions, and what makes some of their actions important were understood, there would be no understanding of their actions. It might be known what they did, but knowledge of the significance of their deeds would be lacking.

Understanding the context for, the reasons behind, and the importance of actions matters because it reveals what the agents' possibilities were and what led them to realise one among their various possibilities. It is the nature of this type of understanding that it attempts to illuminate the significance of what happened by considering what might have happened. The assumption behind it is that the significance of a particular action emerges only by viewing it against the background of competing possibilities and by identifying the agents' reasons for attempting to realise one of these possibilities.

Moral imagination is an essential element of this understanding because it is the activity by which the attempt is made to re-create the possibilities particular agents have faced. But this is a complicated matter. It must involve ascertaining both the possibilities that were available to the agents and the possibilities the agents believed themselves to have. Both are needed for understanding the significance of particular actions, but it is necessary to keep them separate, otherwise the reasons agents give for realising a particular one among their possibilities could not be evaluated.

It is a further complication that not even for thoroughly reasonable agents do these two sets of possibilities coincide, since even they may lack all sorts of information that is generally available in their context. If they had it, their beliefs about their possibilities would change accordingly, but they are not blameworthy for not having it, for their ignorance is not self-inflicted. Of course, few agents, if any, are thoroughly reasonable. The beliefs they form about their possibilities may be mistaken, and often these mistakes could and should have been avoided by them. It is therefore essential to evaluating the reasons agents give for their actions to form some conception of what beliefs about their possibilities were reasonable for them to have, given the available possibilities. Understanding the significance of particular actions thus requires the imaginative re-creation of three sets of possibilities: those that were generally available in the agents' context, those that the agents could reasonably have been expected to believe themselves to have, and those that the agents actually believed themselves to have.

This threefold imaginative re-creation of possibilities goes beyond the bare knowledge *that* there were such-and-such possibilities. To know that much does not require imagination. To understand the significance of particular actions – the attractions, risks, novelty, general regard, emotive connotations, prestige, and so on – associated with the possibilities must be appreciated, and appreciated as they appear to the agents. The understanding of significance, therefore, cannot be merely cognitive, it must also have a large affective component capable of conveying the appeal the relevant possibilities had for the agent. A cognitively and effectively informed imagination is needed to re-create the richness of the possibilities whose significance is to be understood. Only against that background does it begin to become understandable why agents realise a particular one among their possibilities.

Yet the imaginative re-creation of the background is still insufficient for understanding the significance of actions. For there is also the question of the evaluation of the reasons agents give for what they do. The most straightforward situation is when the possibilities the agents actually believe themselves to have coincide with the possibilities reasonable agents would have in that context, and the agents give as their reason that the attraction of the possibility they realised outweighed the attraction of its competitors. In such a case, having recreated the agents' possibilities, it is possible to appreciate how one of them could have been found to possess greater attraction for the agent than others. And then it would be right to claim that the significance of the agent's action was understood.

But what if it turns out, as it often does, that some of the beliefs the agents have about their possibilities are unreasonable? It may be that their possibilities are more or less numerous than they believe, or that they find possibilities attractive or unattractive because they ignore readily available features whose acknowledgement would incline them in another direction, or that they are deceiving themselves, or that their beliefs are misled by anger, fear, fantasy, spite or envy. In such cases, knowing the reasons the agents give is not enough for understanding the significance of their actions. The search for understanding, then, must go beyond these reasons and explore the question of why there is a discrepancy between what the agents believe about their possibilities and what is reasonable to believe about them. By understanding why the agents are unreasonable, it is possible to come to understand the significance of their actions, even though their significance is hidden from the agents themselves.

This sketch of the workings of imagination may make it seem dauntingly difficult. But this appearance is deceptive. The kind of understanding described above is routinely achieved by ethnographers in describing the conduct of agents in other cultures; by historians in describing the situations in which various personages have acted; by novelists, playwrights and biographers who aim to describe the predicaments their characters face; by all those who try to enter sympathetically into the frame of mind of someone they want to know intimately so as to understand the significance of his or her conduct; and by all those again who try to make palpable to themselves what it would be like to realise their own possibilities and live according to them, so that they may shape their future in as informed a manner as possible.

Two aspects of moral imagination

Moral imagination has both an exploratory and a corrective aspect. To begin with the exploratory one, people are usually born into a tradition, and as they try more or less consciously, with greater or lesser success, to make their lives good, they find their aspirations and opportunities defined by the possibilities their tradition provides. They have a vague sense of what they value and they attempt to realise it by seeking some non-Procrustean fit between what they take to be valuable and the possibilities they are aware of having. Part of the exploratory aspect of moral imagination is that of agents trying to acquaint themselves with these possibilities.

This process should not be mistaken for the situation when people who are standing outside of a tradition are initiated into its ways. People do not begin with a self-generated initial conception of a good life and then develop it along conventionally accredited ways. Their first rudimentary view is already couched in terms they have learned from their tradition, since the identification and conceptualisation of what they value already presuppose an evaluative vocabulary, which they possess, if at all, only if they have learned it from their tradition. Initiation into the tradition, therefore, consists in becoming articulate about themselves and their surroundings by learning to view both through the available possibilities. Finding a fit between how they think it would be good to live and how they *can* live is thus a matter of identifying those among their possibilities which attract them because they think that they allow the development and perhaps the realisation of what they regard as valuable. It would be a mistake to suppose, however, that they cannot free themselves from the consequences of this unavoidable conditioning. For moral imagination enables them to carry the exploration of possibilities beyond the confines of their tradition.

The scope of moral imagination enlarges as people become acquainted with possibilities other than those that exist in their tradition. Through the development of a historical perspective, an understanding of other cultures, and immersion in literature (especially novels, plays and biographies), people come to appreciate that the possibilities available to them do not exhaust the possibilities of life, but merely form that small subset of them to which the contingencies of their upbringing have given them access. As they acquire imaginative understanding of new possibilities, so they grow in breadth. And breadth contributes to the enlargement of their own possibilities in two ways.

The first is simply by increasing the number of possibilities they have. History, ethnography and literature reveal ways of living and acting that they can adapt to their circumstances, and thereby enrich their possibilities. But it often happens that the new possibilities people learn about are so remote from their circumstances as to make it impractical even to attempt to adopt them as their own. Yet they can still enrich them in a second way. The increasing breadth of moral imagination helps people to appreciate their own possibilities by providing a point of view from which they can better evaluate them. Breadth allows them to step outside of their tradition and view it from an external vantage point, not by committing them to it, but by providing a basis for contrast and comparison. On that basis, they can come to see better the dangers, pitfalls and losses that they confront by committing themselves to some among their own possibilities.

They may come to see then, for instance, that from the point of view of an aristocratic tradition, which they have no wish to revive, their commitment to equality incurs the heavy cost of discouraging personal excellence, or that from the point of view of a puritanical tradition, which they are happy to consign to history, the sexual revolution tends to undermine the sort of intimacy that exists among exclusive sexual partners. These costs of equality and sexual liberation are not easily seen by those who are immersed in their commitments to them because they have nothing with which they could contrast the way they live. The point, of course, is not that if they appreciate the costs, they will weaken their commitment to realising some possibilities; rather, by appreciating the costs they will be able to work for the realisation of the possibilities in a more reasonable way.

The exploratory aspect of moral imagination contributes to growth in breadth. Breadth enlarges the field of possibilities the tradition initially provides. And the new possibilities, derived from exposure to other traditions, usually through history, ethnography and literature, enable people to view critically the possibilities with which they start, by serving as a basis for contrast and comparison.[5]

The exploratory aspect of moral imagination is forward looking, for it concerns the question of which of the available possibilities should be realised in the future. This is the usual way of thinking about moral imagination. Yet it is not the only way. The corrective aspect of moral imagination reveals an equally important question, but it is one that directs moral imagination backward, toward the agents' past (see Wollheim 1984). This other question is about how reasonable individuals have been in their evaluations of the possibilities open to them. Answering it requires looking backward from the present, for it was in the past that they have formed their views about what their present possibilities are. The desirable character trait for exploring their possibilities is breadth. But there is also another desirable character trait needed for correcting the evaluations of the possibilities, and that is depth. Depth is needed because people are prone to make mistakes in evaluating their possibilities.

In discussing imaginative understanding in general, it has emerged that it requires the re-creation of three sets of possibilities: those generally available in the agents' context, those that agents would believe themselves to have, if they were thoroughly reasonable, and those that agents actually believe themselves to have. The corrective aspect of moral imagination involves overcoming the gap between the last two. This is a necessary task due to the natural propensity of agents to err in evaluating their possibilities. The sources of this type of error are numerous. For the present purposes, it will suffice merely to indicate some of the more obvious ones, before going on to discuss how the corrective aspect of moral imagination can help to avoid them.

The tacit assumption in the argument so far has been that the exercise of moral imagination is good because it improves people's view of their possibilities. But observation of the way people actually conduct themselves belies this assumption. Keeping their possibilities in the focus of their attention is burdensome. Life, after all, cannot be a permanent revolution. Adventurousness of spirit is fine and good, but life largely consists in performing everyday, routine, unadventurous tasks. Even creative artists, explorers and other free spirits must shop for groceries, have their cars serviced, balance their bank accounts, and negotiate with countless people on whom they rely for various services. After the embarrassing stage of adolescent rebelliousness is over, people cannot help conforming to the conventions of their tradition, if they want to get on with their lives. And getting on means, for the vast majority, to live according to some small subset of conventional possibilities. They settle into them – and settle for them – and it is nothing but unwelcome irritation to have to form some attitudes toward possibilities that people other than themselves may conceivably entertain.

Step by innocuous step they are thus led down the path to narrow-mindedness. They learn to live by exclusion, by saying 'no' to the examination of possibilities that may make their lives better. They suppress their dissatisfactions with the life they have settled for, and call its suppression a sign of maturity. In this manner, they deprive themselves of the possibility of improving their lives. This understandable propensity toward laziness of spirit, which constricts their own horizons and makes them willing to stay with the familiar, is one source of the mistakes people tend to make about their possibilities: they ignore many they could have, if they were more reasonable.

One kind of imaginative activity was earlier identified as the falsification of some aspect of reality by fantasising that the facts are other than they are. Another common source of error that leads agents to mistaken beliefs about their possibilities is the confusion between fantasising about them and exploring them imaginatively. The confusion is understandable since both fantasy and imaginative exploration concentrate on currently unrealised possibilities. Furthermore, both are emotionally charged since the envisaged possibilities are coloured by the agents' hopes and fears about how their lives may go. It is natural to have strong feelings on that subject.

Envisaging some possibilities may change from imaginative exploration into fantasy when feelings become disproportionately strong. Instead of merely colouring the way the agents see the relevant possibilities, the feelings may come to alter the agents' beliefs about what they are. Their hopes and fears may become so assertive as to force their attention only on aspects of their possibilities that seem salient from their point of view. They lead them to ignore, overlook or forget about other equally salient aspects, but their salience is obscured by the feelings that rule them. In this way, hope may lead them not to take cognisance of the signs of infidelity in the person they love, or it may cause them to miss the seamy underside of the glamorous life they have embarked upon with great ambition. Similarly, fear may make them see opportunities as threats, it may make them over-estimate risks in possible ways of life, or it may cause them to deny their own abilities in order to avoid the prospect of failure. The damaging effect of fantasy is to motivate them to explore unsuitable possibilities or to undermine their motivation to explore suitable ones. Fantasy can have this effect because it derives its force from feelings whose strength is disproportionate to the possibilities that elicit them. Imaginative exploration is free from this defect if the feelings associated with the envisaged possibilities are appropriate reactions to their objects.

Another source of error in the beliefs people hold about their possibilities is a particular form of self-deception. The fundamental reason why people should concentrate on their possibilities is to make their life better. They can do so only by attempting to realise possibilities which, they believe, would improve their lot. This, of course, requires the possession of some standard with reference to which they select the possibilities whose realisation they seek. This standard is their conception of a good life. It enables people not merely to distinguish between attractive and unattractive possibilities, but to select those among the attractive ones which conform to their conception of a good life. The application of this standard involves a reflective evaluation of available possibilities. The object of this reflection is to enable agents to control the satisfaction of their wants. It leads them to ask both what they want then and there and whether what they want contributes to living as they think they should. It thus includes the consideration of the long-range consequences of selecting and pursuing particular possibilities. The reflective evaluation that conformity to the standard calls for is, therefore, a form of self-control.[6]

The exercise of this form of self-control, however, inevitably produces a conflict in the agents, for it leads them to refrain from pursuing possibilities they find attractive. Self-deception occurs in the context of this conflict. It is a device by which people disguise from themselves the reasons against realising attractive possibilities that conflict with their conception of a good life. Its mechanism is to underplay the significance of violating the standard set by their conception of a good life by convincing themselves of the harmlessness of pursuing a possibility that is incompatible with the standard. They say that one compromise over principle will not make them faithless, that a little padding of the expense account will not break the Treasury, or that one broken promise will not turn them into moral lepers. And they believe what they say because in the forefront of their attention is the satisfaction derived from acting on the deviant possibility, and not the more remote satisfaction that conformity to their conception of a good life would produce. They contrive in this manner to go against what they themselves believe are the possibilities they should aim to realise.

Narrow-mindedness, fantasy and self-deception all involve the falsification of facts relevant to the evaluation of one's possibilities. The corrective aspect of moral imagination is to avoid such falsification, and thus to overcome obstacles to a realistic estimate of what people can do to make their lives better. The way to arrive at such an estimate is through the imaginative recreation of past situations in which they faced the possibilities then available to them. The advantage derivable from such a retrospective view is that the loss of immediacy, the absence of much emotional tension, the knowledge that there is little they can do about their past conduct, all remove many of the obstacles that stood in the way of realism when the recreated situation was alive and present. As a result, they may come to a better understanding of why it was that they valued some possibilities sufficiently to act on them. The context of this understanding is partly constituted of people coming to see, in this retrospective way, what had been responsible in them for the discrepancy between what was reasonable for them to believe about their possibilities and what they actually believed about them. They thus come to understand why their past evaluations were less than thoroughly reasonable.

This imaginative correction, if it becomes habitual, takes as its object very many of the past situations the agents have faced. It is not surprising if in the course of its exercise there emerge patterns constituted of the ways people tend to evaluate their possibilities. Awareness of these patterns enables them to articulate to themselves what it is in them that has made them less reasonable than they might have been: they have been too fearful of risks, too much inclined to favour competitive possibilities, too sluggish emotionally, and so on. In possession of these articulated patterns of the unreasonable evaluations to which they are prone, they can guard against their recurrence in situations they currently face.

The habitual exercise of retroactive moral imagination also makes it possible for people to articulate patterns of their preferences for certain kinds of possibilities. These patterns, then, may be seen as representing their more enduring values. If they are conscious of them, they can more reasonably approach, in yet another way, their present dispositions in their present situations by seeing them as continuations of or deviations from these enduring patterns. And if they contemplate deviations, then the question naturally occurs of why they would be inclined to go against their values in the present case. There may or may not be a good answer, but asking the question, made possible by retroactive moral imagination having become habitual, acts as a guard against present error.

The agents' knowledge of these two patterns, of their characteristic mistakes and values, is a species of self-knowledge. It is bound to have a moral component, since the kinds of mistakes and values people come to know that they are given to making and holding concern possibilities that are involved in making their lives better. If they have this type of self-knowledge, they have a coherent view of an important part of themselves, they have reasonable beliefs about the kinds of possibilities whose realisation would improve their lives, and they are aware of the mistakes they are prone to making. They gain a more reasonable conception of a good life. Those in possession of such a conception may be described as having a kind of depth. This, then, is the sense in which the habitual exercise of the corrective aspect of moral imagination may contribute to people's growth in depth.

The preceding account is intended to make evident the necessity of moral imagination to living a good life. For a good life depends on the realisation of possibilities that are rightly valued by agents, and moral imagination is one indispensable means by which they may come to value their possibilities in a reasonable manner. Without an adequate breadth and depth of understanding their available possibilities, the agents' adoption of any of them would be haphazard. Since conceptions of a good life are composed of the possibilities that agents adopt from among the ones their tradition makes available, moral imagination must be recognised as a necessary part of living a good life. Moral imagination, however, is not an inborn skill; it needs to be cultivated. Doing so is one task of moral education.

Moral education

These concluding remarks about moral education will have to be brief and general. They state three aims of a pluralistically conceived moral education, but they do not go into details. The first two stress limits and possibilities. In stressing limits, pluralistic moral education differs from a relativistic one; and in stressing possibilities, it differs from a monistic one.

The first aim of moral education is to nurture a lively appreciation of the possibilities of life, but not of all possibilities. The education is moral, so it is committed to the evaluation of possibilities under the aspect of good and evil. The moral status of numerous possibilities is of course controversial. Yet there can be no reasonable doubt that there are also obviously good and evil possibilities. The possibilities whose moral status is uncontroversial concern primary values. These values, it will be remembered, are derived from human needs whose satisfaction is a minimum requirement of all reasonable conceptions of a good life. The satisfaction of these needs is normally good, and depriving people of available satisfactions is normally evil.

The qualification that the primary values hold normally is intended as a reminder that even they are conditional. The claim of any primary value may be defeated by sufficiently strong countervailing reasons. But these reasons themselves derive their strength from safeguarding the requirements for the realisation of all reasonable conceptions of a good life.

Moral education therefore must include placing limits upon which possibilities may be reasonably adopted. These limits are the deep conventions of a tradition. They will be acceptable to all sufficiently reasonable people because they protect the requirements of living a good life, however it is conceived, provided only that it stays within the limits. Part of the role of moral imagination is to make palpable the common humanity, the shared needs and the consequent vulnerability of all human beings, regardless of how remote or strange they appear to be from the vantage point of a particular tradition.

The second aim of moral education is to present the possibilities of a tradition as ways of enriching people's lives rather than as pre-established rigid patterns imposed upon reluctant individuals. The possibilities are patterns, to be sure, but in a pluralistic society they are neither rigid nor imposed. They are patterns set by good lives that actual or imaginatively created people have lived. They thus appear to reasonable agents as possible ways in which they themselves could make their lives good. Such possibilities strike those who understand them as riches to be enjoyed rather than as conventions from which they should liberate themselves. They should be seen as the currency of inherited cultural wealth, not as shackles fastened by the dead hand of the past. It is another part of the role of moral imagination to reveal the attractions of these possibilities.

The possibilities are not rigid patterns. They are not blueprints that must be strictly followed if the pieces of a life are to fit together. They are, rather, suggestions about cultivating some general dispositions, such as creativity, adventurousness, service to the needy, political activism, loving attention to intimates, or athletic prowess. These dispositions can be instantiated in a wide variety of different actions, contexts and personal styles. There is no suggestion here that the adoption of one of these possibilities requires the surrender of the agent's individuality. To adopt such a possibility is to try to find a fit between the general loose pattern and the character and circumstances of the agent.[7]

Nor are the possibilities imposed on the agents who adopt them. In a pluralistic society, the available possibilities are far more numerous than even the most experimental agent could adopt in a lifetime. The adoption of a possibility is a matter of selection from among many available alternatives. And even if some people come to feel that they have no options because they must live in a certain way – as a painter, a rebel, a farmer – the necessity is internal, not the result of blatant or subtle coercion. It is dictated by the agents' discovery of what they are about, not by successful indoctrination.

Moral education, however, must have yet a third aim, beyond teaching the adherence to limits set by deep conventions and finding the possibilities according to which it would be good to live. This aim is to train the character of the agents so that living within the limits and according to the possibilities has become natural to them. Lives cannot be good if they involve the agents in constant internal struggles to keep themselves doing what they reasonably decided they ought to be doing. Lives become good when these struggles are over and the agents spontaneously conduct themselves according to their conceptions of a good life. This comes about when they have succeeded in making habitual the character traits upon whose exercise the goodness of their lives depends. There is, of course, much more that needs to be said about this Aristotelian aim of moral education, but it cannot be said here (see Kekes 1990).

The sketch of these three aims of moral education – the recognition of limits, the adoption of possibilities, and the development of character – is the sketch of an ideal. Reality, of course, falls short of it, and, as it happens, the gap is large enough to silence any easy optimism about the future. But if the future is to be made better, then it must be understood what is wrong with the present and in what direction improvement lies. The ideal is meant to provide the standard by which the existing faults can be identified and remedied.

Notes

1 The following descriptions of pluralism and moral imagination draw on Kekes (1993).
2 For example John Rawls (1971 and 1993), Dworkin (1977 and 1985), Brandt (1979), Nagel (1979 and 1991), Williams (1981), Hampshire (1983 and 1989), Baier (1985), Taylor (1985 and 1989), Nussbaum (1986), Raz (1986), Larmore (1987), Stocker (1990), Lukes (1991) and Rescher (1993).

3 For further discussion, see Kekes (1993: ch. 3).
4 For some of the many discussions of moral imagination, see Johnson (1993), Lovibond (1983) and Novitz (1987).
5 On this topic, see Trilling (1979), Geertz (1983a, 1983b) and Gunn (1987).
6 For an exploration of this topic, see Taylor (1976) and Frankfurt (1988).
7 This is the topic of Kekes (1989).

References

Baier, A. (1985) *Postures of Mind*, Minneapolis: University of Minnesota Press.
Berlin, I. (1969) *Four Essays on Liberty*, Oxford: Oxford University Press.
Brandt, R. B. (1979) *A Theory of the Right and the Good*, Oxford: Clarendon Press.
Donagan, A. (1977) *The Theory of Morality*, Chicago: University of Chicago Press.
Dworkin, R. (1977) *Taking Rights Seriously*, Cambridge, MA: Harvard University Press.
—— (1985) *A Matter of Principle*, Cambridge, MA: Harvard University Press.
Frankfurt, B. G. (1988) *The Importance of What We Care About*, Cambridge: Cambridge University Press.
Geertz, C. (1983a) 'Found in translation: on the social history of the moral imagination', in *Local Knowledge*, New York: Basic Books.
—— (1983b) 'From the native's point of view', in *Local Knowledge*, New York: Basic Books.
—— (1984) 'Anti anti-relativism', *American Anthropologist* 2: 263–78.
Gewirth, A. (1978) *Reason and Morality*, Chicago: University of Chicago Press.
Gunn, G. (1987) *The Culture of Criticism and the Criticism of Culture*, New York: Oxford University Press.
Hampshire, S. (1983) *Morality and Conflict*, Cambridge, MA: Harvard University Press.
—— (1989) *Innocence and Experience*, Cambridge, MA: Harvard University Press.
Hare, R. H. (1952) *The Language of Morals*, Oxford: Clarendon Press.
—— (1963) *Freedom and Reason*, Oxford: Clarendon Press.
—— (1981) *Moral Thinking*, Oxford: Clarendon Press.
Harman, G. (1975) 'Moral relativism defended', *Philosophical Review* 84: 3–22.
Johnson, M. (1993) *Moral Imagination*, Chicago: University of Chicago Press.
Kekes, J. (1989) *Moral Tradition and Individuality*, Princeton, NJ: Princeton University Press.
—— (1990) *Facing Evil*, Princeton, NJ: Princeton University Press.
—— (1993) *The Morality of Pluralism*, Princeton, NJ: Princeton University Press.
Larmore, C. (1987) *Patterns of Moral Complexity*, Cambridge: Cambridge University Press.
Lovibond, S. (1983) *Realism and Imagination in Ethics*, Minneapolis: University of Minnesota Press.
Lukes, S. (1991) *Moral Conflicts and Politics*, Oxford: Clarendon Press.
Margolis, J. (1991) *The Truth About Relativism*, Boston, MA: Blackwell.
Nagel, T. (1979) *Mortal Questions*, Cambridge: Cambridge University Press.
—— (1991) *Equality and Partiality*, New York: Oxford University Press.
Novitz, D. (1987) *Knowledge, Fiction and Imagination*, Philadelphia, PA: Temple University Press.
Nussbaum, M. (1986) *The Fragility of Goodness*, Cambridge: Cambridge University Press.

Oakeshott, M. (1991) *Nationalism in Politics* (new and expanded edition), Indianapolis: Liberty Press.

Rawls, J. (1971) *A Theory of Justice*, Cambridge: Harvard University Press.

—— (1993) *Political Liberalism*, New York: Columbia University Press.

Raz, J. (1986) *The Morality of Freedom*, Oxford: Clarendon Press.

Rescher, N. (1993) *Pluralism*, Oxford: Clarendon Press.

Rorty, R. (1982) *Consequences of Pragmatism*, Minneapolis: University of Minnesota Press.

—— (1989) *Contingency, Irony, and Solidarity*, Cambridge: Cambridge University Press.

Stocker, M. (1990) *Plural and Conflicting Values*, Oxford: Clarendon Press.

Taylor, C. (1976) 'Responsibility for self', in A. O. Rorty (ed.) *The Identities of Persons*, Berkeley: University of California Press.

—— (1985) *Human Agency and Language: Philosophical Papers 1*, Cambridge: Cambridge University Press.

—— (1989) *Sources of the Self*, Cambridge, MA: Harvard University Press.

Trilling, L. (1979) 'Why we read Jane Austen', in *The Last Decade*, New York: Harcourt, Brace.

Walzer, M. (1983) *Spheres of Justice*, New York: Basic Books.

Williams, B. (1981) *Moral Luck*, Cambridge: Cambridge University Press.

Wollheim, R. (1984) *The Thread of Life*, Cambridge, MA: Harvard University Press.

10

POSTMODERNISM AND THE EDUCATION OF CHARACTER

Michael Luntley

Moral realism and character education in a postmodern world

Suppose there is no such thing as timeless truth. Suppose the Enlightenment ideas of timeless truth and universal reason by which we were supposed to access truth are untenable. Suppose that there are no general principles formulable in advance that can shape our process of belief formation, for belief formation and defence are shaped by the contingencies of particular situations. Suppose further that no single conceptualisation of human experience can be privileged and that we have to endorse a pluralism regarding the different types of concepts that are required in order to make the best ongoing sense of ourselves. There is no such thing as the world's own story, there are only the local particular narratives that we employ in reflecting on ourselves and our world. Suppose, in short, that all the things that excite postmodernists are true: contingency and pluralism are rampant in our practices of belief formation and defence. What I want to argue in this chapter is that, from the point of view of a moral realist, the above suppositions are harmless. By 'moral realism' I mean the belief that ethical judgements are answerable to truth and falsity, and our reasoning with them consists in a responsiveness to how things are. So construed, moral realism and a realist account of the nature of moral education not only survive but flourish against the backdrop of the suppositions that are fashionably thought to herald only relativism and irrationalism. Truth may not be timeless but it can be timely, and moral education should be thought of as an education of the character necessary for timely judgement.

Adherence to the metaphysics of timeless truth and universal reason makes it tempting to theorise moral education in one of two ways: either as an instruction in doctrine – the body of timeless true propositions of morality – or as the development of a cognitive capacity to recognise and employ general principles from which the truth is derivable. Such principles could be thought of in either a Kantian or a naturalistic manner. In the absence, however, of the metaphysics of timeless truth we cannot think of moral education as either doctrinal instruction or as the instruction in general principles that underpin moral thought. If truth is at best only timely, it might seem that the moral educator has no choice left but to offer young people a record of what their culture/community/society currently think. Even if this opinion is expressed in terms of offering young people the opportunity to 'discover' themselves by locating themselves in their community, the opinion amounts to a flaccid relativism that gives no account of how and why someone could rationally exit their community, should they find it wanting.[1] On such an approach moral education would be in danger of being doctrinal without the support of the thought that the doctrines had a claim to truth. By placing the emphasis of moral education on the idea of the education of character I want to show how a robust realism can be sensitive to the contingencies of belief formation and reason, and that it can avoid the relativistic communitarianism that many people seem to think is the only option once we forgo the transcendent standards of belief and reason that the Enlightenment promised.

The general scope for realism in the face of the loss of Enlightenment ideas of truth and reason is no great surprise.[2] What I want to concentrate on in this chapter is the development of a particularist account of moral reasons and moral judgement. Particularism is the doctrine that the rational force of any given belief or desire is a function of how that belief/desire fits into the context of other beliefs/desires. The rational force of any given belief/desire is then particular to the context in which it operates and there are no general principles governing its role in ethical reasoning. The rational impact of a given belief will vary from context to context in a way that is not predictable (see Dancy 1993: 60). The version of particularism I shall defend is, however, more radical than this. The lack of general principles in ethical reasoning is not just a function of our inability to predict the rational impact of a belief/desire from one situation to another; it is a consequence of our inability to subject the pattern of our ethical reasons to ongoing amendment and interrogation. There are no general ethical principles, because we have the ability to make a difference and change the patterns by which we live and reason about our behaviour.

Given the particularist denial of general principles, there can be no scope for thinking of moral education as the learning of general rules of conduct. In place of this, according to my model, moral education becomes an education of character. I use the word 'character' as a theoretical term. I shall distinguish different conceptions of character below, but in general the idea of character is meant to capture the following thought: there are capacities for belief and for reasoning with belief that have a contingent basis in the way the subject is situated in the world. There are two aspects of the idea of capacities for belief that are important to my concept of character. First, these are capacities for belief the basis for which is contingent: not all subjects are naturally guaranteed the capacities for belief in which I am interested. Some such capacities for belief have a natural basis, for example the capacity for colour beliefs is grounded in a natural ability to respond to electromagnetic radiation within certain parameters, even if not everyone enjoys that capacity. The interesting cases are capacities for belief whose basis is non-natural, or at least not wholly natural; I shall suggest that the capacity for ethical judgement is of this more complex kind. Second, the capacities for belief in which I am interested are capacities grounded in the subject's situatedness or being in the world. This feature of the capacities for belief turns on the non-codifiability of the beliefs in question; they are beliefs that are not fully codifiable in language. It is because of this non-codifiability that having a belief about a colour, for example, is not analysable in terms of an attitude to a sentence, but as an attitude to how things are. I want to suggest that ethical judgements involve beliefs that are definable only in terms of our orientation to the environment appropriately conceived.

By 'character' I mean the sum of a subject's capacities for belief. By saying that moral education is an education of character I am saying that the capacity for ethical judgement and ethical reasoning is a skill that has to be acquired, honed and sustained. In the absence of general principles to guide ethical judgement, what is required for ethical thought and behaviour is the character to continue our ethical dialogues and reasoning in a skilful manner, one that nevertheless makes room for the thought that ethical judgements are candidates for truth.

I believe that the model of moral education and ethical judgement that I explore is intrinsically interesting and worth understanding and defending. The point of my argument can, however, be understood in a more modest light. If the position that I sketch is possible, then regardless of whether or not you think it attractive, this does at least show how much is recoverable from a set of assumptions that most people seem to think entail only irrationalism. It reveals the feebleness of the supposed postmodernist threat to a belief in the power of reason and the availability of an objective concept of truth.

My argument is as much concerned with metaphysics as with the nature of moral education *per se*. It is an argument about the conditions of possibility for a realist construal of moral education in the face of a set of assumptions that are commonly thought to call such a possibility into question. If the argument is correct, the absence of detail on the precise workings of moral education will not matter, for the argument legitimises a concept of moral education that, properly understood, turns out to be very close to our common sense understanding of what we are doing when we bring up young people to understand ethical thought and behaviour. Moral education is not a training in doctrine, an instruction in the catechism of learning right from wrong; still less is it a training in general principles that are suited for guiding

the initiates through life. Moral education is a messier affair. It is an education of character, an education of the capacities for belief that turn us from
novice to competent judge in matters of value. It is a cumbersome protracted
process in which young people acquire the character to become judges
equipped with a sensibility that renders them capable of passing judgement
upon the particular contingencies of life, a judgement that is susceptible for
evaluation by the ordinary standards of truth and falsity. And this faculty of
judgement is, in part, a creative faculty by which we have to respond to the
novelties that history throws at us; it is a faculty by which the educated person
helps negotiate and shape the world through which he or she must live. Moral
education, according to such a vision, is a nurturing of young people into a
position of shared responsibility for the way we make our world and the values
by which we live. Despite the intrusion of such contingency and novelty, the
whole process is one susceptible of a realist construal, because the art of judgement that lies at the heart of this conception is the art of judging truly. The
metaphysical enterprise is to see how so much contingency and creativity is
compatible with the business of judging truly. That enterprise is an enterprise of legitimisation.

The fact that I spend so much time on the metaphysical legitimisation of
the idea of education of character calls for a brief defence. As I write, there
has been considerable attention to the idea of moral education, much of
it spilling over the media in a wide-ranging debate about the condition of
modern society.[3] It is no mere academic arrogance to complain of the mind-
numbingly banal exchange of pieties that has passed for debate in recent months.
None of the debate in the UK media has proceeded beyond a level of sophistication that would embarrass a first-year undergraduate. At worst, the idea
of moral education seems to have been mistaken for a last minute add-on, a
further area of theoretical knowledge that a careless civil servant had left off
the agenda when the National Curriculum was set. At best, the working
assumption has seemed to be that moral education falls either into the category of doctrinal instruction or an instruction in general principles of
reasoning with which children can then confront whatever life throws their
way. The latter, of course, has become something of an entrenched orthodoxy amongst a large section of British educationalists.[4] The simplistic models
of morals – let alone moral education – that have informed recent discussion have survived only because of the resilience of a number of deep-rooted
philosophical assumptions, especially concerning the nature of reasons. If we
are to get a clear sight of an alternative conception of the nature of ethical
judgement – as well as moral education – that is alive to the complexities
of our moral experience, then we need to be clear about a number of basic
issues.

There is a further point in favour of this reasoning. There are no infor-
mative general principles that it could be the task of moral education to
pass on. According to my account, the morally educated young person is

someone with the character to make sensible judgements about how to continue human culture and history and solve whatever novel problems they come to face. Given the particularism that I support, it cannot be part of my job *qua* philosopher to offer instruction on how to live. Particularism underpins a radical democratic impulse: one of the hardest things in a democracy and one of the hardest things in being a parent is to acknowledge the difference between how life is here and how it is elsewhere, the difference between how it was for us and how it might be in the future. The democratic spirit both in politics and good parenting requires the ability to let go and acknowledge that the best advice one can sometimes give to those who occupy different places and different times is to say, 'Whatever else you do, make a better job of it than we did.'

In the next two sections I briefly defend the assumptions that are basic to my position, firstly concerning the nature of truth and reason, and, secondly, the idea that ethical judgements are perspectival because dependent on a contingent capacity for belief.

Particularism and the patterning of reasons

Particularism holds that the rational force of a belief is a function of how it fits into the context of other beliefs and, as such, may vary from context to context. Now, suppose you thought that wherever one thing is a reason for another it must be possible to give an account of why this is the case; that is to say, the relation 'x is a reason for y' cannot be a bare existent, because for any pair of items (beliefs and beliefs, or beliefs/desires and actions) that satisfy this relation it must be possible to show how their instantiation fits some pattern. Let us call this requirement the *reflexivity of reasons*.[5] A particularist account of reasons would appear to undermine the reflexivity of reasons. It certainly challenges a natural and powerful way in which many people have assumed one has to meet the requirement of reflexivity by adopting a subsumptive theory of reasons. A subsumptive theory of reasons holds that if a belief is a reason for a belief/action it must be possible to subsume the relationship between the former and latter under a general principle. Particularism denies a subsumptive theory of reasons but still accommodates the idea of the patterning of reasons that flows from the reflexivity requirement. In this section I want to clarify how this is possible by distinguishing a number of basic platitudes about reasons, the endorsement of which falls short of a subsumptive theory of reasons.

I shall assume that the reflexivity of reasons is a legitimate constraint on reasons. The idea that it forces a subsumptive theory of reasons is the intuitively appealing thought that the buck has to stop somewhere as one reflects on a reason and looks for its antecedent reason, and where else can the buck stop other than in a general principle? Now, I am prepared to accept that my kind of particularism, although endorsing the reflexivity of reasons, admits that the buck never finally stops. This means that the exercise of giving reasons for our reasons has no ultimate and universally applicable measure; but that, of course, is just to note that such particularism disavows an Enlightenment thirst for ultimate standards. It does not mean that there are no such things as standards for reasons, nor that the standards cannot involve an orientation to the truth.

I suggest that the intuitively appealing thought that the reflexivity of reasons requires a subsumptive theory of reasons arises from a misreading of a legitimate demand that reasons exhibit a connectivity with one another, a connectivity that is required in order to capture the *detachability of reasons*. The detachability of reasons is the requirement that the normative impact of reasons is, in some way, detachable from whoever offers the reason, and when and where they offer it. There are, I think, a number of different points that need to be made in cashing out this metaphor of the detachability of reasons, but I suggest that the intuitive hostility to particularism arises, in part, from an over-zealous interpretation of what is at issue in acknowledging the detachability of reasons.

The subsumptive theory arises from thinking that by demanding the reflexivity of reasons one demands that beliefs stand in relations of connections such that the pattern of connections is detachable from the subjects or agents concerned. Now, I think it is right to hold that the reflexivity of reasons entails a notion of the detachability of reasons, but that the latter is open to different interpretations. The idea (typical of consequentialist theories that treat all reasons as agent-neutral reasons), that the detachability of reasons amounts to beliefs standing in patterns of connections that are describable independently of the agent, is more than is demanded by observing the unavoidable and minimal account of the detachability of reasons.

Agent-neutral accounts of reasons treat the rational impact of a belief as something that applies to a position within an abstract topography of reasons, not to a particular agent. Such an account of the detachability of reasons treats the rational impact of a reason as something, like your council tax, that applies to a position not to you, and the position is thought of as a place within a topography of connections that is describable independently of the agents who are subject to reasons.

This is not the place to enter into a detailed argument about the metaphysics of reasons, but let me outline a minimal reading of the detachability of reasons that arises from the idea of the reflexivity of reasons. Suppose A utters sentence S and in so doing expresses a belief that provides B with a reason for belief/action. S has a rational impact upon B. The first grade of detachability of reasons comes from noting that if we ask for a reason why S has this rational impact, it is not enough to say, 'Because A uttered S'. In other words the rational impact of this sentence upon B does not consist solely in the fact that A uttered it. The reflexivity of reasons requires that there must be more to be said than merely that.[6]

The second grade of the detachability of reasons shows why the rational impact of S upon B cannot consist simply in the fact that A uttered S. The obvious thought is that it is the content of S that carries the normative force of reasons, not the fact that it was A who uttered it. The reason why B ought to respond to the rational impact of S is because the content of S is a bearer of objective truth values, where this means (at least) that the truth value obtains independently of anyone thinking that it does. The second grade of detachability of reasons turns then on the detachability of truth, the idea that the belief contents that engage us rationally do so in virtue of this possession of truth values that are independent of our will.[7]

But now, if all cases of giving reasons turn on the contents of what is said because the contents are bearers of objective truth values, this introduces a further grade of the detachability of reasons; it introduces the idea that the connections that obtain between one belief and another are patterned. It does not, however, require that the patterning of reasons define a topography detachable from the agents concerned, and so it does not threaten the particularist. The notion of the patterning of reasons that the third grade of detachability introduces is this. In order for S to have a rational impact upon B it must engage the inferential structure of B's beliefs and desires. The rational force of S's impact upon B resides in the content of S having an objective truth value insofar as its truth value enforces a systematic redistribution of truth values over B's beliefs, given B's desires. The only way we have to account for a content having this effect upon a set of beliefs is in terms of there being a common structure to the beliefs in question. It is the systematicity of belief contents (the fact that beliefs are composed of a combinatorial structure that can be reorganised in systematic ways) that accounts for the inferential bearing any single belief has upon others. This means that if S has a rational impact upon B it must be by virtue of some pattern of structure discernible in both the content of S and in B's beliefs. It follows from this that if S has a rational impact upon B then it would have the same rational impact upon anyone else with just the same belief set (and desires) as B, for if the rational impact of S consists in the way its component structure engages the component structure of B's beliefs, then S will engage any belief set with just the same structure. This, however, is no more than the minimal and banal universalist claim that the impact of S upon B's beliefs operates by the mediation of a universally quantified sentence. For example, if S is a sentence of simple subject–predicate form, 'a is F', then for it to impact upon B's beliefs, not only must B possess beliefs about a and beliefs about F-ness, but she must also hold some universally quantified belief that instantiates the schema:

All F's . . . are G

where the dots signify that the qualifications permissible upon the antecedent have no fixed limit. Of course, if the universal sentence is the simple 'All Fs are G', then we have a general principle in operation, but this is not a requirement that flows from the patterning of reasons. The patterning of reasons is compatible with a particularism that acknowledges that the universal sentence involved in connecting S with B's belief set might be so qualified as to apply only to B. More interestingly, the properties involved in formulating this universal sentence might be properties that are agent-relative and so guaranteed to apply only to B.[8]

The perspectival nature of ethical reasoning

As already stated, there are capacities for belief that are grounded in the subject's situatedness or being in the world. Such capacities generate beliefs that are perspectival in the sense that the belief content is not fully codifiable linguistically. This means that such a belief cannot be theorised as an attitude to a sentence; it must be theorised as an attitude to the environment. Beliefs that figure in agent-relative reasons are an extreme example of this phenomenon, for they are beliefs that involve an attitude of the subject to herself. But the notion of agent-relative reasons is just one example of a more general phenomenon.

Well-documented accounts of beliefs that are perspectival in the above sense include perceptual demonstrative beliefs about material objects expressed with the singular terms 'this' and 'that'.[9] Understanding the singular desire expressed when someone says 'I want that', requires that in addition to understanding their words, you have to share perceptually their environment; you have to be located perceptually in the same environment. Replacing the demonstrative 'that' with a description does not capture the original belief, for altering the form from the demonstrative to the descriptive changes the rational impact of the sentence, it engages differently with other beliefs.

A related case of the perspectivalness of belief concerns colour beliefs. One might think that the belief expressed by 'The apple is red' is not fully codifiable because the ability to understand the sentence requires not only a grasp of rules of linguistic usage but also the capacity to have colour experiences. A more extreme example would be a combination of the first two in the case of the belief expressed by the sentence 'I want that shade of blue.' In all these cases, beliefs are expressed whose content is perspectival in the sense that they are not fully coded linguistically. To put the point in the most abstract way, the uncodifiability obtains because grasp of the content requires an experiential openness to the environment. Quite how the 'experiental openness to the environment' is conceived will vary from case to case. In the case of colour beliefs there is the option of treating this in terms of possession of qualia, an option that does not make sense in the case of perceptual demonstratives about material objects, nor, I suspect, in the complex case of demonstrative thoughts about colour shades. In general, the idea that beliefs are perspectival is compatible with them being answerable to truth and falsity if we can make sense of the idea of being mistaken with such beliefs where this involves a conception of states of affairs independent of will. In the case of perceptual demonstratives about material objects this is easily achieved, for in that case the experiential openness to the environment cannot be conceived of in any other way than as a literal openness to how things are. A naive realist about colours will also have available a conception of that which is independent of will in terms of an environment replete with colour properties.[10]

The account of ethical belief I want to employ in my account of character is the idea of ethical belief as perspectival in the sense that the content of such beliefs is not fully codifiable because it is relativised to the sensibility, the operation of the sentiments. The thought then is that just as in the demonstrative case, understanding the belief expressed requires a capacity for locating oneself perceptually in the world: in the colour case, understanding the belief requires a capacity for a particular type of experiential orientation in the world; in the ethical case, understanding requires a capacity for locating oneself by the faculty of sensibility in an environment peopled with fellow creatures of sentiment. The experiential orientation of the ethical is an orientation of the sentiments.

The possibility that such perspectivalness is compatible with ethical judgements being answerable to plain truth should be familiar.[11] I want to explore the option for allowing that even under the most radical construal of the way that ethical judgement is conditional upon contingent configurations of our sensibility, answerability to plain truth is still applicable. I shall not then dwell here on the general point of the compatibility of the kind of subjectivism that is acknowledged by making ethical judgement perspectival with respect to sensibility and answerability to plain truth. Before considering the extreme case, there is, however, one further feature of the kind of perspectivalness that I am working with that warrants attention.

If ethical judgements are perspectival in the above sense, moral reasoning is a form of narrative reasoning. I say that moral reasoning is 'narrative' because it is a form of reasoning that cannot be studied as a formal syntactic structure. This is not to deny that any given piece of valid ethical reasoning will be valid insofar as it instantiates a formal pattern; the point is only that the items that instantiate that pattern cannot themselves be defined formally. Put another way, the items that figure in the patterns of ethical reasoning are not sentences, for the content of ethical judgements are not fully codifiable linguistically. Ethical reasoning requires that ethical judgements instantiate patterns, but the ethical judgements that instantiate such patterns are items whose individuation requires a sensibility in orientation to its environment. This means that what makes something a valid ethical argument cannot be isolated and represented as a linguistic sequence. The point is not peculiar to ethical judgement. It is a feature of all arguments that employ linguistic units whose content is context-sensitive. The validity of ethical arguments turns not on the context-insensitive properties of a string of linguistic items; it turns on the context-sensitive properties of the string. The structure of a valid ethical argument is not a linguistic structure; it is, in part, a structure of sensibility. This introduces a special notion of narrative: the idea that ethical arguments involve a relighting of the sensibility. Being presented with an ethical argument is not, as in the case of mathematical arguments, being presented with a formally definable string of symbols; it is a matter of being presented with an engagement of the sensibility (Baier and Luntley 1995). Put abstractly, because the content of the judgement is individuated in part by the subject's orientation in his or her environment, and because the validity of the argument requires that we employ the same content at the appropriate points in the argument, the reconstruction of the argument requires the reconstruction of the orientation that the subject enjoyed. This is why in setting out one's reasons for action one often needs to employ rich and thick descriptions of the situation. The salient features that make the action reasonable may lie deep in the particularities of the description of the situation. If this thought is anywhere near right, it already has profound implications for the way we conceive of moral education.

The idea that moral education might be built around an abstract exercise of critical thinking, in which pupils might learn the art of abstracting from the particular to find a general principle, is anathema to the point of view just expressed. Pupils subjected to such a programme would be at risk of losing the very sensitivity to the salient particularities, the engagement of the sentiments in the many varied and detailed nuances of configurations, that are typical of the alert educated sensibility. The abstractionist approach is in danger of blunting rather than sharpening our moral sense. Of course, the key insight that prompts so many proponents of critical thinking programmes and, more generally, those who have seized upon Hare's work as a basis for moral education, is the insight that where there is a valid moral reason it must be possible to state why the reason is valid. The mistake is to think that the only way that this can be done is by showing how the proffered reason instantiates a general principle. The detachability of reasons does not demand this. What it demands is simply that where S is a reason for B, that it is a reason should be defensible by showing how S's engagement with B's belief and desires is patterned. This is a requirement of generality, but it is the requirement that the engagement of S with B's beliefs be an engagement that would lock into A's beliefs if they were of just the same configuration. It does not follow from this that the configuration of B's beliefs that makes them susceptible to S as expressing a reason for action should be a configuration that fits in a stable pattern that is part of a general topography of the connectedness of reasons, let alone that it should fit a general principle.

In summary, the model I am employing is a model in which giving a reason for an action can, and very often does, involve a narrative reconstruction of the details of one's orientation in the predicament at issue. If what one gives is a reason, it must be possible to detect the systematic patterning of the orientation that reveals how the impact of the reason upon one's beliefs and desires is not an impact that is, in Hume's terms, an 'original existent'. A reason does not just happen, it is something that keys into the systematic connectedness of our sensible orientation to the environment. Without the extra requirement that the keying-in of the reason should instantiate a general principle, the way is left open for the thought that the best account available of why S is a good reason amounts to more of the same; that is, the further narrative reconstruction of one's orientation. That will, of course, unveil further respects in which one's orientation has a systematic structure that makes it potentially alike the orientations of others. But none of this entails that at any point in the process light will, and only can, finally dawn when the structure of one's orientation is seen to instantiate general patterns that are discernible in everyone's orientation. To the objection that this means that there is no entry point to the narrative unfolding of reasons for the uninitiated, for one must already be party to the sort of narrative reconstruction of sensible orientations before the offering of such narratives engages one's sympathy, there is no better reply than to ask, 'Just who is the strange character who is uninitiated in the play of the sentiments?' It really is no objection to an option in moral theory to complain that the account of ethical judgement leaves Callicles cold.

Two conceptions of character

Suppose the brief account of the nature of ethical judgement that I sketched in the previous section is correct. Although many people seem to think that such perspectivalness threatens the truth-aptness of ethical judgement, that is simply an error. The idea that judgement can be both perspectival and truth-apt should be commonplace. What I want to pursue is the thought that this possibility is not closed off by the most radical intrusion of contingency into our account of the sensibility that makes ethical judgement perspectival. To this end I want to distinguish two different conceptions of the idea of character and the claim that moral education is an education of character. I shall call the first a naturalistic conception of character.

Suppose that one thought that the sensibility by reference to which ethical judgement is to be understood was grounded in human nature. So, understanding ethical judgements depends on possession of the appropriate faculty of sensibility and, furthermore, this is a faculty – a capacity for belief – that is not to be understood as the operation of brute passions – a sort of emotive colouring upon an experiential confrontation with the environment that is in its own terms inert. Instead, the faculty of sensibility introduces what can only be called an 'enlarged faculty of reason'.[12] According to this account, it would seem appropriate to think of moral education as an education of character in the sense that it is an education that inculcates this enlarged faculty of reason. Coming to be a morally educated person would then be a coming to acquire the faculty of sensibility that made ethical judgement possible; it would be a coming to see the world in terms lighted up by the operation of sensibility. The purpose of moral education would be to bring young people within the operation of this enlarged faculty of reason. To call this an education of character seems appropriate, for although the sensibility is a faculty of reason answerable to plain truth, the operation of this faculty does not conform to the narrow model of cognition on which cognitive processes are modelled in terms of operation upon symbols. The operation of the faculty of sensibility is the operation of a faculty of judgement that, although possessing the systematicity required of any faculty that aims at truth, is a systematicity of judgements whose identity conditions are embedded within the operation of the sentiments.[13]

If, however, one assumes that the faculty of sensibility is grounded in human nature either because one assumes – as Hume might have done – that, as an empirical fact, there is only one way that human nature develops, or because one assumes – as Aristotle perhaps did – that as a metaphysical fact, there is only one telos that guides the development of human nature, then the character that moral education develops would be uniform. With such an approach, the emphasis on judgement rather than law in our account of the nature of ethical judgement and education would be dependent on the epistemological difficulty of foreseeing all the particular situations to which a sensible character might be asked to respond. In the absence of any guarantee that the world has, as it were, only a limited menu of options to set before us, one could not with any confidence assume that there would be useful generalisations on which to base the task of moral education.

Such a concept of moral education as an education of character supports a form of particularism about ethical judgement, but it is an epistemological particularism. It is a particularism that holds that the lack of generalisations to figure centrally in the task of moral education is a function of our ignorance of all the possibilities. To put the point in the light of the detachability of reasons, such a concept of character is compatible with the idea that not only is there a pattern to anything that counts as a moral reason, but that the pattern is a consequence of the general structure of human nature. There is, if you like, a general recipe for living well that is grounded in the constancy of human nature. The particularism is only a function of our inability to predict how that recipe will apply in the varied contingencies of life. According to this option, there are such things as general rules of conduct, but we are incapable (most of the time) of anticipating their correct application.

I do not find such a conception of character plausible. In the remainder of this chapter I want to explore the scope for a more radical and contingent conception of character that is not grounded in truths about human nature. Nevertheless, I shall show how accommodating such contingency is compatible with the idea that the faculty of sensibility is answerable to plain truth. If so, this supports a model of moral education as the education of character which, despite the contingency at play in the account of character, is compatible with a moral realism that conforms to the constraints on truth and reason adumbrated in the second section. Let me first note a further idea that distinguishes a contingent model of character from a non-contingent model.

It has become commonplace to observe that the activity of exchanging reasons with one another, even if constrained only by the minimal platitudes about the detachability of reasons and truth that I have endorsed, nevertheless seems to presuppose certain higher-order values. Exchanging reasons with one another is an activity of conversation, a dialogic practice that brings with it its own procedural norms. Let us call these the conversational virtues. They include respect, sympathy, truth and care. One can hardly engage in a conversational exchange of reasons for action without some respect for the other's point of view, a readiness to consider their orientation as something worth understanding. This, in turn, requires some operation of sympathy and a care for how things are from the other's point of view. A degree of trust is also required, for at the least, it amounts to the idea that one is entitled to hold the other to what they have said. If your conversant is free to change the meaning of their words halfway through a conversation, or to assume that holding a judgement to be true is something that involves no commitment to continuing to hold it true in ten minutes' time, even when no change in evidence (or whatever) has taken place, then such a person is not recognisably a party to conversations. They would be random sentence producers, but not people engaged in a dialogic pursuit of reasons, truth, and so on.

My suspicion is that the conversational virtues are genuine virtues, but that their content is so abstract that the injunction to observe them is banal. That should not be surprising if they are virtues that are constitutive of the very idea of engaging in a conversation of reasons: one cannot be enjoined to observe such virtues, for one must already acknowledge them before one could be party to any conversational exchange whatsoever. Being party to these virtues is a condition for the possibility of conversational exchanges. A programme of moral education built around the stricture to observe the conversational virtues would be a very short programme indeed! The difficult task is to build a programme that gives exercise in the activity of conversing about reasons where this is thought of as the narrative reconstruction of sensible orientations. That exercise is, however, an exercise that requires that young people be given a richness of experience that enables them to explore the operation of the sentiments. Of course, insofar as their exploration is a reasonable one, it will be one that meets the abstract conversational virtues. But that it does so will not be because the exploration of the sentiments is derived from the general virtues; it will be because any reasonable exploration will have to be patterned. Observing the conversational virtues will not drive or guide the exploration, though: because it meets the patterning required by the detachability of reasons, any reasonable exploration will observe the conversational virtues.

A further way of distinguishing a contingent conception of character from a non-contingent conception concerns the relationship between the abstract conversational virtues and the particular values uncovered by what I have called the exploration of the sentiments. If one thought it was possible to derive particular virtues that offered concrete guidance on how to live from the abstract conversational virtues, then one would have no reason to endorse a contingent conception of character. The idea that there is a useful derivation of this sort to be made is distinctive of Habermas's work. Attempting this move does not require a naturalistic account of human nature, although that could provide an alternative basis for the derivation in which the conversational virtues were naturalistically grounded, as opposed to transcendentally grounded as I suggested. Either way, scepticism about the potential for deriving anything interesting out of the conversational virtues once more opens the possibility for a contingent conception of character and of sensibility, in terms of which ethical judgement has to be understood.

Character as the capacity to respond to contingencies

A contingent conception of character supports a more radical particularism than the epistemological variety supported by a naturalistic conception of character. Suppose that the reason why we cannot formulate general principles that anticipate reasonable action is because agents make a difference. The patterns that exist in our reasonable behaviour are not natural patterns, they are patterns that we make and that we sustain. The fact that the patterns are not natural means that in our actions we are not playthings of natural law. Acting for a reason is not acting in a way that instantiates a natural law; it is acting in a way that is patterned but in which the patterning is itself something susceptible to reasonable interrogation, emendation and sustenance. This introduces a radical contingency into our conception of character, for the patterning of character is no longer grounded in universal truths about human nature. Although the intrusion of contingency is radical, and although it captures something that many self-proclaimed 'postmodernists' would endorse, it is important not to overstate the contingency at play here.[14]

The patterning of our reasons is something that is itself susceptible to reasonable interrogation, emendation and sustenance. The contingency that this introduces is not an 'anything goes' contingency in which a pattern could change overnight for no good reason as a result of a chance occurrence. The idea is that the patterning of our reasons is something that is subject to reasonable interrogation; that is to say, we have to give reasons for changes in the patterning of our reasons. That can then look circular, as though there is no real contingency at play in the form of particularism that allows that agents can make a difference. That there looks to be a problem here is grounded in our deep-rooted tendency to misunderstand the demand of the patterning of reasons.

The particularism that I am proposing is built on the observation that agents make a difference. The objection that I am considering says that either agents make a difference by chance contingencies – non-rational changes to the patterns of reasons – or they make a difference by giving a reason for the difference. On the former option, the difference made cannot be a contribution of reasons and so does not support a particularist account of character as the faculty of sensible reasoning. On the latter option, the idea that reasons are given for changes in the patterns of reasons means that this cannot really amount to a change in the patterns of reasons, for the reason appealed to is maintained across the change in the patterning that is altered. In other words, the objector thinks that the latter option amounts only to a local change in the pattern of reasons, a change made possible by the continuing endorsement of more global patterns of reasons. The dilemma presented here is not real, for the second option misdescribes the procedure of giving reasons for changes in the patterning of our reasons.

If you assume that the patterning of reasons is ultimately grounded in a subsumptive model of rationality in which all reasons can be ordered in a hierarchy and local reasons are subsumable as instantiations of more general reasons, and so on, then of course the idea that one gives a reason for a change in the patterning of one's reasons can only be thought of as a local alteration made to bring local reasons into line with the more general reasons that drive the whole system of rationality. According to such a model, there is no change in the patterning of reasons, there is only the correction of a local reason in order to conform to a general reason. But this assumption about the nature of the patterning of reasons is illicit. It is the assumption that is typical of an Enlightenment concept of rationality, but it is not required by the mere recognition of the patterning of reasons. As I argued in the second section, the patterning of reasons requires that where S is a reason for B it must exhibit a generality, but this does not require that the pattern into which S fits is one that is formulable in advance as a general principle, nor that it is a pattern subsumable under a set of general universal principles of the patterning of all reasons. There are such general principles – we can call them 'logic' – but logic gives no advice on how to live or what to think.

The platitude of the patterning of reasons that I defended in the second section already accommodates a particularist account of reasons which allows the radical option that the patterns manifest in our reasoning are part of a complex dynamic non-linear system of rationality. If our reasoning conforms only to the minimal platitudes that I proposed in the second section, then there is such a thing as contingency to the patternings of our reasons. It is not the contingency of chance interruptions to our reasoning; it is the contingency of a radical interruption, but where the interruption is prompted not because our reasoning was out of line with a general principle, but because someone was able to tell a reasonable story about a better way of proceeding. The complexity and dynamic character of our reasoning allows the possibility that there will be scope for novel changes in the patternings of our reasons. Once we read the patterning of reasons in the manner of the minimalist platitudes I offered, we can occupy the site between the Enlightenment conception of reasons as forming an axiomatic and formal system that is, in principle, stateable in advance of all particularities, and the nihilistic nightmare scenario in which no reason is left at all, or our conversations become subject to all manner of chance interruptions. There is a deep-seated blindness to the idea of genuine creativity with reasons. It is curable only by shaking off the rigid model of subsumptive rationality in favour of the minimalist account of the patterning of reasons that I have acknowledged.

To put matters another way, the idea that the patterning of our reasons can itself be something that is subject to reasonable interrogation is compatible with moral realism insofar as the sustaining of our patterns of reasons is achieved not by mere mimicry, but by a dialogic or conversational sustaining. If this is anywhere near right, the model of moral education that it supports is quite unlike most of the options in the literature. Moral education cannot be a training in doctrine, a mimicry of how the elders behave. It cannot be a learning of a set of general rules that will then guide the initiate through life. It can only be a gradual and particularist education of character, the character of sensibility with the capacity to judge creatively and correctly about what to do next. The creativity of exercise (the possibility that the patterning of reasons is subject to reasonable interrogation) means that in being so educated one takes on a share of the responsibility for sustaining our patterns of reasons. Indeed, according to the model I am describing, moral education is not an extra, a 'bolt-on' to the otherwise instrumental business of acquiring examination certificates and so on, it is central to the very idea of bringing young people into agency. In moral education we bring young people within the ongoing conversation about the contingencies that confront us. We equip them with the character to respond to contingencies that we cannot yet conceive, but we leave them, we hope, with a character to make timely judgements about how to proceed. The whole activity is not unlike bringing someone into a music ensemble that is improvising a score. The most basic injunction is not the boring 'Do as we did', but 'Try and make something better.' And all we can offer young people to equip them to respond to this injunction is a detailed particular experience of the exploration of sentiments and of the responsibility of making judgements about how to continue.

Character education: the way forward

I have articulated the basic outlines of my conception of character and of its particularist reasoning about values. The position I have outlined is, I hope, recognisable to anyone who has ever indulged their reflection upon the activities of bringing up children, let alone providing moral education within a formal environment. If the resulting picture seems familiar, I take that as a bonus, for my project has been to legitimise an activity that most sensitive educators already knew to be far more complex than either the postmodernist sceptics or the establishment worriers ever allowed. The task of legitimisation may be abstract and painstaking, but the reward is a recovery of, and right to inhabit, a common ground that acknowledges the particularity of the creative art of passing judgement and giving reason for what we do, a common ground from which we acknowledge that we can and do make a difference. Before closing with a few remarks on the consequences of my conception of the education of character for education in general, I want to present a simple example to illustrate the ordinariness of the conception that I am advocating.

The difficulty most people have with my position concerns the compatibility of the perspectivalness and particularism of judgement with the idea that judgement is answerable before the tribunal of plain truth. The following example shows how familiar that compatibility really is. Consider the case of financial truths; think about the state of your own personal finances. Most people are prone to adopt a realist attitude to judgements about their personal finances. Judgements about one's credit status wear all the appearances of judgements whose truth value obtains independent will. There are brute facts of the matter concerning whether or not you can afford a new hi-fi, car or expensive night out. Despite the apparently brutal independence of will that the truth of such judgements enjoy, it is clear that judgements about one's financial status are perspectival judgements. Indeed, the whole of economics constitutes a perspectival discourse, a discourse that only makes sense from the point of view of human creatures who have indulged in various complex acts of promising.[15] This means that financial discourse, with which we have an uncomplicated familiarity, is a discourse that is perspectival in just the manner I have been describing and also a discourse for which we unproblematically assume a realist truth predicate is licit. The complexity of these two features is particularly clear in the observation that despite the robustness of facts about one's credit status, these are facts that can be altered by negotiation and interrogation; they are facts whose sustenance requires our continued willingness to play the game and honour our promises.

The role of negotiation is complex and does not necessarily depend on negotiation by the immediate parties to a particular financial exchange. For example, if the government agrees with its central bankers to change base rate this immediately changes everyone's credit status. Something happens, behind our backs, but the fact that the change is made in such a fashion does not impugn the robustness of the financial facts. More transparently, one can negotiate changes in one's credit status by oneself, and that activity can involve the kind of creativity that I spoke of with regard to the particularity of reasons. Negotiating an extended credit line at the bank is an exercise in creatively restructuring the web of obligations that one has to honour. It is not something that happens according to hard-and-fast rules that make it predictable in advance that the negotiation will go in one general pattern or another. The negotiations will be patterned and the resulting position will be patterned, for that is a requirement that the activity is reason-governed, but neither the negotiations nor the result are predictable as instantiations of general rules.

Of course, if someone objects that we do not have to honour the promissory relations that constitute the modern economic order, they are right in the sense that there is no fundamental necessity that these promises persist. The promises involved are not, as it were, part of the fabric of the cosmos. We insult no one and nothing, other than ourselves, if we break our financial promises. But this observation is no objection to the general position I have described. It amounts to no more than the recognition that the facts that constitute our economic realm are perspectival facts, they are facts that depend on the contingencies of real human history. From the point of view of the cosmos, from within the world's own story, there are no such things as overdrafts and credit cards. That undoubted piece of metaphysical truth is, I suggest, not a shocking insight that prompts despair; it is the platitudinous realisation that the Enlightenment project is over. If we want to get ourselves right, if we want to understand our predicaments both economic and moral, then we should not be looking any further than the view from within our perspectival conceptions of the points and purposes of human life, perspectives that can be subject to negotiation and interrogation. The educated person, let alone the morally educated person, needs then not just a record of the structures of the perspectives so far created within human history. Such a record, which amounts to a study of the ancestors' doctrine, is adequate only for a mimicry of the past; on its own it is no basis for the critical interrogation of the past required in order to face the contingencies of the future. The only thing that will do as a basis for responding to the contingencies of the future is a faculty of judgement that answers to the general outline structure that I described for the faculty of sensibility. Education in such a faculty is an education of character, as I have used that term.

What of the robustness of character? Could our moral world, like the economic, not break down irrevocably? Of course, it could. Therein lies the contingency that postmodernists find so impressive. The robustness of our ethical judgement is a function of our ongoing deliberations about matters that impress on the sentiments; it is a function of how we continue to explore the sentiments. Such fragility of the ethical is a direct consequence of giving up the idea that there is such a thing as the world's own story and that it contains a recipe for living well. Measured by such standards the ethical is extraordinarily fragile, but in the face of the rejection of such standards, this observation is not threatening. And despite the lack of any direct derivation of particular ethical values from the general conversational virtues, the existence of such virtues provides one important bulwark against the worry about the robustness of the ethical. What the existence of the conversational virtues reveals is that, like it or not, as long as we indulge in conversations of any kind, we have to admit that we are creatures who are inescapably bound by normative concepts of obligation and trust. The very act of assertion is understandable only by acknowledging that the speaker is committed to certain things being thus and so; the very act of conversational exchange binds us in relations of trust, care and sympathy. These abstract virtues may not offer much guidance in working out the particularities of life, but they do show how deeply we inhabit a world that is bound together with normative ideas of obligation and trust. The idea that our ethical world might fall apart because we no longer acknowledge ideas of obligation in general is simply not imaginable, for inhabiting a world of obligations is a condition for assertion and conversation. What is imaginable is that we might, with good reason, amend our obligations, ditch some, and invent new ones. But the fact that we can imagine this does not show that we are teetering on the edge of a cataclysmic void; it shows only that we are adequately prepared to face up to the contingencies that the future throws our way and to respond creatively and reasonably to the ongoing task of sustaining the ethical.

A moral education that took such preparation as its goal could not be an afterthought to the general educational process. It would be central to the task of educating agents, rather than training operatives for the labour market. It could be the basis for a renewed humanism in education that found no difficulty in placing the imagination, the arts, the creative exercises of rational self-expression right at the heart of our curriculum. Such a model is, despite its realism and sense of truth in the ethical, also deeply democratic and individualistic. Its central message is that in place of the servile training and mimicry of what history's elites have thought and done, moral education is the preparation of active and equal participants in the ongoing conversation that is human culture.[16]

Notes

1 The anti-Kantian position defended in Sandel (1982) would be a good example of a communitarianism in which moral education would be a process of discovery.

2 For an elementary account of the defence of realism see Luntley (1995).

3 The UK media debated moral education extensively throughout the latter half of 1996.

4 This orthodoxy has been informed largely by Hare's work on moral reasoning (1981).

5 The reflexivity of reasons is not the requirement that if something is a reason for belief/action then it should be possible to give a reason why this is so, for that demands that one always be able to give a reason for one's reasons, and that

is too strong. By 'the reflexivity of reasons' I mean the weaker requirement that if something is a reason for belief/action it should be possible to defend its status as a reason, as opposed to a chance connection, by showing how the relation of being a reason fits into a pattern.

6 As formulated, the point in the text is compatible with the idea that what else needs to be said could be that A possesses theoretical or practical authority. If, however, one thinks that authority has to be subject to dialogic or practical inter- rogation then that will still require the second grade of detachability, for to subject the authority to such a requirement is to say that ultimately it is the context of S that matters, not who said it. For present purposes, all that is required is the conditional claim that if all reasons operate by virtue of the content of claims at issue rather than by virtue of who offers them, this does not commit us to an account of the detachability of reasons that is incompatible with particularism. Thanks to Andrew Williams for forcing me to clarify my thoughts on this point.

7 'Independent of our will' because this ensures that something that has an objec- tive truth value is also the sort of thing that one can be mistaken about, for one cannot assign truth values to contents at will. I here draw upon David Wiggins's work on the marks of truth in laying down the minimal notions of truth and reason that I am appealing to (Wiggins 1991: esp. essay V).

8 Dancy's defence of particularism is flawed, in part, by his lack of attention to the difference between universalism and generalism about reasons. It is the latter that the particularist objects to; the former is a mere logical requirement that patterns the connections between the two items that instantiate the relation 'x is a reason for y' (see Crisp 1993: 181–90 for a clear discussion of this point in Dancy's book).

9 See Evans (1982: ch. 6) for the classic contemporary discussion of such beliefs; see also Luntley (1998: ch. 11) for an introduction to the issues in this field.

10 See Campbell (1992) for a defence of a naive realism that draws on the analogy between demonstrative thoughts and colour thoughts.

11 See Wiggins (1991), also Baier's reading of Hume especially in the symposium 'Moral sentiments and the difference they make' (Baier and Luntley 1995), and also in Luntley (1995).

12 See Luntley (in Baier and Luntley 1995) for a discussion of the narrative char- acter of moral reasoning, given the particularism that comes from relativisation to the sentiments. In that essay I used the analogy with spacial reasoning to make the point that to reconstruct a piece of spacial reasoning using perceptual demon- stratives, to a certain extent one has to reconstruct the space, the background against which one's use of perceptual demonstratives makes sense. Similarly, I suggested that in giving an account of a piece of moral reasoning one has to reconstruct the moral environment, the surround of sentiments and sympathy that is required in order for the ethical judgements at play to possess the content necessary for the reasoning to go through. The concept of narrative that I am employing is not a concept that is used to label reasoning that is lacking in rigour or that uses what some have been tempted to call 'floppy' logic. The reasoning is as rigorous as any contained in any other domain of human discourse; the issue concerns only the way that the items that, as it were, get moved around when one performs this reasoning, are items that are not disengageable from the context of their employment which, in the moral case, is the activation of sentiments.

13 Again, see Baier and Luntley (1995) for more details on this sort of approach.

14 The postmodernist I have in mind is, of course, Rorty (1991).

15 There is much that needs to be said about the ontology of economic facts, but I do not have time to pursue the investigation here. Suffice to say that there is

a *prima facie* case for saying that the ontology of money consists in a complex web of promises. In the modern world money is credit: the undertaking by the Governor of the Bank of England, printed on every UK banknote, promising to 'pay the bearer the sum of . . .' is not a metaphor; cash is just government-backed credit.

16 An earlier version of this chapter was presented at the conference 'Morals for the Millennium', Lancaster University, July 1996, organised by the *Journal for Moral Education*. Thanks to those present for many useful ideas and suggestions. Thanks also to Terry McLaughlin and Mark Halstead for comments on a later draft, and to Andrew Williams, Margaret Archer and Angie Hobbs for comments and criticism on various presentations/drafts of this and related material.

References

Baier, A. and Luntley, M. (1995) 'Moral sentiments and the difference they make', in *Proceedings of the Aristotelian Society, supplementary volume*, 69: 31–45.

Campbell, J. (1992) 'A native view of colours', in D. Charles and K. Lennon (eds) *Reduction, Explanation and Realism*, Oxford: Oxford University Press.

Crisp, R. (1993) 'Motivation, universality and the good: critical notice of J. Dancy *Moral Reasons*', *Ratio* 6(2): 181–90.

Dancy, J. (1993) *Moral Reasons*, Oxford: Blackwell.

Evans, G. (1982) *The Varieties of Reference*, Oxford: Oxford University Press.

Hare, R. M. (1981) *Moral Thinking: Its Levels, Method and Point*, Oxford: Clarendon Press.

Luntley, M. (1995) *Reason, Truth and Self: The Post-modern Reconditioned*, London: Routledge.

—— (1998) *Contemporary Philosophy of Thought and Language*, Oxford: Blackwell.

Rorty, R. (1991) *Contingency, Irony and Solidarity*, Cambridge: Cambridge University Press.

Sandel, M. (1982) *Liberalism and the Limits of Justice*, Cambridge: Cambridge University Press.

Wiggins, D. (1991, reprinted from 1987) *Needs, Values, Truth: Essays in the Philosophy of Value*, Oxford: Blackwell.

11

AGAINST RELATIVISM

Marianne Talbot

Moral relativism seems to have become in the eyes of many of the educational establishment, and certainly for most school-leavers, the unquestioned dogma that sets the standard for moral debate. But moral relativism – at least in the forms in which it has become fashionable – is not only false, it is a theory whose widespread acceptance would be disastrous for society. My concern in this chapter is to offer several explanations of why these forms of moral relativism have become so fashionable – and why they shouldn't have become so fashionable for these reasons – in the hope that such an understanding will start to reverse the process. I shall conclude with one argument for moral absolutism.[1]

Moral relativism and what is wrong with it

Moral relativism is the view that there is no absolute moral truth, the view that all moral beliefs and the statements that express them[2] are true only in relation to some moral system or other, rather in the way that all beliefs about the time, along with the statements that express these beliefs, are true only in relation to some time zone or other. So just as 'it's 2 o'clock' is true (or false) only in relation to some time zone, so, to the moral relativist, 'doing A is wrong' is true (or false) only in relation to some moral system.[3]

The fact that, to a moral relativist, moral truth is system-relative means that there are different types of moral relativism, depending upon different views of what counts as a moral system. So there are types of moral relativism according to which moral systems are constituted of the beliefs of individuals, and there are types of moral relativism according to which moral systems are constituted of the beliefs of interest groups, communities or nations. The larger the group whose beliefs are said by a form of moral relativism to constitute a moral system, the more like moral absolutism that form of moral relativism is.[4]

The forms of moral relativism that have become fashionable are those forms according to which moral systems are constituted of the beliefs either of individuals or of some community.[5] In the first case, moral beliefs are comparable to beliefs such as 'sardines are tasty' because they are true (or false) only in relation to an individual: just as it can be true for you but false for me that sardines are tasty, so, according to this form of moral relativism, an action can be morally right for you but morally wrong for me. In the second case, moral beliefs are comparable to beliefs such as 'everyone should drive on the left' because they are true (or false) only in relation to some community: just as it can be true in England but false in France that everyone should drive on the left, so an action might be morally wrong in England but morally right in France.

Moral absolutism on the other hand, is the view that there is absolute moral truth, the view that moral beliefs, and the statements that express them, are true (or false) *simpliciter*, in just the same way that beliefs such as 'the universe started with a big bang' is true or false *simpliciter*.

Moral relativism[6] is false, or so I claim, because it can offer only an impoverished account of moral error, of the fact that we can go wrong in our moral judgements. A moral relativist can, of course, like everyone else see internal inconsistency in a moral system as evidence for error, but he cannot recognise inconsistency between two different systems as evidence for error; he cannot, in fact, even make sense of the idea that two different moral systems could be *inconsistent*.[7] If moral beliefs are true or false only in relation to individuals, for example, in the way that the belief that sardines are tasty is true or false only in relation to individuals, then the claim that you are wrong in your moral judgements will be comparable to the claim that you are wrong in your judgements about the tastiness of sardines: it will be the claim that you are wrong *by my lights*.

So if you believe that mugging the elderly is permissible or that Hitler was onto a good thing, and these beliefs are consistent with the rest of your moral system, then the moral relativist cannot say that you are wrong *simpliciter* to believe this, he can say only that you are wrong by his lights. And this, of course, is a different thing entirely because it allows that, relative to at least one moral system, mugging the elderly *is* morally permissible. The absolutist can, and will, deny that mugging the elderly could ever be morally permissible for anyone.[8]

Similarly, if a community believes that it is permissible to execute writers for speaking their minds or to abort foetuses because they are female, and these beliefs are consistent with the rest of the moral beliefs of that community, the moral relativist cannot say that this community is wrong *simpliciter* to believe this, he can say only that this community is wrong *by our lights*. And again this is a different thing entirely because it allows that, relative to at least one moral system, executing writers for speaking their minds, or aborting foetuses because they are female, is morally permissible.[9]

The difficulty for the moral relativists is that we simply do not believe that mugging the elderly or executing writers for speaking their minds is morally permissible for anyone or for any community. And what is more, disagreements of this kind matter to us: we want to be able to *say* that mugging the elderly or executing writers for speaking their minds is impermissible, that these behaviours are morally wrong, whoever performs them. Moral relativism, however, can make no sense of this.

But then why has moral relativism become so fashionable?

The arguments

The argument from moral disagreement

One confusion that leads to the adoption of moral relativism is the view that the very existence of moral disagreement suffices to show that moral relativism is true. So people will say that English people differ in their moral beliefs from Eskimos, or that we in the 1990s differ in our moral beliefs from those who lived in the 1890s, therefore morality must be relative.

The first difficulty with this argument is that even if it is true that there are differences in the moral beliefs of the English and the Eskimos, it need not be true that the values that underlie these moral beliefs differ, or, therefore, that the fundamental moral beliefs of the English and the Eskimos differ. So, for example, whilst the Eskimos believe (if they do) that the elderly should be gently put to death, and the English believe (if they do) that the elderly should be kept alive as long as possible, both these beliefs might be differing applications of the belief that the elderly should be respected and protected, applications that differ as a result of a difference in the circumstances in which these values are applied.

Consider two genetically identical plants brought up in quite different circumstances: one of them on a sunny windowsill with sufficient (but not too much) water and food, the other in a darkened cupboard, watered only by a small leak in the roof. These plants will look very different indeed, but this difference is wholly consistent with the genetic identity of the plants. Similarly, the different circumstances in which the Eskimos and the English act on their common belief that the elderly should be respected and protected might result in very different responses to this belief. We should no more be misled by differing beliefs about how we should act into thinking that these beliefs are, of necessity, the result of a difference in our fundamental values, than we should be misled by a difference in the appearance of two plants into thinking this difference is the result of a difference in genetic endowment. The question of whether there really *is* a fundamental difference is a question that can be established only after deeper examination. Absolutists believe that deeper examination would show that all apparent moral differences are the result of differences in the circumstances in which the same moral values are being applied.[10]

The second problem with this confusion lies in the fact that it ignores the possibility that the English (or the Eskimos), or that we (or the Victorians) are (or were) *wrong* to hold the moral beliefs they hold (held). It is, of course, important in making the claim that someone is morally wrong that we exercise due humility and always consider the possibility that we are *ourselves* wrong, but if you believe something and I believe something inconsistent with what you believe, then our first thought should be that one (or both) of us is *wrong*. We do think, now, that those generations who believed that slavery was morally permissible were wrong, and our great-grandchildren may well say, of us, 'they ate *meat*' with all the horror we reserve for 'they believed in *slavery*'. But here another confusion arises . . .

The argument from respect

Another reason for today's widespread acceptance of moral relativism can be traced to the increasingly widespread belief that it is morally wrong to say, of another, that *they* are wrong. Young people, in particular, seem to think that we respect the opinion of another only if we refuse to consider the possibility that that person might be wrong (and they are convinced that we should always respect the opinions of others, about which more below).

The difficulty here lies in the claim that we respect the opinions of another only insofar as we refuse to consider, never mind convey to that person, the possibility that they might be wrong. Once this belief is in place, argument – the method by which rational animals cooperate in the search for truth – is going to seem not only unpleasant but actually wrong: worse, in fact, because given that this belief is believed to follow from what appears to be taken as a *moral* truth, that everyone's opinion must be respected, argument will seem not only unpleasant but *morally* wrong. There can be no better reason for avoiding argument than this.

Once this belief is in place, whenever disagreement looms (and we can be sure that it will) there are only two paths open to us: we can form the belief that we are *ourselves* wrong, or we can find some way of believing that both of us are right. To take the former path too often, however, will inevitably result in a loss of self-respect, to the belief that one's own opinion is not to be respected and to an internal inconsistency. The only consistent (and indeed psychologically healthy) path to take, therefore, once this belief is in place, is the path that leads inexorably to relativism: the path on which both parties are deemed to be right (relative, of course, to their own moral systems).

If we adopt moral relativism for this reason, of course, then not only will we have embraced a moral doctrine that is not obviously true,[11] we will also have left unquestioned a belief whose consequences will be disastrous.

The belief that we respect the opinions of others only insofar as we refuse to consider the possibility that they might be wrong will not only prevent our discovering the truth about moral relativism, it will eventually erode the value that we currently – and correctly – place on discovering the truth. Insofar as we see argument – the method by which we cooperate in the search for the truth – as morally reprehensible, as incompatible with the moral truth that everyone's opinion ought to be respected, we shall have to reject the view that we should engage in the search for truth.

Serious stuff. So serious in fact that it is important to understand that I am not suggesting that acceptance of moral relativism will result in the denial of the value of truth, I am suggesting that to accept the belief that we respect the opinion of others only insofar as we refuse to believe that they are wrong will lead to the denial of the value of truth. And I am also suggesting that this belief is one of the beliefs behind today's widespread acceptance of moral relativism.

There is no reason to accept this belief. Quite apart from the appalling consequences of accepting it (which cannot, of course, be a *reason* for rejecting it), it is false: it is perfectly possible to respect the opinion of another whilst simultaneously considering the possibility that he might be wrong. To err, after all, is only human. The very capacity to form beliefs – the capacity for reason – brings with it the capacity for error: in striving for truth, we do not, we cannot always succeed. To form the belief that a person (possibly oneself) has, on an occasion, formed a false belief is wholly consistent, therefore, with valuing that person and with respecting his opinion.

And not only is forming the belief that a person might be wrong on an occasion wholly consistent with respecting that person's opinion, *expressing* that belief is also consistent with respecting that person's opinion. Not only can we consistently think that a person might be wrong on an occasion, we can even *tell* him, on that occasion, that we think he might be wrong: there is nothing disrespectful in suggesting to another human being that he might be wrong about something. This seems so obvious, in fact, that it is interesting to ask why people should have formed the belief that we respect the opinion of others only insofar as we refuse to consider the possibility that they might be wrong.

The answer, it seems to me, lies in the fact that people have confused the true belief that, faced with a disagreement, we should always consider the possibility that the other is right, with the false belief that, faced with a disagreement, we should never consider the possibility that the other is wrong. In fact, of course, I exhibit my respect for you by being prepared to engage with you in argument, in making it clear, by being prepared to argue with you, that I see you as a worthy collaborator in the search for truth.[12]

The belief that we respect the opinion of others only insofar as we refuse even to consider the possibility that they are wrong is false. And as such we cannot correctly derive moral relativism (or any other form of relativism) from it. But that we do is, I think, explained in part by the following:

The 'argument' from the dislike of argument

The adoption of moral relativism enables us to treat a disagreement – something that *matters* – as a difference – as something that doesn't matter. The adoption of a relativistic stance enables the parties to what threatens to become a disagreement to claim that both parties are right (each of them, of course, relative to their own moral system). And given our dislike of argument, and in particular our dislike of arguments about right and wrong, the fact that the adoption of moral relativism can defuse such arguments can make it seem very attractive.[13]

The problem with adopting moral relativism because it enables us to avoid argument, of course, is that if moral relativism is false, both parties fall into error. Both parties are wrong to embrace the belief that moral truth is relative to a moral system if, in fact, moral truth is absolute. The dislike of argument will have resulted in both parties adopting, for fear of falling out, the false belief that both parties are right (relative to their own moral systems).[14]

This false belief, however, will now prevent these parties from discovering even the truth about moral relativism. It is, after all, by virtue of our acknowledging the differences between us and by virtue of our attempting, through argument, to find the source of this difference, that we discover the truth. If neither party to an apparent difference takes advantage of the opportunity offered by the discovery of this difference to correct, confirm or extend their own moral understanding by arguing with the other, then even if, by chance, one or other of them comes upon moral truth, this could not be said to be moral knowledge: it is moral luck.

I submit that it would be far better for us to learn how to engage in moral argument (and in the cooperative search for moral truth) without falling out, than to adopt a theory that might well be false simply for fear of falling out.

A confusion about belief

Another confusion that can lead (especially in the context of the confusions outlined above, to the adoption of moral relativism) is a logical blunder, a confusion between two very different claims: the claim that it is true, of someone, that he has a certain belief, and the claim that it is true, of a belief that is had by someone, that *it* is true.

So, for example, if you believe that there are three books on the table and there *are* three books on the table, then it is true, of you, that you believe that there are three books on the table, and it is also true, of the table, that it has three books on it. In such a case it is also true, of your belief, that it is true. If, on the other hand, you believe this yet there are only two books on the table, then it is still true, of you, that you believe that there are three books on the table, but it is false, of the table, that it has three books on it.

In such a case it is true, of your belief, that it is false.[15] The claim 'you believe that there are three books on the table' and the claim 'there are three books on the table' are true and false independently of each other.

The situation with moral beliefs is exactly the same as the situation with beliefs about books on the table. It might be true, of Fred, that he believes that mugging the elderly is morally acceptable, yet false, of mugging the elderly, that it is morally acceptable. In such a situation it is true of Fred's belief, that it is false. So it might be true, for example, to say 'For Fred, mugging the elderly is morally acceptable' (meaning that it is true to say, *of Fred*, that he believes mugging the elderly is morally acceptable), without its being true to say, of *mugging the elderly*, that it is morally acceptable.

But to the moral relativist the claim 'For Fred, mugging the elderly is morally acceptable' need not simply be a statement about Fred and his beliefs, it may also be a statement about mugging the elderly; for the moral relativist who believes that moral beliefs are true only in relation to the moral systems of individuals if Fred believes that mugging the elderly is morally acceptable and this belief is consistent with the rest of Fred's moral system, then mugging the elderly is morally acceptable – relative to Fred's moral system. Fred doesn't have a false belief, in other words, he simply has a different moral system: there is no *disagreement* between Fred and those whose moral systems portray mugging the elderly as wrong, only a *difference* similar to the difference between people for whom it is true and people for whom it is false that sardines are tasty.

To the absolutist, of course, mugging the elderly is wrong *simpliciter*: if Fred believes that it is acceptable then Fred has a false belief, and if this belief is consistent with the rest of Fred's moral system then Fred's moral system is abhorrent. The absolutist might not condemn Fred for having this belief or even for having this moral system – there are all sorts of reasons why someone might form this belief or embrace such a moral system and not all of them are the result of moral turpitude, but he will certainly condemn Fred's belief because, he will say, it is false, and if this belief is consistent with the rest of Fred's moral system then the absolutist will also condemn Fred's moral system.

The point is that if we want to embrace the view that mugging the elderly is morally permissible (relative, of course, to some moral system), then we ought to have an argument for it, we should not embrace this view simply on the basis of the fact that moral beliefs differ from person to person, simply on the basis of the fact that some people *believe* that mugging the elderly is morally permissible.

Relativism and (absolute) truth-in-a-situation

The final (bad) reason for embracing moral relativism consists in the belief that moral absolutism must be false because no moral belief can reasonably be believed to be true (or false) *simpliciter* in the way that the belief 'the universe started with a big bang' is true (or false) *simpliciter*; there will always be numerous situations in which, for example, the belief 'telling lies is wrong' is false. The need to add *ceteris paribus* clauses to everyday moral beliefs such as 'lying is wrong' before we get something that can reasonably be believed to be generally true, constitutes evidence, it is thought, for the fact that such beliefs are only true for a restricted range of situations. And this, it might be said, is the belief that moral truth is relative: relative, in this case, to a situation.

But the view that certain everyday moral precepts are true only in a restricted range of situations is not, and it does not entail, moral relativism, the view that there are no absolute moral truths. This is because it is wholly consistent with this view not only that these moral precepts are, in these situations, absolutely true, but also that what restricts the range of situations in which these everyday moral precepts are (absolutely) true is the absolute truth of certain more fundamental moral precepts.

So, for example, if in a particular situation the moral precept 'lying is wrong' is true, then that precept is true for everyone in that situation, the precept 'in this situation lying is wrong' is an absolute truth because anyone who lies in this situation fails to do his moral duty. Even if such a person believes that what he is doing is right, he has fallen into moral error, he holds a false belief about what is morally permissible. And similarly, if in a particular situation the moral precept 'lying is wrong' is false, then that precept is false for everyone in that situation; anyone who fails to lie in this situation fails to do his duty.[16]

And behind the fact that everyday moral precepts such as 'lying is wrong' are true only in a restricted range of situations is the fact that there are more fundamental moral principles, principles that trump the principle 'lying is wrong' because whenever conflict occurs it is this principle that gives way. A candidate in this case, for a more fundamental moral principle, is the principle 'preserve life'. But even the principle 'it is wrong to tell lies except when doing so will preserve life' is true only in a restricted range of situations: sometimes it would be wrong to tell a lie even to save a life (consider the situation in which you are threatened with death unless you recant your belief in liberty, equality or justice).

The beliefs that are candidates for the rock bottom principles that are true without restriction, the beliefs that restrict the range of situations in which other, less fundamental, moral precepts are (absolutely) true, are far more general than beliefs such as 'lying is wrong' or 'promises must be kept'; they are more general, even, than beliefs such as 'preserve life'. They are so general, indeed, that they are virtually no guide to action at all (in the absence of knowledge of many other things). One candidate for a fundamental moral principle, for example, is the utilitarian principle: 'actions are right in proportion as they tend to promote happiness, wrong as they tend to produce the reverse of happiness' (Mill 1972: 6). Another is that from which is derived the Kantian principle: 'Act only on that maxim through which you can at the same time will that it should become universal law' (Kant 1991: 84); yet another is that from which is derived the principle: 'Do as you would be done by.' And this brings me to my argument for absolutism.

An argument for absolutism

The five confusions identified above usually work together to produce moral relativism. Our observations of apparent diversity in moral belief and our true belief that we must respect the opinions of others, work together with the false belief that we respect the opinion of others only insofar as we refuse to believe that they are wrong, and with our confusions about the nature of belief and about the situation-relativity of beliefs, to produce the belief that argument about moral matters is itself wrong because it is a sufficient condition of a moral belief's being true that someone sincerely holds it.

But insofar as we believe, and (I would venture to suggest) as everyone of goodwill believes, that every person regardless of race, sex, age, sexuality, ethnic or religious background is intrinsically valuable, then we must *deny* the claim that it is a sufficient condition of a moral belief's being true that someone, or some society, sincerely holds it, because we must treat as false any moral belief that is inconsistent with the belief that every person is intrinsically valuable. It is, I shall argue, this fundamental belief that constrains the moral differences that can be treated simply as moral differences, rather than as differences that are evidence for moral error. It is also, I believe, this belief that is behind the belief that everyone's opinion ought to be respected.

There is, I believe, an internal inconsistency in the position of many of those who adopt moral relativism. Moral relativism cannot be derived from the belief that everyone is intrinsically valuable, therefore their opinions ought to be respected, so long as these beliefs are believed to be *absolute moral truths*. And many of those who find disagreement about moral matters distasteful, or even morally wrong, do so, apparently, because they believe that these beliefs are absolute moral truths: we should refuse to form the belief that another might be wrong, they appear to think, because *as everyone is intrinsically valuable*, we must at all times treat others with respect (and this involves refusing to form the belief that they are wrong).[17]

I submit that those who treat this belief – the belief that everyone is intrinsically valuable – as an absolute moral truth are right to do so: it *is* the case that everyone, every single human being, irrespective of race, sex, age, sexuality, ethnic or religious background, is intrinsically valuable.[18] And this is why we should accept moral absolutism. This absolute truth places an absolute constraint on which moral beliefs can be accepted as true and upon which systems can be counted as moral. No belief that is inconsistent with this belief can be true and no system that is inconsistent with this belief can be moral.

This allows for different moral systems, of course, because it allows for the fact that differences in circumstances can generate different ways of exhibiting the fact that we value people. But our accepting the (absolute) truth of beliefs that differ in this manner is wholly consistent with our condemning as morally wrong, as false *simpliciter*, the belief that (for example) writers should be put to death for expressing their opinions or the belief that mugging the elderly can be morally permissible. If we do want to insist that these beliefs might be true relative to some moral system then we need to reject, as an absolute truth, the belief that everyone is intrinsically valuable. To embrace this belief as an absolute moral truth is to be committed to denying the 'anything goes' of the moral relativism that is so widely accepted today: we cannot be moral relativists whilst believing that it is absolutely true that everyone is intrinsically valuable.

This argument for moral absolutism is not, of course, original. The belief that everyone is intrinsically valuable is little more than a different formulation of the belief that every rational animal is an end in himself, the absolute truth underpinning Kant's moral system. Kant, of course, was an arch-absolutist who believed that the fact that every rational animal is an end in himself generates a categorical imperative, a moral precept that binds each and every one of us at every time and in every place, namely: 'Act in such a way that you always treat humanity, whether in your own person, or in the person of another, never simply as a means, but always at the same time, as an end' (Kant 1991: 91). This, according to Kant, is the fundamental moral precept that generates all the others and that restricts the situations in which these other moral precepts are true.

If the belief that every person is intrinsically valuable is an absolute moral truth, then every single one of us (regardless of race, sex, age, sexuality, ethnic or religious background) is bound never to treat another (regardless of race, sex, age, sexuality, ethnic or religious background) simply as a means to his own ends, and any action that violates this fundamental moral precept is wrong. It is simply false, I submit, that anything goes, and it is also false that moral truth, at this fundamental level, is system-relative.

Whither moral education?

It is fashionable these days in discussing moral education to ask 'if we are to teach values, *whose* values are we to teach?' This question is often asked rhetorically as if to silence anyone who believes that values should be taught, and certainly it is used to label as naive anyone who thinks that there could be any values we all hold in common.

I believe that there *are* values that we hold in common irrespective of our race, sex, age, sexuality, ethnic or religious background,[19] and I believe that all these values can be traced back to the fundamental value of personhood, to the fact that every person, including oneself, is intrinsically valuable and must be treated as such. We may not – indeed do not – agree on the source of this fundamental value or the values derived from it, upon how they should be applied in behaviour or upon how they – the derived values – should be ordered, but this should not tempt us to conclude that we do not – or need not – agree on the fundamental value itself, and upon many if not most of those values we derive from it.

We have, for the past decade or so, in this country concentrated on recognising and celebrating the differences between us. There was, and is, very good reason for this and we should continue to recognise and celebrate these differences. But we ought not to do this at the expense of simultaneously recognising and celebrating the *sameness* that makes all these differences, in one very important sense, unimportant. It is, I believe, in virtue of our common humanity that each of us recognises – or ought to recognise – in others, something of intrinsic value, something whose feelings, desires and goals must constrain our pursuit of our own feelings, desires and goals. Young people, I submit, have both the right and the duty to understand this.

Notes

1 I am grateful to John Foster, Edward Harcourt and Don Rowe for discussion on these and other issues.

2 From now on I shall talk about moral *beliefs* without mentioning the statements that express them.

3 For an account of moral relativism by a moral relativist, see Harman and Jarvis-Thomson (1996).

4 The key difference between relativism and absolutism remains so long as the relativist insists that moral truth is relative to some system or other.

5 The word 'community' here is intended to signal recognition of the fact that some of those who embrace moral relativism recognise that the more radical forms of relativism are untenable, that the group whose beliefs can be said to form a moral system must be composed of more than an individual. There are many different shades of this form of relativism.

6 In its fashionable form – I shall leave out this qualification from now on.

7 Any more than two beliefs about time could be inconsistent if each was relative to a different time zone.

8 The absolutist could give all sorts of reasons for this. He might say, for example, that any system allowing the mugging of the elderly would be impermissible because it would be inconsistent with what Kekes calls the 'primary values required for a good life' (see Kekes in this volume), or he might say that no such system could produce the greatest happiness for the greatest number. He might also adopt the view I adopt at the end of this chapter.

9 Just what counts as a 'community' is another problem for this form of relativism. How, for example, are we to deal with the disaffected youngster who denies that he is a member of *our* community? Are we to allow that our moral truths are irrelevant to him?

10 I think that this distinction between the values – or fundamental moral beliefs – underlying our everyday moral beliefs and the everyday beliefs themselves, is one that goes unnoticed too often – see, for example, Alistair MacIntyre in this volume. Even as an absolutist I acknowledge the possibility that even were we

to hold constant *all* the facts we would still find moral disagreement. I do not, however, think, as the relativist does, that this *would* be the case. I reject utterly, however, the idea that the appearance of disagreement that we see around us suffices to show that there is fundamental moral disagreement, hence my talk of 'knee-jerk relativism'.

11 And not only, in fact, a *moral* doctrine. The belief that argument is wrong will lead to the adoption of a much more general relativism. I take as support for my view that these confusions are behind moral relativism the fact that today's knee-jerk relativism is a general relativism and not just a moral relativism.

12 That the first belief – the belief that faced with disagreement we should always consider the possibility that the other is right – is true can be seen from our response to those who do not do this. Such people will either arrogantly refuse even to listen to us if they disagree with us, or they will patronise us by pretending to agree. Our fear of being thought such a person causes us, I suspect, to over-compensate. The only appropriate response, however, to the fear of being thought such a person, is to make sure (a) that we express agreement, but (b) that we do so in an appropriate manner.

13 Two types of argument can be defused in this way: arguments about which type of issues are to count as moral issues (for example, is the permissibility of sex before marriage a moral issue or an issue of personal taste), or arguments about the permissibility of particular actions.

14 And we must not forget the other false beliefs that will be left in place: imagine agreeing, for fear of falling out, with someone who believes that gassing Jews is morally permissible.

15 Alternatively it might be true, *of the table*, that there are three books on it, but false, *of you*, that you believe that there are three books on it, either because you falsely believe that there are two books on it (in which case it is true, of your belief, that it is false), or because you have no beliefs about the table at all (in which case there is no truth about your belief).

16 So consider the person who, asked by the Nazis whether there are any Jews in the area, fails to say there are not (irrespective of whether or not there are). We might not condemn *him* for saying this (depending upon the situation) but we should not go so far as to say that what he *did* was not wrong.

17 Such an attempt is, in fact, the mirror image of the attempt (dubbed 'vulgar relativism' in Williams 1972: 22–6) to derive an absolute principle – we should never interfere with the views of others – from moral relativism. I am suggesting that just as we cannot derive an absolute truth from moral relativism, so we cannot derive moral relativism from an absolutist premise.

18 We might think that this is false on the grounds that we do not want to say that people like, say, Frederick West or Hitler, are of intrinsic value. Our belief that even these people are of intrinsic value would be manifested in our deeming them innocent until proven guilty and giving them a fair trial and, if proven guilty, punishing them in a way that is neither cruel or unusual, in the belief that even they, perhaps, are capable of redemption.

19 Although I think that it is often difficult to discover what these common values are, not least because some people believe it is unsophisticated to admit to embracing them.

References

Harman, G. and Jarvis-Thomson, J. (1996) *Moral Relativism and Moral Objectivity*, Oxford: Blackwell.

Kant, I. (1991) *The Moral Law*, tr. H. J. Paton, London: Routledge.
Mill, J. S. (1972) *Utilitarianism* (first published 1859), London: Dent.
Williams, B. (1972) *Morality: An Introduction to Ethics*, New York: Harper Row.

12

THE ARTS, MORALITY AND POSTMODERNISM

David Best

Section 1: The arts and morality

Preface

There are marked differences among the various art forms in many respects, and in particular with respect to the principal concern of this chapter, namely the relationship between the arts and morality. It is very surprising how the traditional, unquestioned assumption persists that the arts comprise a homogeneous set of disciplines or activities, or a generic unit. While there are similarities, there are also significant differences.[1] The traditional assumption that there is a single province or attitude of the aesthetic – or worse, the Aesthetic – which includes the arts and, for instance, appreciation of the beauties of nature, is even more fundamentally confused and educationally damaging, yet it remains largely unquestioned.[2]

Moral considerations arise most clearly in literature, theatre and film, but not so clearly in many works in the visual arts, music and dance. Nevertheless, in each of these last there are obvious and significant examples of works with deep moral themes, such as much of Francis Bacon, some of Goya, Picasso's *Guernica*; Gorecki's *Symphony of Sorrowful Songs*, and, perhaps less obviously, but profoundly, in much of the contemporary work of Arvo Pärt.

Introduction

A question of fundamental importance to philosophy of the arts, and especially to the arts in education, is that of the relationship of the arts to society. One's understanding of a work, and with it one's emotional response, in relevant cases, may be inseparable from the aspects of life which are its subject matter, or to which implicit reference is made. Frequently this central characteristic of the arts involves moral evaluation. For example, the works of

Ibsen, D. H. Lawrence and James Joyce have been censored and banned because of their allegedly harmful moral attitudes, and certain plays of Shakespeare have either not been performed, or have been sanitised, because of their ribald or other supposedly immoral character. For example, *King Lear* was considerably altered by Tate, to give it a more morally acceptable happy ending, and this version held the stage for a century and a half. For F. R. Leavis moral seriousness was a principal criterion of literary merit. The same criterion provoked the remark that Barbara Cartland's novels actually impede an understanding of the human condition. The implicit criticism here is that such sentimental, escapist novels lack integrity: the moral is inseparable from the artistic criticism.

Educationally, this characteristic clearly involves considerable responsibility. For while enriching art and approaches to art, taught well, can have a significant constructive influence, so some kinds of art and approaches to art can be commensurately potentially harmful. The moral implications for the teacher are inescapable. Some subjectivists would like to believe that they can opt out of this responsibility, indeed some seem to regard it as a moral obligation to do so. Yet to do *nothing* is morally reprehensible if this should amount to failing to provide fresh and enriching understanding and feeling which students could otherwise have achieved: to that extent they have been deprived. No teacher can avoid the crucial moral responsibility of deciding what to teach and how to teach it. In relation to the arts, such decisions frequently involve considerations of subject matter inseparable from significant moral questions. (Of course, other subjects, such as history, also inevitably involve such moral implications.)

Clearly this makes great demands on the teacher's objectivity, for he or she must be constantly alert to avoid imposing prejudices, and instead should stimulate the progressive development of the student's own attitudes, conceptions and feelings.

Polarisation

So far I have begged an important question, since some strongly deny that the arts can express moral issues. This raises the central question of this chapter, which will be elucidated by examining a polarisation of views.

Those at one pole emphasise the potential influence of the arts on understanding of and attitudes to life generally: they conclude that the meaning and value of the arts consist in the purposes they serve, including especially their moral purposes. For instance, throughout history the arts have expressed or raised powerful and incisive moral, social and political questions. It is a recognition of this highly significant characteristic which provokes totalitarian régimes to censor, imprison, torture and execute artists: such regimes fear the potentially powerful moral influence of the arts. Indeed, so prevalent and disturbing are brutal attempts to suppress artistic freedom that recently there has been formed the Association Internationale de Défense des Artistes (AIDA), based in the Netherlands.

There is a striking paradox: at least in most Western countries, it is assumed that nothing significant can be learned from the arts, and thus they are marginalised in the curriculum: yet it is precisely the powerful possibilities of learning from the arts which makes them so threatening to authoritarian regimes.

By contrast with this purposive view, those at the opposite pole correctly point out that to insist that the value and meaning of the arts consist in the purposes they serve is to deny any *intrinsic* value to the arts. For in that case the arts are reduced to mere means to ends. For example, the moral purposes or ends attributed to the arts could be achieved by other, non-artistic, means, such as sermons, political speeches or journalism, and thus, on the purposive thesis, the arts as such would have no intrinsic value. Consequently many reject the notion of moral meaning and value in the arts, and insist that they are autonomous, having no reference to extrinsic values such as those involved in the life of society. Autonomists insist that artistic meanings and values are exclusively internal to the traditions, conventions or practices of the arts themselves.

There is almost inevitably a confused sliding between these two poles, even by the advocates of these opposing conceptions of art, since there is important truth in each.

The conflict is generated by an underlying misconception shared by both groups. This is a familiar situation in philosophy: the rejection of the theory is still a theory on the same level, whereas the conflict arises from an unrecognised, fallacious presupposition that infects both thesis and antithesis.

Purposive or autonomous

Let us examine the opposing conceptions more carefully. Tolstoy (1930: 120) expresses a view that is still very common, namely that the arts are trivialised unless it is recognised that the value of art lies in 'the purpose it may serve in the life of man'. For Tolstoy the value of art resides in its moral purpose; thus, a good work of art is one that expresses morally good feelings from which morally good lessons can be learned. Currently, a similar conception is expressed in the concern that postmodernism has brought about a decline in moral purpose in the arts.

By contrast, the autonomist contends that it is the purposive account that trivialises the arts by reducing them to mere message-carriers since, as was mentioned above, the purpose could be achieved in other ways. Hence the autonomist rejects the purposive view in order to emphasise the intrinsic value of the arts. This conception of the arts as exclusively self-contained, having no relation to life in general, appears to be endorsed by Hampshire:

> The canons of success and failure are in this sense internal to the work itself ... In so far as the perfection of a work is assessed by some external criterion, it is not being assessed as a work of art, but rather as a technical achievement in the solution of some problem ... Nothing but holding an object still in attention, by itself and for its own sake, would count as having an aesthetic interest in it.
>
> (Hampshire 1954: 162)

The autonomist view amounts to a denial that the arts can involve moral issues. Thus, Peter Brooke, the theatre director, once said: 'Culture has never done anyone any good whatsoever', and 'No work of art has ever made a better man.' Similarly, Hirst (1980: 6) says that 'the role of the arts in education is to aestheticise people'. This is a view which he still holds (see his paper, 1989: 38–43, and also the incisive reply by McFee 1989: 33–7). Quite apart from the current issue, this notion that the purpose of the arts is 'to aestheticise people' is not only extremely unclear, but, so far as one can understand it, seems to display a remarkable lack of understanding of the character of the arts, and trivialises their educational potential. Similarly, 'a distinguished educational pundit' is quoted (*Observer*, 24 January 1982) as saying sharply: 'The arts are marvellous, but moral they are not.'

In his essay 'The decay of lying', Oscar Wilde writes: 'to art's subject matter we should be more or less indifferent' (Wilde 1966: 976); and in 'The critic as artist' he writes: 'the sphere of Art and the sphere of Ethics are absolutely distinct and separate' (*ibid.*: 1048). In the preface to *The Picture of Dorian Gray*, he states that 'no artist has ethical sympathies', from which he concludes that, since it cannot be said legitimately to have any purpose, 'all art is quite useless' (*ibid.*: 17).

This conception is common, and it is shared by some good philosophers. For example, it underlies Ruth Saw's (1962: 239) drawing a distinction, in literature, between reading something 'for its own sake' and reading it 'for the sake of its meaning'. Clearly, this is a confusion, for what sense can it make to speak of *reading* something *not* for its *meaning*, but 'for its own sake'? It is an incoherent distinction, for to read something necessarily implies that what is read has meaning. Although I can look at, I cannot *read* ancient Egyptian hieroglyphics, although some Egyptologists can. Ruth Saw seems to be led into this incoherence precisely because of the misconception we are now considering, for she wants to insist that literary art has intrinsic value, which, she assumes, implies rejecting the notion of *meaning*, since that could not be exclusively intrinsic.

What underlies and creates this intractable problem is the assumption of an inadequate and misleading conception of meaning. As R. W. Beardsmore puts it, 'a work of art is not a means by which some independently identifiable message is communicated, it is not a sign or even a collection of signs which indicate some independently identifiable state of affairs' (Beardsmore 1971: 37).

However, if the autonomist thesis should imply a denial that *any* external factor can be relevant to the meaning and evaluation of the work of art itself, it can easily be refuted. For example, it would make no sense to suggest that a knowledge of French is irrelevant to critical appreciation of Verlaine's poetry, since without some grasp of the language one could not understand it even in the most obvious sense. Moreover, some comprehension of the socio-historical context is required in order to understand and evaluate works of art. For example, Chaucer's work cannot be understood without some comprehension of the social and religious life of his time. The meanings of some of the terms used by Shakespeare have changed because of social changes, and one may have to learn their meaning, given by that different context, before one can fully understand his plays. Clearly, it makes no sense to regard literary works as isolated from the rest of life. This point about language is of far greater significance than is often realised (and this misconception underlies the confusion of both the autonomist and the purposive theses), since to understand a language necessarily involves an implicit understanding of a social context. To put it briefly, to understand a poem is to understand a language, which is to understand a culture, a social context.

Moreover, a work cannot be understood in isolation from its artistic context. For example, it would be difficult to make sense of the notion that Stravinsky's music might have been written in the twelfth century. A discord, characteristic of Bartók, would be either very puzzling, or perhaps of immense significance, in Haydn.

Artistic innovation can be understood as such only in its context. Some of Turner's later painting may be seen as a precursor of modern abstract expressionism. And the remarkable progressions in some of Guesaldo's madrigals are in a form often used by much more modern composers. But the strikingly innovative character of these works can be identified as such only against the background of the contemporary artistic context.

Artistic meaning depends upon relations with social and artistic context to such an extent that it becomes unintelligible to regard such contexts as 'external': thus the autonomist thesis cannot even be coherently stated. It is as incoherent as suggesting that the meaning of a sentence could be considered in isolation from the rest of language and social context.

Source of confusion

What generates the confused conflict is the shared presupposition that either art serves some purpose, or its value is exclusively intrinsic, and therefore purposeless. Yet, on the one hand, it is obviously mistaken to assert that the arts have no meaning or value other than serving an external purpose; and, on the other hand, it is obviously mistaken to assert that artistic meaning is exclusively intrinsic, and therefore isolated from moral, social and other issues.

There is an important sense in which the arts are non-purposive, but this characteristic is commonly misunderstood, for it certainly does not imply that therefore there is no point or value in art. To say that an activity has no purpose does not necessarily imply that it is purposeless, in the generally assumed sense that led Oscar Wilde to declare that all art is quite useless. Indeed, the generally unquestioned presupposition I am criticising is clearly implied by the assumption that 'purposeless' is equivalent to 'valueless'. For it is taken to be axiomatic that if an activity or object should have no purpose, then it has no value. It is precisely that mistaken assumption that creates the confusion and conflict we are considering.

To put the point another way, the source of confusion is the use of the language of purpose in this context. Yet it is difficult to avoid this use, because it is commonly assumed that, in general, any activity or object can intelligibly be said to have value or meaning only in relation to its independently identifiable purpose. In cases where there is a purpose, value does depend on it. For example, a painting considered solely as an investment would be evaluated according to its degree of success in achieving maximum capital appreciation. Where the attainment of the purpose is the overriding consideration, the means of attaining it is relatively unimportant. For instance, the artistic quality of the painting would not matter so long as the purpose, of capital appreciation, were achieved. Similarly, if someone should wish to improve his car's petrol consumption by changing the carburettor, the design of the new one would be unimportant as long as it achieved the purpose of giving maximum mileage per litre.

This reveals the unintelligibility of supposing that an account of artistic meaning can be given in purposive terms, that the value or meaning of every object or activity *must* be identifiable as a purpose distinct from that object or activity, which is the means by which the purpose is to be achieved. Yet where artistic meaning or value is concerned, the distinction between purpose or end – and means of achieving it – is inapplicable. For instance, the question 'What is the purpose of George Eliot's *Middlemarch?*' could be answered comprehensively only in terms of the novel itself. It may be objected that this is not entirely true, since the purpose of some novels can be identified independently. For instance, the objection may run, the purpose of many novels, films, plays, etc. could be identified as exposing certain deleterious social conditions, as in the case of much of Dickens. But this objection misses the point I made earlier, for if the purpose is the external one of exposing those social conditions, then in principle it could equally well, or perhaps better, be achieved by other means, such as the publication of a social survey or a political speech. The report of the social survey is evaluated by reference to its efficiency in achieving its purpose of effectively conveying the information, whereas this would be totally inappropriate as a criterion for evaluating a novel. To put the point another way, the precise form and style of writing of the report is unimportant except insofar as it affects the purpose: of efficiently conveying the information. One report could be as good as another, even though the style of writing were inferior. It would make no sense to suppose that there could be a parallel situation in the arts, where, for example, one poem might be said to be as good as another although not so well written. This is an aspect of the problem of form and content. Briefly, in the arts there is a logical connection between the particular form of expression and its content, i.e. what is expressed in that form; at least to a very large extent, a change of form of expression necessarily involves a change in what is expressed.

It is important to recognise that this is a logical point. Even if one style of writing the report should be the clearest and most efficient, this is a contingent matter, since it is always possible in principle that a better way could be devised. But it would make no sense to suggest that the content or meaning of Dickens's *Hard Times* could be more effectively expressed in another style of writing.

Thus, in this case, the question becomes: 'What is the purpose of this particular way of exposing these social conditions?' The purpose cannot be identified as 'exposing such and such social conditions', but only as 'exposing such and such social conditions *uniquely in this way*.' And to give a comprehensive account of what is meant by this purpose would require nothing less than reproducing the whole novel. The end, or purpose, can be identified only in terms of the means, or manner of achieving it; which is another way of saying that the presupposition encapsulated in the question – that artistic meaning or value is to be identified by the purpose served by the work of art – is unintelligible. In short, the only way to answer the question 'What is the purpose of this work of art?', is to reject the question as confused. It involves tendentious misconception even to discuss questions of artistic meaning and value in the language of purpose: it is rather like asking what is the weight in kilograms of heavy sarcasm or light entertainment. Or, to cite another common and insidious confusion of our age, it is like talking of the measurement (as opposed to assessment) of educational progress.

It may be objected that since I argue that a work of art can be considered only in terms of itself, and that there is no independent standard or purpose by which it can be evaluated, how can it be criticised; what is the character of critical appreciation? There is a great deal to be said about the common misapprehension that to engage in critical reasoning is to generalise (see Bambrough 1973: 42–3). I have considered this question more fully elsewhere (see Best 1993a: *passim* and esp. ch. 3). We shall touch on the issue again later, but at this point it is sufficient for my argument to recognise that critical appreciation consists largely in giving reasons why particular features contribute so effectively to or detract from *this particular* work of art. There is no end or purpose that is independent of the means of achieving it: any suggested improvement is offered in terms of that particular work of art.[3] I consider the question of particularity elsewhere (see Best 1983, 1993a: ch. 11).

Although criticism refers only to the particularity of a work, that does not necessarily imply that every detail is a defining feature of it. To say that any feature is irrelevant is *ipso facto* a criticism of a work of art: but a feature may be relevant without being irreplaceable. In this sense, necessarily there will be contingent aspects.

The notion of irrelevance, failing or criticism is *internal* to the work, so that to criticise an aspect as irrelevant (and therefore an artistic failing) is implicitly to conceive of and compare it with an ideal model of *this* work: it is to contend that the work would be more effective if this aspect were omitted.

For example, Collingwood (1938: 123) contends that Beethoven, despite his undoubted genius, tends to 'rant', and his (at least, inchoate) recognition of this tendency induced him to write many string quartets where, by the nature of the instruments, he was unable to succumb to that indulgence. For instance, the criticism might be that some of his symphonies would be improved if the ending were omitted or reduced, since the music would be intensified by the consequent compression. That is, it might be argued that Beethoven sometimes fails to recognise that the most effective thing to do at the end is to stop. This criticism amounts to contending that, for example, the Fifth Symphony would be more effective if written in this way: the criticism is internal to that piece of music.

Similarly, Collingwood also criticises as 'rant' Hardy's writing, at the end of *Tess of the d'Urbervilles*: 'Justice was done, and the President of the Immortals, in the Aeschylean phrase, had ended his sport with Tess.' When Wittgenstein says that the bass moves too much, it is only in terms of that particular piece of music that the remark makes sense (Moore 1955).

Another way of expressing my main point here is to say that every feature of a work of art is relevant to the artistic evaluation of it, whereas when we are evaluating something in terms of a means to achieve an end or a purpose, there are irrelevant features of the means, or equally effective alternative means, of achieving that purpose. To say that x is an irrelevant feature is always a criticism of a work of art, whereas this is not true of a functional object. For example, a hammer has the purpose of driving in nails, and it is no criticism to say that the material from which the handle is made is irrelevant, as long as the hammer achieves its purpose with maximum efficiency. By contrast, to say that a scene in a Shakespeare play is irrelevant does indeed constitute a criticism of the play.

In this section, then, I have tried to show that the widely prevalent presupposition that an activity or object can be evaluated only in terms of a purpose is the source of considerable confusion. To put the point misleadingly, there is a distinction between a purpose that is identifiable independently of the means of achieving it, and a 'purpose' that is logically inseparable. And the latter cannot intelligibly be regarded as a purpose at all.

With respect to artistic value and meaning, the language of purpose is seriously misleading, and the imposition of it involves damaging and incoherent consequences. For either it leads to the conclusion that a work of art must be a mere substitutable means to achieve an independently identifiable purpose (often a moral purpose), which implies that the arts have no value in themselves; or it leads to the incoherent claim that art has *only* intrinsic value, is thus completely separate from the life of society, and is therefore 'useless'. Both theses caricature and trivialise the character of the arts, and overlook the immense contribution they have made to many societies, over centuries: both theses fail to recognise the immense educational potential of the arts. Yet there is an important truth in each thesis.

This is a classic example of the way philosophical conflict often arises. Each proponent is so impressed by an important insight into an area of enquiry that he over-emphasises it to the point of denying the equally important insight of the other, and thereby incurs an obvious mistake.

Meaning in the arts

Artistic meaning cannot, then, be characterised in terms of purpose, and it makes no sense to suppose that therefore art is exclusively self-contained. I have, I hope, established that (for example) there is moral meaning in, while not being the purpose of, many works of art: what a work of art expresses about morality cannot be distinguished from the way in which it is expressed. There is a great deal to be said about this crucial characteristic, which has immense significance for what can be learned from the arts. In the space available I can offer only an outline: I have written elsewhere in greater detail on the issue.

The arts can significantly *contribute* to moral understanding by revealing what certain situations *amount to*: they can bring *home* to us the force of, for example, moral dilemmas. It is often believed that moral learning is exclusively concerned with the acquisition and application of general principles. But this assumption is grossly over-simple. Sometimes the very insistence on adhering rigidly to moral principles is itself a moral failing.

For example, in Ibsen's *Ghosts*, Pastor Manders is a sincere man, deeply entrenched in conventional contemporary attitudes and strict religious and moral principles that circumscribe his thinking and feeling. He is suddenly confronted with a tragic situation whose complexity is beyond his comprehension, because it is not even intelligible in the language of the over-simple doctrinaire attitudes that largely constitute what he thinks he is. Many years previously Mrs Alving had left her husband to go to live with Pastor Manders. He had sent her back, proclaiming, righteously, that it would have been a sin for her to stay with him. Her riposte now is that it had been a sin for her *not* to stay.

The use of the word 'sin' in this apparently contradictory way was a shocking flash of insight into moral considerations that were beyond, but (and this is crucial) not *totally* beyond, his understanding. To put the matter with full paradoxical force, Pastor Manders was in effect being told that, in these circumstances, it was a sin *not* to live in sin. He was being confronted with the cataclysmic possibility that living strictly to moral principles, no matter what the circumstances, may be morally reprehensible.

Such a possibility was deeply disturbing, not only to Pastor Manders, but to contemporary society. For it threatened the security of living by adherence to simple, rigid moral principles, and revealed that moral understanding is more complex and subtle. This use of language was an alarming way to expand his horizons of moral understanding, but he was unable or unwilling to follow through the shaft of insight which penetrated that rigid wall of inflexible security. Because of this, and other challenges to unquestioned moral attitudes, the play so outraged contemporary society that Ibsen could not have it performed in Norway for nine years, and booksellers even returned their stocks of the text.

A work of art can give us a clearer comprehension of a moral situation, so that we can see it in a new light. What has been learned cannot adequately be stated in propositions. After the ghost of Hamlet's father has revealed the truth of his treacherous murder, Hamlet cries: 'My tables, – meet it is I set it down, That one may smile and smile and be a villain.' Hamlet has learned a powerful lesson. But what has he learned? If, in order to answer that question, we were to consider only what he has *written*, then we might well echo Horatio: 'There needs no ghost, my lord, come from the grave to tell us this.' For of course we all know, and Hamlet knew very well *before* this deeply moving incident, that villains can smile deceptively. Yet the full force of what it *amounts to* may be brought home to us by a particular incident.

Paradoxically, Hamlet felt impelled to write down what he had learned because he did not want to forget the full vividly illuminating force of it: he did not want it to retreat again into the bland generality of what he knew before. More prosaically, the force of the point may strike us as a consequence of being cheated by a plausibly charming car salesman.

This is the kind of moral learning characteristic of the arts. It consists not so much of what can be stated – although partly that – as in a change of understanding and attitude. It should be emphasised, in view of some current, regrettably regressive trends in education, that this crucial characteristic of learning applies not only to the arts but to learning generally. The development of constructive, creative attitudes to learning, the increase of understanding, is unlikely to be achieved, and indeed is more likely to be stifled, by the tick-box, measurement approaches that now infect education. In this, as in many other ways, education generally has much to learn from the arts.

Dickens's novel *Nicholas Nickleby* was a powerful indictment of the appalling conditions, the cruelty and indifference, which typified many of the boarding schools of the early nineteenth century. Several boys, for instance, went blind from gross neglect. Dickens visited some of these schools in Yorkshire. His novel brought home to people what it was like to be compelled to live in such schools. It is clear evidence of the power of the kind of learning involved in the arts that on the publication of the novel conditions improved rapidly: it has been said that the influence of *Nicholas Nickleby* 'passed like a whirlwind over the schools of the North'. This was achieved not, or not primarily, by giving information, but by offering incisive insights into, understanding of, situations that were morally insupportable.

James Joyce's exquisitely sensitive short story 'The Dead' brings out with poignant sadness aspects of the many-faceted character of love, loss, the awefull chill of what might have been. It clearly reveals the character of the arts to which I am trying to draw attention that the description I have just given is so inadequate. One needs to read the story.

Similarly, we are all aware of the tragic consequences of irreconcilable differences among those earnestly involved in an idealistic movement, and of the cynical manipulation of those differences. But a work of art, such as Ken Loach's film *Land and Freedom*, can bring out these issues in poignant personal terms, which could not be adequately stated.

There are numerous such examples. Richard Hamilton's painting *Just What Is It Which Makes Today's Homes So Different, So Appealing?*, Mike Leigh's play *Abigail's Party*, Samuel Beckett's *Happy Days*, bring out the stultifying effect on human possibilities of thought and feeling brought about by the conditioning cliché-banalities purveyed by television, advertising and the popular press. (We shall return to the issue of how such media form and limit human potential.) Again, none can be adequately characterised in statements, and, although I have crudely described them in similar terms, it would make no sense to say that they are substitutable.

Similarly, the perceptive French film *Un Coeur en Hiver* reveals something of the perplexing heterogeneity of emotional relationships; the Canadian film *A Company of Strangers*, brings out, *inter alia*, the truth of the saying that there is at least one novel in each of us. The pace of this film is so remarkably slow that it took some of us time to adjust to it, because the films with which we are familiar are so much faster paced. Many students in the audience when I saw this film became quickly impatient, chatted, fidgeted, and even left. Yet *what* the film was expressing could not, logically, have been expressed otherwise. Mike Leigh's current (as I write) film *Secrets and Lies* explores in personal terms some of the many-hued complexities of family relationships. The Icelandic film *Children of Nature* subtly, but with refreshing frankness, humour and avoidance of any shred of sentimentality, expresses the feelings and problems of old age, the craving for identity rooted in early environment. Samuel Beckett's television films *Quad* and *Quad 2* present a stark vision of life, which could not remotely be captured in another form, and certainly what is expressed could not be verbally stated.

Each of these works of art has a moral meaning that could not be expressed in any other way: each offers a perspective, a fresh understanding: each reveals something of the immensely complex, subtly varied character of morality.

Section 2: Postmodernism

Perhaps the greatest difficulty in discussing postmodernism is the impossibility of discerning any clear account of what it is. As Carr (1995: 123) puts it, there are numerous postmodernisms: 'each theorising the meaning of postmodernity in a different way'. To compound the difficulty, much of the literature on postmodernism is characterised by arcane obscurantism, a porridge of abstract verbosity. Indeed, I confess to scepticism even about the term 'postmodernism'. What comes next? I have already read of 'post-post-structuralism' (Pride 1993). One can envisage post^{21}-modernism, or even post^n-modernism. Moreover, it has become fashionable, trendy, so that some people, perhaps especially in the arts, but also in academic life, use it as a label behind which they can attempt to justify vapid, pretentious work by accusing those who can see no value in it as 'behind the times'. One is also suspicious of the claims that the 'texts' (as they call them) are difficult or even impenetrable because English-speaking readers are unused to their 'heightened intellectualism and theoretical denseness' (Usher and Edwards 1994: 18). One suspects that this is just an excuse for a failure of clarity and that, as so often, a mystique is created by high-sounding obscurity. (One is reminded of the pomposity-puncturing American phrase 'doing a snow-job'.) This is a great pity since some versions of postmodernism are very critical, as I am, of the obscurantism that has bedevilled for centuries philosophy of the arts, and the arts in education. For example, one arts-education theorist[4] asserts that artistic experience is 'very mysterious', 'drug-like', requiring introspective delving into 'tranced consciousness', and thus becoming 'tribally grounded in some universal', which is 'a form of transcendence'. He even concludes that all artistic experience is religious! Small wonder that, some years ago, one philosopher referred to the whole field of aesthetics as the natural home of rapturous and soporific effusion.

It is a pity that some versions of postmodernism, while justifiably rejecting the unintelligible vocabulary of such traditional attempts to 'support' the arts in terms, for example, of supernatural, metaphysical universals, themselves adopt an inscrutably esoteric vocabulary in opposition to it. The peddling of such gnomic utterances becomes a badge of acceptance in both cults, but one strongly suspects that even (perhaps especially) the members of each cult are unsure what they mean.

It was necessary to introduce the preceding cautionary note because I do not pretend that my conception of postmodernism is accurate. Postmodernism, by its very nature, is hostile to any clear account of itself: it critically questions and subverts the very possibility of systematic theory. 'Perhaps it is best understood as a state of mind, a critical, self-referential posture and style, a different way of seeing and working, rather than a fixed body of ideas, a clearly worked-out position' (Usher and Edwards 1994: 2). My conception consists in what I understand, from reading and discussion, to be a broad consensus of the principal aspects of postmodernism. I should add that, because of restrictions of space, I can offer only a brief survey of a topic, or congeries of topics, which would repay more detailed consideration.

The postmodernist rejection of the Kantian notion of philosophical foundations, universal principals, which are independent of socio-historical, cultural context, seems to me entirely justified. I have already quoted one arts-education theorist who remains wedded to this Kantian view. Another is Witkin, who stated explicitly that in order to achieve the requisite, 'direct', 'pure', untrammelled feeling for art it is necessary to erase all memories. This supposition of a 'natural', aboriginal, universal, culture-free artistic experience is unintelligible, as I have argued elsewhere.[5]

Postmodernism emphasises that cultural practices and media, such as especially language and the arts, are the crucial determining factors of human thought and experience. While this seems to me correct, it is certainly not new: many of us have been arguing this way for many years.

The self

The preceding conclusion implies the existence of what postmodernists call the 'fragmented' or 'decentred' self. This is a rejection of the unintelligible notion of an essence of self, or personal identity. In Samuel Beckett's play *Not I*, the character, of whom it is significant of the whole point of the piece that only her mouth is visible, pours out a jumbled stream of incidents that have occurred to her during her life. She appears to be engaged in a desperate but vain search for her essential self. Yet each of the incidents she recounts seems to be only *contingently* related to what she is, since it might not have happened to her, or it might have happened differently. This seems to leave her with nothing that is essential, and therefore with the despairing feeling that she has no real identity. Hence the title, for she finds it confusing and terrifying to refer to herself, since there is nothing to which to refer. Francis Bacon is, I think, making a similar point in his painting *An Accidental Being*.

It is true that if none of the incidents or attributes which is or could be mentioned by Beckett's character applied to her, one could give no sense to the notion of her identity. If all these were removed there would be nothing left. As Wittgenstein (1958: para. 164) put it: 'In order to discover the real artichoke, we divested it of its leaves.' Yet clearly identity can be ascribed to a person on the basis of her actions, attributes, and what has happened to her. That there is no real artichoke when we have divested it of its leaves does not imply that there is no real artichoke: that there is no essence of the self does not imply that there is no self. What is required is a different conception of the self.

Moreover, because each aspect could have been different, it does not follow that every aspect could have been different. Also, not every aspect of a person's personality and life is of equal importance for determining the character of his identity. Of some aspects, one might be justified in saying that they are merely contingent, whereas of others it would be difficult to make sense of the supposition that he could be the same person without them. There will necessarily be considerable imprecision here.

A central criterion for personal identity, for the character of the self, as postmodernists emphasise, is the culture, the language and other social practices of one's environment. To put it succinctly, it would make no sense to suppose that I could be the same I if I had been born and brought up in tenth-century Mongolia.

Language and thought

This question is central for a consideration of morality, for moral values are implicit in culture and social practices, in which language is central. Consider the common notion of a conscious self, which is independent of culture, and which invented language. This dualist or subjectivist theory, still widely prevalent among psychologists, educational and linguistic theorists, and others, is clearly exemplified by the well-known art-educator Elliott Eisner, who writes:

> Humans not only have the capacity to form different kinds of concepts, they also *because of their social nature*, have the need to *externalize* and *share* what has been conceptualized. To achieve such an end, human beings have *invented . . . forms of representation* [which] are the means by which *privately held conceptions* are transferred into *public images* so that the meaning they embody can be shared.
>
> (Eisner 1981: 17–23) (my italics)

Eisner illustrates his theory by reference to language, which, he says, human beings invented in order to externalise and share private feelings and thoughts. This is a clear example of the self described by Descartes: a self whose foundation is consciousness. In his excellent book, Fergus Kerr (1986) aptly refers to this common conception as that of the 'mentalist-individualist'. But it is beset with fatal problems. This is, of course, a complex philosophical question, which I can only sketch here. I have discussed it more fully elsewhere (Best 1993a: 108–15). But although this conception of the self and language remains plausible, it is senseless. For example, if all the mental experiences of A were completely private, how could she communicate them to B? It is no good saying that she could invent words, since in this isolated, solipsistic world B could never know what the words meant. Worse, he could not even know that they were words, since the notion of a word makes sense only *within* an already existing language. Thus, at most, it could be only a meaningless noise. It must be remembered, too, that this problem is not limited to verbal language, for in this isolated world of the mentalist-individualist no one could understand anything that anyone else thought or felt.

The supposition that human beings could have invented language makes no sense. Moreover, it is questionable whether creatures without language or any other form of communication could even count as human beings, since in an important sense the attributes that distinguish human beings from animals would be absent. Across an immensely wide and varied range, the very possibility of feelings and thoughts is given by language.

To put succinctly a point that requires more explication, normally the use of language is *not*, as is generally assumed, a mere symbolic expression of thinking going on previously or concurrently in the mind (about which, as we have seen, nothing could be known anyway); on the contrary, normally the use of language *is* the thinking.

The ability to think without expressing one's thoughts is a secondary acquisition, as becomes clear when we recognise that in such cases the thoughts are formulated in, and identified by, language and other cultural media (such as, centrally, the arts).

Rush Rhees says: 'What do we learn when we learn language? A list of verbal expressions would be no answer' (Rhees 1969: 135). To learn a language is to learn to participate in a whole way of life, and with it to acquire an immense and varied range of feelings and thoughts. And language is the most influential of a whole interconnected complex of cultural practices that define personality, identity, the self.

On the mentalist-individualist, subjectivist conception, espoused for instance by Eisner, even if it were to make sense (which, as we have seen, it does not), the relevant thoughts, concepts, feelings are already *there* 'in the mind' (since birth? before birth?), and language and the arts provide merely the means to express them. This, of course, would carry the extremely implausible implication that the unborn child is already remarkably gifted intellectually. The thesis for which I am arguing not only makes sense, unlike this subjectivist conception, but has significant educational implications: for linguistic and artistic media are not mere message-carriers of pre-existing subjective concepts and feelings; understanding the arts provides not merely the means of expressing mental experiences; on the contrary, far more strongly, the acquisition of artistic and linguistic practices uniquely gives the *experiences themselves*. So that, for instance, educating artistic understanding *is* educating artistic feeling. Moreover, as I argued earlier, moral values are intrinsic to certain works of art, so that a work of art may cast a fresh light on moral issues: it may bring greater understanding of aspects of life generally.

Kerr says: 'The locus of meanings is not the epistemological solitude of individual consciousness but the practical exchanges that constitute the public world which we inhabit together' (Kerr 1986: 58). Yet it is difficult to free ourselves from the alienating power of this deeply pervasive metaphysical conception of the self. Despite the powerful arguments that show, in my view indisputably, the unintelligibility of the presupposition that individual consciousness is the foundation of the self, it is difficult to grasp the full implication of the notion that the self is, at least to a very large extent, a cultural construct.

According to the traditional mentalist-individualist, subjectivist conception of the conscious self, exemplified by Eisner, human beings, incarcerated in their isolated logical privacy, created language, the arts, and other cultural practices in order to express and communicate previously existing feelings and concepts. What I am arguing, by contrast, is that *language and cultural practices create human beings*. That is, the thoughts and feelings characteristic of human beings are *created*, at least to a very large extent, by language and cultural practices.

We need to eradicate the deeply embedded but incoherent notion of mentalist-individualist consciousness: we need to free ourselves to accept 'the *conversation* which *we* are' (Kerr 1986: 115 and *passim*).

Unfortunately, I have insufficient space in which to explore adequately the considerable and significant implications of this conception: I can offer only some lines of thought. But I hope that it is clear that postmodernism agrees with my emphasis on the powerfully defining influence of culture, linguistic, artistic and other social practices and media.

Power of the media

In my view, the most important insight of postmodernism is the way it extends the conclusions of the previous section into an emphasis on the influence of what are called these days 'the media', by which I mean especially television, film, radio, popular newspapers, modern communications and information technology, and their language and attitudes. Postmodernists are, I think, right to draw attention to this new aspect of our current way of life, although I do not altogether agree with the consequences sketched out by some postmodernists. I do not agree, for instance, that we are helpless against these admittedly very powerful tides. However, I may be unduly optimistic. At least postmodernism has the great merit of making us aware of the trend: and to be aware is a necessary condition for resistance or change of direction. This is part of postmodernism's commendable inclusion of *itself* as a target for criticism, or deconstruction.

A casualty of such criticism is the notion of 'objective', value-neutral truth. There is much to be said in favour of postmodernist deconstruction of commonly held notions of absolute truth, and of, by contrast, the emphasis on underlying interpretation or conceptualisation. I shall return to this crucial issue. However, although I have considerable sympathy with postmodernism in this respect, some postmodernists, it seems to me, go too far in rejecting altogether the notion of truth, insisting that interpretation is all. This, and the supposed helplessness to which I referred above, raise what may be the most crucial questions for morality and education, namely: does the rejection of moral absolutes imply that we have to accept nihilism? Are there no values, or are all values merely a matter of personal idiosyncrasy?

To illustrate, consider the film *Schindler's List*.[6] According to postmodernism, popular culture in the form of the media is taking over the memories and official historical versions of the Holocaust (as of other historical events). In comparing their memories with what was portrayed in the film, the actual survivors found it seriously misleading. Yet the film version will probably become generally accepted as the definitive version. In a media-saturated age, people all over the world can, and probably do, have the same dominant conception of the Holocaust: in postmodernist jargon the film will become the 'master narrative', just as, to a large extent, films such as *Apocalypse Now* and *The Deer Hunter* have probably become for many people the accepted versions of the Vietnam War.

Historians tend to cling to the idea that books offer authentic history, but postmodernism, with considerable justification, insists that popular culture, and especially the media, are seriously challenging this. A crucial issue here is that of the limits, if any, of representation (see Friedlander 1992). One can fully appreciate the taboo for many years, and especially by the Jewish community, on *any* representation of the Holocaust, which was regarded, justifiably, as unrepresentable. Any representation is inevitably partial, from a particular perspective: it has been said that the Holocaust was a horror of such unimaginable proportions that it should be surrounded by a ring of fire, which it would be deeply immoral to transgress.

When the survivors have passed away, the truth about it will be given by accounts in books, films and so on, and the ways in which it is perceived may be very different. Some say that we shall progressively achieve a more comprehensive understanding, whereas others emphasise the danger, indeed the inevitability, of rewriting history.

Objectivity

This brings out sharply postmodernists' emphasis on the myth of objectivity. Their rejection as senseless of the prevalent, unquestioned conception of objectivity construed as *absolute* is to some extent similar to my own conception of objectivity. However, there are crucial differences, for postmodernists assume that this implies a rejection of the notion of objectivity altogether. This is a crucial issue, which I have been arguing for years. To put it far too briefly, I too reject the myth of 'objectivity', i.e. the traditional and still-prevalent assumption that there are objective truths that are universal, absolute and completely independent of human conception. But this is *not* to deny objectivity in a more coherent sense, namely as that for which sound reasons can be offered which refer to qualities of the *object*; this definition concedes nothing to subjectivism. Now, of course, it may be objected that I have simply transferred the problem to what counts as 'sound'. Not so. What counts as a sound reason will depend on the context; and within the same cultural context, and even the same discipline or area of discourse (for example, of physics), this allows for conflicting but equally objective judgements. Yet equally, some judgements can be invalid because they are not supportable by such reasons. For far too long, the misleading notion of objectivity as absolute and universal has, at least implicitly, distorted educational policy: education, conceived as the acquisition of facts and useful skills, has hardened the creative arteries to the point of terminal thrombosis. Implicit in that conception is the intellectual authoritarianism of deductive and inductive reasons, as the only (or at least the paradigm) kinds. But I contend that what I sometimes call 'interpretative reasons' are more important, and they *underlie*, give sense to, deductive and inductive reasoning (see Best 1993a for a more comprehensive account of interpretative reasoning). Thus interpretative reasoning is equally important in the sciences: such reasons may offer not only a different perspective or understanding, but also a different implicit evaluation. Herman Bondi, the eminent astronomer and theoretical physicist writes: 'Certain experiments that were interpreted in a particular way in their day we now interpret quite differently – but they were claimed as facts in those days' (Bondi 1972: 225). For this reason he does not like to use the word 'fact', since it implies an absolute truth, which is inapplicable in the sciences. Sir Hans Kornberg, Professor of Biochemistry at Cambridge University, wrote more recently: 'The great joy of scientific research is to see what other people may already have seen, but to be the first to notice it' (Kornberg 1992: 21).

I have insufficient space to explicate the important distinction between interpretation and the underlying conceptual context within which interpretation makes sense. Suffice it to say that what I mean by 'interpretative reasoning' applies to both.

It may seem that my insistence on the interpretation or conceptualisation that necessarily underlies and gives sense to fact, truth and objectivity concedes that there can be no sense in objectivity and truth; that it is all a matter of individual interpretation and evaluation. On the contrary, what it does show is, to repeat, that we need a different conception of *objectivity* as that which *is open to different conceptions, interpretations and evaluations*. That there is no 'essence' of the artichoke does not imply that there is no artichoke; that there is no 'essence' of the self does not imply that there is no self, or personal identity; that there is no absolute, universal objectivity, independent of human conception, does not imply that there can be no objectivity.

To put briefly a point that requires more elaboration: a coherent conception of objectivity has to encompass an indefinite but *not unlimited* possibility of valid interpretation.

Of course there can be, and characteristically is, considerable argument about where the limits have been transgressed. The film *Schindler's List* is more concerned with survival than with death. If the perspective of the Holocaust should be based on the film, then it will enshrine as authoritative an optimistic ending, that will be understood as the historical truth about the Holocaust. Yet fewer than four thousand Jews now live in Poland, compared with three million before the war. Despite the incalculable, unimaginable suffering and slaughter, the central message of the film is of a redemptive aspect of the Holocaust. Does this not transgress the limits? Spielberg, the director, altered or omitted many historical facts. For instance, Schindler was a Nazi spy who was in prison in Czechoslovakia for two years; he had a long history of affiliation with the Nazis. These facts were not mentioned in the film.

The film has given rise to sharp and painful debate about what can count as a valid perspective, and whether a film has the authority to portray history. Criticisms have included: 'Is it acceptable to make a film about a good Nazi, rather than about the hideous, largely anonymous agonies and deaths of six million Jews?'

Yet the very existence of this debate concedes the crucial distinction for which I am arguing: there are limits of valid interpretation, limits to what can count as true, even though those limits may have very fuzzy and changeable edges.

News media

Advertising, the popular press and television influence thought, and therefore define personality, to an incalculable extent. In a paper entitled 'How much am I?' (Best 1985) I tried to show how the materialism-dominated culture in which we live has the defining effect of turning the question 'Who am I?' into the question of the title, i.e. the character of the self is defined in materialistic terms.

In a recent radio discussion, the film director Ken Loach rejected as senseless the distinction in his work between fiction and fact. He was criticised for giving a 'fictional' partial perception of the Spanish Civil War in his film *Land and Freedom*. His reply was that *any* supposed 'factual' account would inevitably offer an equally partial perspective. The notion of 'the truth' about the war in Bosnia is illusory. There is an indefinite number of possible perspectives, each of which may be true: indefinite, but *not unlimited*. Some accounts may be false.

Nevertheless, this aspect of postmodernism seems to me important and salutary. The ethos, the projection of the news media, centres on (and even fabricates) dramatic and sentimental situations while ignoring others; thus moral thoughts and feelings are prescribed within stereotyped, cliché limits. Morality is reduced, constricted, debased: in reducing the possibility of the varied criteria for what can count as a moral issue, the media are *ipso facto* reducing possibilities of personal individuality.

In this respect, television has a considerable influence, in that it fails to present anything of the immense subtlety and sensitively varied criteria of moral conceptions that can be found, by contrast and for example, in James Joyce, Shakespeare, Tolstoy, Dostoevsky, George Eliot and Mike Leigh's films. The news on the media has *become*, to a considerable extent, shallow art, like a cheap novel, or slushy film. Snippets of real human tragedies are presented in kaleidoscopic sequence, and thus inoculate against serious moral and emotional impact and development. One is reminded of Oscar Wilde:

> The intellectual and emotional life of ordinary people is a very contemptible affair. Just as they borrow their ideas from a sort of circulating library of thought . . . and send them back soiled at the end of each week, so they always try to get their emotions on credit, and refuse to pay the bill when it comes in.
>
> (Hart-Davies 1962: 501)

Complicit in this ethos is that of the personality cult, in which even news readers are 'elevated' to the status of film stars, and are thus regarded as lending authority to the circulating clichés of thought and feeling.

To cite them again, Becket's *Happy Days*, Hamilton's painting: *Just What Is It Which Makes Today's Homes So Different, So Appealing?*, Mike Leigh's *Abigail's Party* and much of the work of Harold Pinter (to mention only a few such examples), reveal the defining influence on thought and personality of the media. In effect, what can *count* as a happy day for Winnie is logically limited by the pile of cliché in which she is buried.

However, there is still room for the notion of truth: one can recognise shallow, escapist falsity, and one can offer alternative visions of life, and with them alternative possibilities of thought, feeling and the self. Beckett's stark vision, for instance in *Waiting for Godot*, *Endgame*, *Act Without Words* and *Quad* are incisive antidotes to Cartlandesque sentimental escapism. Beckett, regarded by many as typical of postmodernism, can be seen as making important *moral* points in his art.

In this respect the arts can play a vital part in educating moral sensibility.

Conclusion

The theses of the two sections of this chapter are closely complementary. The character of the moral learning possible in the arts reflects the differences of perception and interpretation which are central to a more coherent conception of objectivity and rationality.

The warnings implicit in postmodernism are important and salutary. But, in my view, we are not helpless. There may be no moral absolutes, but that is not to say that there are no limits, and therefore that morality, if it should make sense at all, amounts merely to subjective preference.

Moreover, my thesis reveals clearly where the principal emphasis should be, in all aspects of education – an emphasis directly contrary to current trends. Instead of clinging to the cripplingly false security of the assumption that education consists in learning facts about unquestionable truths, we should *welcome*, as many leading theoretical scientists do, the *liberation* of the refreshing inevitability of uncertainty. We should not resist, but accept *eagerly*, with a vivid sense of release, that *uncertainty* is the bedrock truth about the human condition. Which is to say that the central emphasis in education should be on creativity, open-mindedness. That is the most important lesson to be learned from the learning, including the moral and emotional learning, which is characteristic of the arts.

Notes

1 I have exposed the myth of generic arts in several places, for example Best (1995a).
2 For a discussion of this issue philosophically, see Best (1993a: ch. 12). I consider its important educational implications in Best (1984, 1996a).
3 Critical appreciation of an artist's work (or a genre), while more general, of course involves the same considerations.
4 Abbs (1992). See also my reply (Best 1993b). Abbs extended this thesis of 'justifying' the arts in terms of supernatural metaphysical universals and subjective introspection in Abbs (1994). See my critical replies (Best 1995b, 1996b).
5 See my three papers mentioned in note 4 above. See also Best (1993a: *passim*, esp. chs 1 and 3).
6 I am greatly indebted to Yosefa Loshitzky, of the University of Jerusalem, for many of the points that follow, which were included in an extremely interesting and incisive talk and subsequent private conversation. See Loshitzky (1997).

References

Abbs, P. (1992) 'Making the art beat faster', *Times Higher Educational Supplement* 18 September: 10.
—— (1994) 'The primacy of the aesthetic: an understanding of the nature of aesthetic experience in relationship to works of art' *Curriculum*, 15(1): 21–6.
Bambrough, J. R. (1973) 'To reason is to generalise', *The Listener* 89(2285): 11 January.
Beardsmore, R. W. (1971) *Art and Morality*, London: Macmillan.
Best, D. (1983) 'Logic, particularity and art', *British Journal of Aesthetics* 23(4): 306–18.
—— (1984) 'The dangers of "aesthetic education" ', *Oxford Review of Education* 11(1): 159–68.
—— (1985) 'How much am I?' *Educational Research and Perspectives*: December.
—— (1993a) *The Rationality of Feeling*, London: Falmer Press.

—— (1993b) 'Minds at work in an empire of the senses', *Times Higher Educational Supplement* 19 February: 16.

—— (1995a) 'The dangers of generic arts: philosophical confusions and practical expediency', *Journal of Aesthetic Education* 29(2): 79–93.

—— (1995b) 'Educating artistic response', *Curriculum* 16(1): 12–21.

—— (1996a) 'Values in the arts', in J. M. Halstead and M. J. Taylor (eds) *Values in Education and Education in Values*, London: Falmer Press.

—— (1996b) 'Understanding artistic experience: some vital pointers for research', *NADIE Journal* (National Association for Drama in Education, Australia) 20(2): 41–53.

Bondi, H. (1972) 'The achievements of Karl Popper', *The Listener* 88(2265): 225–9.

Carr, W. (1995) *For Education: Towards Critical Educational Enquiry*, Buckingham: Open University Press.

Collingwood, R. G. (1938) *The Principles of Art*, Oxford: Clarendon Press.

Eisner, E. (1981) 'The role of the arts in cognition and curriculum', *Report of INSEA World Congress, Rotterdam*, Amsterdam: De Trommel.

Friedlander, S. (1992) *Probing the Limits of Representation: Nazism and the Final Solution*, Cambridge, MA: Harvard University Press.

Hampshire, S. (1954) 'Logic and appreciation', in W. R. Elton (ed.) *Aesthetics and Language*, Oxford: Blackwell.

Hart-Davies, R. (1962) *The Letters of Oscar Wilde*, London: Hart-Davies.

Hirst, P. (1980) *Transcript of a Symposium, 'Education with the Arts in Mind'*, Wakefield: Bretton Hall.

—— (1989) 'The concepts of physical education and dance education', *Collected Conference Papers in Dance*, vol. 4 (ed. G. Curle), London: NATFHE.

Kerr, F. (1986) *Theology after Wittgenstein*, Oxford: Blackwell.

Kornberg, H. (1993) Article in *CAM: Cambridge University Alumni Magazine*, Michaelmas term: 21–3.

Loshitzky, Y. (1997) *Spielberg's Holocaust: Critical Perspectives on 'Schindler's List'*, Indianapolis: Indiana University Press.

McFee, G. (1989) 'Reply to Professor Hirst', *Collected Conference Papers in Dance*, vol. 4 (ed. G. Curle), London: NATFHE.

Moore, G. E. (1955) 'Wittgenstein's lectures at Cambridge, 1930–32', *Mind* 64: 1–27.

Pride, A. (1993) 'Ethics, criticism and creativity in post-post-structuralist classroom', paper delivered at the AATE Conference, 5 July.

Rhees, R. (1969) *Without Answers*, London: Routledge.

Saw, R. (1962) 'Art and the language of the emotions', *Proceedings of the Aristotelian Society*, supp. vol. 36: 181–94.

Tolstoy, L. (1930) *What is Art?* tr. A. Maude, London: Oxford University Press.

Usher, R. and Edwards, R. (1994) *Post-Modernism and Education*, London: Routledge.

Wilde, O. (1966) *Complete Works*, ed. V. Holland, London: Collins.

Wittgenstein, L. (1958) *Philosophical Investigations*, Oxford: Blackwell.

Part V

MORAL MOTIVATION

13

'BEHAVING MORALLY AS A POINT OF PRINCIPLE'

A proper aim of moral education?

Graham Haydon

Moral motivation

Does morality involve some special kind of motivation? And if it does, is it a kind of motivation educators should be trying to encourage?

There is no distinctive kind of motivation which leads people to act in ways that are not wrong, if we mean by that simply that their action does not violate any moral norms. I may on various occasions act from unthinking habit, or from calculated self-interest, or from affection for another, or 'on the spur of the moment' for no articulated reason – and in any of these cases it may be that there is nothing wrong in what I do. But it may also be that there is nothing distinctively moral in what I do. There is a way of thinking about morality which holds that to act morally in a positive sense *is* to act from a particular kind of motivation. It is this idea, that there is a distinctive moral motivation, that I want to explore in this chapter. I shall start by recognising that in recent times some critics have been sceptical about the value of morality itself. Part of any such radical case against morality must be that a distinctively moral motivation, if it exists at all, is unnecessary or undesirable; I shall argue here that, even though it may not be easy to make sense of this kind of motivation, it does exist and cannot readily be dispensed with.

The relevance of these issues to moral education will, I hope, be clear. If morality itself, incorporating a distinctive kind of motivation, is less important than many people have assumed – if, indeed, we might even be better off without morality – then it could well be argued that we should not be educating people in morality at all. Indeed, John White (1990) has argued that we should replace 'moral education' by what he calls an education in altruism – where the notion of altruism suggests a kind of motivation that is different from the specifically moral motivation I have in mind. If an education in altruism were sufficient, the problem of making sense of a specifically moral motivation would be purely academic; whereas if education does have good reason to try to promote a specifically moral motivation, it must also try to make that kind of motivation intelligible.

Since the word 'morality' may itself convey different things to different people, we need to ask: 'On what understanding of morality could it be an intelligible, and even perhaps a plausible, claim that we would be better off without morality?' I shall illustrate the answer by reference to Marx. There was clearly an ethical impulse behind much of Marx's writings; he was not just doing value-free social science, whatever he may sometimes have claimed. But he saw morality as a form of alienation. Morality was a system of constraints on freedom of action; these constraints were actually a human construct, yet, in common with many other human constructs – including God, in Marx's view, following Feuerbach – they came to be experienced as emanating from something outside of human beings, as an objectively existing power over people. The moral system of constraints presupposed a form of life in which people's interests were constantly in conflict, and within that form of life, the moral system tended to work in favour of the more powerful. Whereas if people lived in a form of society in which their interests were in harmony, they would not need the constraints of morality to keep them from conflict.

Even within the earliest Marxist writings, the term 'morality' was used in different ways; thus Engels was able to say that only in a post-capitalist society could a 'truly human morality' be attained. What he had in mind, roughly, was a form of society in which people could be motivated by concerns that did not bring them into conflict with each other, either as classes (which would have ceased to exist) or individually. They would cooperate rather than compete, they would promote collective interests rather than undermining each other's individual interests, and they would not, in so acting, be motivated by a sense of moral obligation experienced as some kind of objective and alienating constraint.

More recently Bernard Williams (1985) has argued that we would be better off without 'the morality system', which is characterised by the centrality of obligation. Williams delineates various formal aspects of the way in which the notion of moral obligation functions in this system; so far as motivation is concerned, what is central is a sense of practical necessity attaching to the idea of obligation: the sense that there is something that, morally, I must do or must not do. It is this kind of motivation that is downplayed by White in favour of altruism. Influenced by Williams, White argues that morality brings with it rigidity, a tendency to fanaticism, an unwillingness to compromise, and the pervasive tendency to blame oneself and others for moral defects. Our ethical life, says White (1990: 53), 'does not *have* to be as unlovely as this'.

The conception of morality which writers such as Williams and White call into question is one associated historically with Kant. Kant argued that morality must be grounded in reason. Properly conceived, reason would endorse a system of principles – derived ultimately from one principle, the categorical imperative – which a rational agent would recognise as binding on his or her conduct. A limited acquaintance with Kant's moral philosophy often leads people to equate it with an idea of absolutism: the notion that there are certain highly general principles, such as not telling lies, which must be adhered to without exception.[1] But a morality could, arguably, be Kantian in spirit without this absolutism; in any case it is not necessarily the most central feature of Kant's ethics, nor the one to which the critics I have mentioned most object. What is arguably more important, and what I shall concentrate on here, is a distinctive understanding of the motivation of the moral agent.

We sometimes, even in contemporary discourse, encounter the idea that someone should do a particular thing, not because he or she feels so inclined, and not (directly) because of any awareness of how others will feel, but simply because it is the right thing to do. Similarly, we may encounter the idea that a person should not do something, not because of an aversion to doing it, not through a desire to avoid hurting others, not indeed (directly) as a result of consideration of the feelings or reactions of others, but simply because it would be wrong. It seems to me that one of the central features of morality (that is, of the system which critics such as Williams and White would wish to see replaced) is that it tries to work with some such notion of a distinctively moral reason for action. Such a notion cropped up, for instance, in a discussion document from the National Curriculum Council for England and Wales (NCC 1993, republished as SCAA 1995), which put at the head of its list of the qualities to be developed in moral education 'The will to behave morally as a point of principle.'

In that document (as is typical of much contemporary discussion) the notion of moral action on principle did not stand alone in a pure form. There were elements of apparently quite different approaches to morality, or to what some would prefer to call the broader area of ethical concern. It is common in contemporary discussion to find expressions of a view that is closer to Hume than to Kant, in that the underlying motivation for moral action (and indeed for any action) is taken to rest in the agent's feelings and desires. Approaches to moral education, which are conceived as Kantian, such as that associated with Lawrence Kohlberg (1981), are challenged by an alternative approach, initially associated with Carol Gilligan (1982) and Nel Noddings (1984), which is often now labelled 'an ethic of caring'. Kohlberg himself was perhaps never clear enough about the nature of the motivation we might describe as 'acting on principle', but it is striking that the alternative account finds the underlying motivation of the ethically responsible person in *caring*, which is surely an essentially affective matter. Again, when White suggests that for moral education we should substitute an education in altruism, he is speaking of something that has to be manifested in people's feelings. At a minimum, the altruistic person will sometimes be motivated by compassion, whereas we can imagine a rigid moralist, adhering to Kantian principles, never actually *feeling* compassion.[2]

I want to argue that this notion of a distinctively moral form of motivation is worth holding onto in the face of approaches that may leave too much to contingencies of feelings, even where the feelings involved may themselves be admirable. But if it is desirable that people should be educated so that they will have the capacity to 'behave morally as a point of principle', any such education will still face the challenge that it is by no means obvious how we can make sense of such an idea.

Why do we need moral motivation?

The reader may have some idea, from experience, of what it is to behave morally as a point of principle. Yet I suspect that for most of us this is not a very common experience. Most of the time, I suspect, we do what we want to do; not necessarily what we want to do immediately or with reference only to ourselves, but what we want to do, all things considered, and given our dispositions. 'All things' here include: the interests and wishes of others, especially others whom we care about or feel responsible for; our knowledge that others might disapprove if we acted in certain ways; and our own sense that we would be uncomfortable with ourselves if we did not act in a way that we could feel was justified. None of this amounts to the will to act morally as a point of principle. But then, what *does* that consist in? I think it would be difficult to give to this notion a sense very different from that which Kant gave it; but that does not entail accepting all of Kant's moral philosophy. It is in the first chapter of his *Groundwork* (Kant 1948, first published 1785), where he is still analysing what he calls 'common rational knowledge of morality', that Kant first gives an account of the motive of moral duty, well before he introduces the notion of the categorical imperative, let alone the notoriously difficult conception of the noumenal and phenomenal standpoints. Kant says at one point:

> To help others where one can is a duty, and besides there are many spirits of so sympathetic a temper that, without any further motive of vanity or self-interest, they find an inner pleasure in spreading happiness around them and can take delight in the contentment of others as their own work. Yet I maintain that in such a case an action of this kind, however right and however amiable it may be, has still no genuinely moral worth.
>
> (Kant 1948: 63–4)

Some readers find this passage abhorrent. It seems to suggest that we should not welcome the presence in the world of these people who find pleasure in spreading happiness around them, but should prefer a world populated by people who do good reluctantly, out of a sense of duty. But that is not what Kant is saying. He is concerned to clarify what is entailed in a specifically moral motivation. He does not say that people ought never to act out of anything but a moral motivation. Nor, of course, is the NCC paper claiming this. What they do both claim, though this is not a Kantian way of putting it, is that a specifically moral motivation has a vital place in human life. For what reasons?

From Kant in the same passage of the *Groundwork* we can elicit one answer (he is referring to a person of sympathetic temper as mentioned above, one who – most of the time – enjoys doing good):

> Suppose, then, that the mind of this friend of man were overclouded by sorrows of his own which extinguished all sympathy with the fate of others, but that he still had power to help those in distress, though no longer stirred by the need of others because sufficiently occupied with his own; and suppose that, when no longer moved by any inclination, he tears himself out of this deadly insensibility and does the action without any inclination for the sake of duty alone . . .
>
> (*ibid.*: 64)

We may well think that the world would be a better place if no one were ever in the position here described. But in the real world it does happen that people get depressed, self-absorbed, weighed down by their own problems; and they may cease to feel any benevolence towards or sense of identification with others. If, in that condition, it is still possible for them to 'will to behave morally as a point of principle', is it not better that they should have rather than lack the capacity to be moved in that way?

Let me take another case: a real though artificially constructed one. In some famous – or notorious – experiments by Stanley Milgram, subjects thought that they were inflicting electric shocks on other subjects, people who were innocent victims, except that they were not doing very well in the supposed learning experiment. On the experimenter's instructions, many subjects did what they believed was inflicting high-voltage shocks to the point of causing severe pain and distress. Relatively few subjects refused to go along with the experiment. What sort of motivation could have led to more people refusing to be party to this infliction (as they believed) of suffering?

Here we might answer 'altruism' or 'benevolence', and certainly we can suppose (indeed, we could make it true by definition) that if the experimental subjects had been sufficiently benevolent towards their victims they would not have gone along with the experimenter's instructions. But then we have to conclude that a lot of ordinary people were not sufficiently benevolent. To put it this way is perhaps rather crude. Benevolence or altruism is both a rather diffuse quality and one that can be rather specific in its direction.

These experimental subjects may have been thoroughly benevolent spouses and parents; they may even have felt some benevolence towards the experimenter, not wanting to mess up his experiment. Certainly they had mixed motives in many cases (Milgram 1974 devoted a good deal of attention to the question of their motivation). To go against the experimenter's instructions would have been uncomfortable and embarrassing, would have taken some courage; besides, most subjects will have felt a duty to go along with what the experimenter asked of them.

That last point might incline some of the critics of Kant to suggest that the sense of duty is suspect because it can so easily be misdirected. Altruism is seen as preferable to following authority, acting out of a sense of duty to one's superiors, blindly following tradition, and so on. But Kant was talking, not of a blind sense of duty, or of a duty towards human authorities, but of a sense of moral duty informed by reason. A Kantian sense of the moral law would have led the experimental subjects *not* to believe that they must go along with the experimenter's instructions but to say, 'No. This is immoral, I will not do it.' (Some people, but not many, did respond in that sort of way.)

Suppose that one of the experimental subjects (who were mostly male), perhaps a person of a generally benevolent and kindly disposition, was having an off day. Like the person in Kant's example above, he was depressed and fed up (we can suppose he was taking part in the experiment because he was bored, had nothing better to do, and was getting paid for it). He felt no particular fellow-feeling towards the victim. If anything, so far as feelings go, he felt bloody-minded: if he himself was in such a bad state, why shouldn't someone else suffer too? It seems to me it is just in such a case that the Kantian motivation – the will to act morally as a point of principle, to do what one ought to do just because it is what one ought to do – could operate; and that nothing else, no other sort of motivation, would lead, in such a case, to a refusal to inflict the suffering.

I think the point can be generalised. Whenever one person does something horrible to another person, or to another sentient being – and cases seem to be too frequently reported in the media to need elaboration here – we can ask what kind of moral education, if any, would have made a difference. An education in altruism, if the resulting altruism were strong enough and general enough, would certainly have prevented many of the things we hear of. And the development of altruistic dispositions may lie behind many of the good and positive things we also hear of. But I doubt that we can reasonably expect, this side of Utopia, that altruistic dispositions will be general enough, strong enough and sufficiently resistant to countervailing motivations to eliminate all instances of malevolence or, indeed, to promote as much good in the world as people could achieve. I am suggesting that we also need the kind of motivation summed up, as it happens, in the NCC's wording: the will to behave morally as a point of principle.

That is one kind of reason why we need moral motivation. Another, which I do not have space to go into at length here, arises from reflection on the justice/caring debate initiated by Gilligan in response to Kohlberg. It is roughly this: the existence of a community of altruistic and caring persons would not guarantee justice; and justice, though not everything, is important. Caring, in the first instance, is caring towards particular others. A community of caring persons would be one in which everyone acted in a caring way towards particular others. But this would not, by itself, guarantee that everyone was cared for, or that everyone's needs were met. To ensure this, a more impartial view is also necessary. We need justice, even though it is, in Hume's terms, an artificial rather than a natural virtue; and we need people who care about justice. Caring about justice, though compatible with caring for particular others, is not the same; sometimes doing what is just means making particular others, whom one cares about, worse off than they would otherwise be. The motivation that will bring this about will be *not* caring about particular others, but caring about justice itself. (This direction of the caring towards an idea, rather than towards persons directly, is roughly what makes justice an artificial rather than a natural virtue.) And to care about justice is an instance of what I have been calling moral motivation; it can call on people to act in a particular way, not because they are so inclined, nor from their natural benevolence, but simply because this is what justice requires.

Justice is, I believe, necessary within communities, certainly when they are communities of any size. It may also be necessary as a corrective to too great an immersion in the concrete morality – Hegel's *Sittlichkeit* – of a particular community. We have too much experience of xenophobia and racism to suppose that the *Sittlichkeit* of a particular community can be relied on without some more universal sense of what is owed to all persons simply as persons. To see this, imagine that in Milgram's experiment the experimental subject identifies with the experimenter as one of the same community, but identifies the victim as a member of a different group towards whom the subject is habitually prejudiced.

So far I have been suggesting that even when there are bonds of fellow-feeling within a community which will support altruistic behaviour, a principled sense of morality is still important. But there are many people in the modern world who do not feel part of a concrete community. While education should do what it can to promote a sense of membership of concrete communities, we must also give a moral education to those who may not achieve that sense – who could, in a modern society, turn out to be any of our children. Even if Marx is right that Kantian morality is a morality of alienation, for as long as alienation exists, we still need a morality for that condition.

Such a morality, I am suggesting, involves a specific form of motivation. Perhaps experience can establish that such a motivation sometimes does exist. But it is not enough to see such motivation as an occasional and inexplicable occurrence; if it is to be possible for moral education to treat the development of such motivation as an aim, it has to be interpreted in a way that makes it intelligible – not only to educators but also in some form to pupils. The question of intelligibility arises because this kind of motivation presupposes that the agent is able to have the thought: 'This is what I morally ought to do.' But an agent cannot have that thought, in a sense that will be able actually to feed into motivation, if the thought itself is not intelligible.

The same problem does not arise with the motivation involved in an altruistic disposition. If someone wants to help a fellow-creature (given a realisation that the other is, say, in distress) there is no problem about the intelligibility of this want in itself which could stand in the way of the motivation; the mere want is, as it were, enough. Indeed, it seems quite possible that members of some non-human species are capable of this motivation. But thoughts such as 'This kind of thing is morally wrong' are only available to language-using beings, and such beings, given a degree of scepticism, may well wonder whether that thought actually means anything. If we are trying to educate people to use their reason and think critically, we must expect that they will ask what this idea, the very idea of a moral 'ought', means, and we cannot just assume that they will find an answer. The remainder of this chapter will suggest some directions in which we might look for an answer.

Making sense of morality – religious and secular ways

In a paper that may have had some influence in turning moral philosophers' thoughts towards virtues rather than 'oughts', Elizabeth Anscombe proposed that

> the concepts of obligation, and duty – *moral* obligation and *moral* duty, that is to say – and of what is *morally* right and wrong, and of the *moral* sense of 'ought', ought to be jettisoned if this is psychologically possible; because they are survivals, or derivatives from survivals, from an earlier conception of ethics which no longer generally survives . . .
>
> (Anscombe 1970: 211)

The earlier conception she was referring to was a religiously based conception of morality, in which the moral law was God-given law. Without the general acceptance, she argued, of a belief in God as law-giver, this conception has lost its sense. Similar ideas have been reinforced, among philosophers, by Alasdair MacIntyre (1981). I am suggesting in this chapter that there still is a role for the moral sense of 'ought' and the notion of moral obligation, so that we still do need to make sense of it. It is right that we have to find ways of making sense of it without seeing morality as a system of commands issued by God. It is, however, premature to move from this point to the immediate conclusion that the effort of making sense of moral obligation and motivation has to be carried on within an entirely God-free vocabulary. Theological thinking does at least provide examples of making sense of moral obligation, and it may be that the discourse of moral philosophy here has something to learn from the discourse of theology.

Much theology (this is probably particularly true of Protestant Christian theology) would not treat the sense of obligation as a recognition of commands from God – or at any rate not as that simply or primarily. In twentieth-century theology there is a strong strand of the Kantian emphasis that it must be possible to recognise moral demands, moral right and wrong, independently of acknowledgement of moral demands as God's demands.[3] If religious belief does help to make sense of morality, this need not be because morality is seen as a set of commands from an arbitrary ruler; indeed the Kantian strand would say that such a set of demands, because heteronomous rather than autonomous, could not be morality at all. But religious belief can help to make sense of morality by enabling moral demands to be experienced within a wider framework of meaning that is independently valid, but not for that reason isolated from other aspects of a person's life. And it is to the possession of a unified framework of meaning that we probably have to look if we are to make sense of morality. It seems that, as human beings, we can act in a certain way, not just because doing so serves some self-interested desires (such as avoiding damnation), or even because it serves non-self-interested desires relating to particular others, but because it makes sense to us to act in that way, as part of a life itself understood as part of something larger. Attempts to make sense of morality which are avowedly non-religious may still need to be able to connect a sense of obligation in some way to a wider whole.

Within theology, again, one way of making sense of moral demands without seeing them as arbitrary commands is by identifying the central values with the God which is worshipped. This may be done in more or less radical ways, but in at least some cases it has led to what is essentially a Feuerbachian account of God as a projection of human concerns. A 'projectivist' view seeks to make sense of, or to retain a sense for, religious language and practice within a world, and an intellectual culture in which it is increasingly difficult (at least for many people) to maintain wholeheartedly or with integrity the whole of the older supernatural beliefs that went with such language and practice. Talking of God becomes in such accounts a way of talking about deep human concerns, about what we most care about, about what we recognise as most important in the world. God becomes a projection of human values; but what is most significant for the present argument is that writers who take such a view do not necessarily see themselves as subscribing to atheism. The language and the practice of religion in which they participate still has meaning for them. In both the academic writing of a philosopher of religion such as Don Cupitt (1980) and the autobiographical writing of a parish priest such as Anthony Freeman (1993) one finds the idea that giving up a belief in a literal, supernaturally existent personal God 'out there' need not make a fundamental difference to the life of the believer. It is the language, the practice, the whole 'mind-set' of religion that makes the difference, and this can continue, and can still in fact have very much the same meaning, after the belief in its literal truth has been abandoned.[4]

What is the relevance of all this to our question? It is relevant, I suggest, on two levels. First, it does itself offer us *one* way – one could even say a tried and tested way – in which moral language can have meaning without conceiving it as an expression of God-given law. Of course, it would be a very long way from this observation to arguing that, from where we are now, we ought after all to see moral education as a branch of religious education. For one thing, a major question faces 'projectivist' conceptions of God. Thinkers who have come to such views have started from more traditional or orthodox religious interpretations. The religious language and practices already make sense to them, have meaning for them; it is not so surprising that a change in intellectual interpretation need not destroy that meaning. What is much more doubtful is whether someone who had never held a religious belief on a more traditional interpretation could find any meaning in religious language and practice if, from the beginning, it were presented in an avowedly projectivist way. Since there are indeed in modern society (more so in Britain, incidentally, than in the United States) many who do grow up without encountering religious language and practice from the inside (and since it is not plausible that enforced 'religious worship' in schools can have much effect on that situation), we can hardly advocate religious language, however thoroughly demythologised, as a route towards moral meaning for society at large through the public education system.

Nevertheless, on a second level, the thinking of some modern theologians and philosophers of religion may still be relevant. For even if their particular route is not one that can be advocated for everyone, their attempt is still an *example* of the kind of task we face in moral education. For the question of the meaning that moral language can have within a thoroughly de-supernaturalised world-view is actually very similar to the question about religious language and practice, precisely because a 'projectivist' view can also be taken of moral language and practice. Such views, as regards the moral aspects of the world, go back at least to Hume (1888, first published 1739), who was perhaps the first to argue systematically that we do not really observe moral qualities – of good and bad, right and wrong – *in* the world, but project them *onto* the world. Such a view does not mean that we can simply invent and apply to things whatever moral labels we like; our moral conceptions will certainly reflect in some way underlying human concerns that are real aspects of human nature (of the human condition or of rationality as a quality which humans possess), and it may well be possible to argue that there are good reasons for holding to some particular conceptions of right and wrong and rejecting others; it may be possible in that kind of way to establish a sense in which certain moral claims are objectively valid. But it is hardly controversial that claims about objective rightness and wrongness cannot be settled in anything like the same kind of way that we might settle claims about things, like rocks and planets, that could exist quite independently of any human thought or action. To hold that moral qualities are qualities we project onto the world may not, then, change the meaning of moral terms at all radically. Indeed, this is the claim of the major contemporary proponent of moral projectivism, Simon Blackburn (1993), who calls his account 'quasi-realism': we can go on using moral terms as if they were picking out real, independent qualities in the world, even while aware that these qualities are not really there in the world but are projections of our own concerns.

But it is worth noting why this quasi-realism can work (assuming that claims like Blackburn's are correct). It is because anyone who is likely to take a projectivist view will already be on the inside of moral language and practice. For such a person the answer to the question 'Does taking a projectivist view make any practical difference?' may very well be 'No'. But just as in the case of religion, if we were to present a projectivist reading of morality to someone who had never before encountered moral ideas at all, it is unlikely that the moral claims could be made to stick. Just as someone who had never encountered religious ideas could not react to projectivist views as a welcome way of continuing to make sense of a certain form of language and practice, but only as a language game there was no particular reason for playing at all, so someone who had never been on the inside of morality might well be able to brush aside moral ideas if they could only be presented as projections. And here is an important lesson for moral education. It may indeed be the case that an important function of moral education is to enable people to make sense of morality, not just as a social phenomenon, but in their own lives, and it may enable different people to do this in different ways; but a still more fundamental, and unifying, function may have to be performed by moral education, on a social rather than individual level: to ensure that moral language and practice themselves are kept alive as going concerns. (By 'moral practice' here I mean the practice of employing moral language in a serious way in thinking and talking about one's own conduct and that of others.)

To suggest that moral education – and I am thinking here of what can be done in formal schooling – should have this function is to presuppose that, left to itself, morality as a distinctive practice might not survive. This may seem unlikely, but it is not impossible. (It would have seemed very unlikely once that religion would not survive as a universal set of beliefs and practices.) There probably has been some decline of morality in even a loosely Kantian sense, and as we have seen, some philosophers think that this is a trend to be encouraged. I have suggested, against this, that there is still point in morality, and that its continuation cannot and should not be taken for granted. So one task for moral education is to keep it alive, and another is to help to make sense of it. In this latter task it is possible that moral philosophers and teachers have something to learn from philosophers of religion and theologians. Yet it remains true that, probably for most people, morality will have to be made sense of, if at all, in thoroughly secular terms. So we still need to explore how that might be done.

Kant's own moral philosophy was itself an attempt to make sense of morality independently of theological assumptions. There are still some philosophers who believe that his attempt succeeded, and perhaps they are right. But certainly Kant's attempt is difficult, in the modern world, to follow, and it is unlikely to be intelligible to the average teacher, let alone the average school pupil, in a way that is deep enough to be effective. I say that it is difficult to follow in the modern world because I think that Kant was able to assume in his own day common 'intuitions' (as moral philosophers now call them) that supported his conception and were supported by it. Consider this passage from the *Groundwork*:

> the most ordinary observation shows that when a righteous act is represented as being done with a steadfast mind in complete disregard of any advantage in this or the other world, and even under the greatest temptations of affliction or allurement, it leaves far behind it any similar action affected even in the slightest degree by an alien impulsion and casts it into the shade: it uplifts the soul and rouses a wish that we too could act in this way. Even children of moderate age feel this impression . . .
>
> (Kant 1948: 75)

Moral education, for Kant, would start from this kind of impression. But I wonder how far Kant's observation, if it was correct in his own time and place, is still correct.

I think, then, that we cannot now place our reliance on the detail of Kant's argument. And I want to stress that I am in any case taking a profoundly un-Kantian approach in my own way of advocating the importance of moral motivation. I am suggesting that things will go better, there will be less suffering, more happiness, if a Kantian kind of motivation is available to people.[5] This does not mean that we should expect the specifically moral motivation to be a substitute for altruistic, benevolent dispositions. Moral motivation as a complete substitute would perhaps only be possible, if at all, under one of three conditions: that a Kantian backing for it, as a kind of motivation following logically from full rationality, is understood and accepted; that a theological backing for it is understood and accepted; or that it is simply conditioned into people. The third must, for educators, be unacceptable, as bypassing the use of reason; the other two, even if they do not go against reason, are not fully available to us, and even if they were, moral motivation by itself might indeed carry with it a kind of coldness and rigidity that would be undesirable if it were not tempered by altruistic dispositions. So certainly we should try to foster altruistic dispositions. But I have been arguing that we should also, if we can, foster the moral motivation, as a supplement to altruistic dispositions, because altruism can be too diffuse, or too particularised, or too discontinuous.

How, then, is this motivation to be made intelligible? What can be involved in the thought 'I ought to do this, because it would be wrong not to' – if that is to be a thought that can move someone to action? Or in the thought 'I must not do this, because it would be wrong', if that is to lead to someone refraining from action?

This question has affinities with the old question 'Why should I be moral?', which often in the history of philosophy has been conceived as addressed to the rational individual, as if it were a question that could be answered for an individual, in isolation from any consideration of membership of a community. I do not think that it can be given a satisfactory answer in that way, unless the Kantian answer is valid – and even the Kantian answer does in a way gesture towards community, as we shall see. There does, I think, have to be a kind of sense of community lying behind moral motivation, but it is not necessarily a sense of membership of a real, concrete community.

Of course, a felt sense of community with concrete others can be enormously important, and within the community in which it holds, the felt sense of membership may both make morality as such less important, and may give it the weight it needs when it still is important. If someone is to be able to act morally on principle, it has to be possible to take the principle seriously (and not to see morality as a quaint kind of game some people choose to play); and this is more likely to be possible where real people in a real community realise the importance of morality. So part of an education in morality will be an education *about* morality, because people need to be able to see the importance of morality even if it is a thoroughly natural (as opposed to supernatural) phenomenon. It is no good trying to get people to swallow a 'noble lie': if we are educating people to think, we must expect them to be sceptical and to demand reasons for taking morality seriously. But a cognitive appreciation of the importance of morality may still not have much motivational force if the well-being of real people in a real community has no motivational force. So promoting a real sense of community, in whatever ways that this can be done educationally, will be part of an education in morality as well as part of an education in altruism; the two need not conflict.[6]

I said above, however, that we need the possibility of moral motivation partly because it is a kind of motivation that can operate even where there is no felt sense of community with concrete others. How is this possible? I shall suggest that for someone who was altogether alienated from any sense of human community a principled morality would indeed have no force. But there is the possibility that someone who does not feel part of any concrete community may still be conscious, in a more abstract sense, of membership of a human, moral community. And it may be this consciousness that is able to give the backing to the importance of the principle of moral action.

There are, within moral philosophy, at least three lines of thought which can make this idea less obscure, and which turn out to be inter-related. Annette Baier (anticipated, as she says, by William James) argues (1985) that morality requires in the agent a kind of faith – which for many people today will have to be a secular faith – that a community of moral persons is possible. By acting morally oneself, one demonstrates, to oneself and perhaps to others, that at least one condition of such a community is possible: one demonstrates that the aspiration towards a moral community is not a psychologically hopeless one, since one shows by one's own action that it is possible for people to act justly, to act from a moral motivation. Everyone who acts morally thereby does something to keep the idea of a moral community alive, to preserve the faith that is a condition of morality.

The second line of thought is from Thomas Scanlon (1982), in his defence of a contractualist ethical theory (the kind of theory that is couched in terms of what rational agents could or would agree to as a basis for coexistence). Scanlon suggests that the basic moral motivation is the desire to be able to justify what one does in terms no rational agent could reject. In one way this notion of moral motivation may strike one as narrow. The truly altruistic, caring person perhaps could go through life without constantly having to ask herself whether what she is doing is justified. But this only shows that Scanlon's account is indeed an account of what I have been calling moral motivation. And as he says, this desire to be able to justify what one is doing can be quite strong, and it can be cultivated in moral education (Scanlon suggests that this is largely what moral education is about). The justification in question is not necessarily successful justification to one's actual peers: perhaps, however hard one tries, they will not actually agree that what one is doing is justified, maybe because their prejudices are too strong. Yet one can still have the thought that fully rational persons would not be able to reject the way one is acting. Why should that have any motivational force? Only, I think, because one has a sense of membership of a notional community, rather like that which Baier is talking of. You can see yourself as part of an ideal community, of the community as it ought to be, even if to some degree members of your own concrete community – if you have one – would reject what you are doing. (Think perhaps of what is needed if a teenager is to reject, on moral grounds, the pressure of her peer group to join in with some antisocial behaviour.)

Third, as both Baier and Scanlon recognise, these ideas have affinities with Kant's notion of the 'kingdom of ends'. One should act in such a way that one's action could be a pattern for action for the members of a kingdom of ends – a community of people who respect each other as ends in themselves, who refuse to use each other merely as means. One has here an idea that Kant tries to make intelligible through purely rational argument. Yet it also has – at least it does to me – a certain rhetorical, emotive force. So far as one can grasp what Kant is getting at, it is possible, I think, to be moved by it, even perhaps to find it inspiring. If there is a paradox here, it is not, I think, a vicious one. To grasp what can be grasped, in the modern world, of Kant's justification of morality, one may need to appeal to the imagination as well as using rational argument. The same is likely to be true of any educational attempt to make the very idea of the moral 'ought', as a motive for action, intelligible to pupils. I believe there are reasons that can have weight with people who are, as we all are, partly rational beings, but it may take all of a teacher's skills and many different strategies to bring it about that the sense of morality does indeed have weight. The experience of practising teachers is likely to be more fruitful than my own in coming up with ideas on how to proceed, but teachers need first to understand what it is they are trying to do, and I hope I may have helped in this respect. Though we should do all we can to promote community, altruism, caring, a whole range of virtues, it is too soon, this side of Utopia, to jettison morality with its particular kind of motivation. Yet morality may fade away by default if we cannot find ways to keep it alive. I believe philosophers and practising teachers need to work on together on this challenge.[7]

Notes

1 This is only one of the ideas for which the elastic label 'absolutism' can be used (see Haydon 1997: ch. 3).

2 To some degree, a broadly Humean tendency is manifested in the recent turn in moral philosophy towards 'virtue ethics', though the writers within this tendency more often take their cue from Aristotle than from Hume. Advocates of virtue ethics will often see themselves as presenting an Aristotelian account in contrast to a Kantian one. The point needs to be mentioned here, because while I shall in what follows be suggesting that an aspect of the Kantian approach needs to be retained, I would not want to be read as defending Kant against Aristotle, since I suspect that the contrast between Kant and Aristotle has often been overdrawn. An Aristotelian ethic does not suppose, as some modern accounts seem to, that people ideally would act mainly out of fellow-feeling (in fact a distinctly altruistic motivation does not figure largely in Aristotle); it does, however, concern itself with the basic structure of an agent's desires rather than with adventitious feeling. The NCC document's 'will to act morally as a point of principle' may not be alien to Aristotle's ethics, even though the modern phrase could not be translated exactly into Aristotle's vocabulary. Certainly Aristotle believed that the possession of the virtues involved acting according to the right rule or principle, and he has the conception of doing what is noble for its own sake. One can imagine that if Aristotle and Kant could converse now, they might agree on a good deal, including some notion of 'how the upright gentleman behaves' (where the gender reference is deliberate).

3 A striking example is the first chapter of Tillich (1964). For a detailed philosophical discussion, within the analytical tradition, of the relation between morality (conceived in a Kantian way) and religion, see Maclagan (1961).

4 There have been many twists and turns in Cupitt's writing over the years. He discusses projectivism explicitly in connection with Feuerbach in Cupitt (1985).

5 In effect, I am suggesting a consequentialist, utilitarian reason for encouraging a Kantian conception of moral motivation. It is worth stressing that the kind of motivation I am concerned with here – doing something on principle because it is the moral thing to do – is open to a consequentialist (who thinks that the thing that morally must be done is the thing that will have the best consequences), as well as to the deontologist (who thinks that there are certain sorts of thing that must be done, or not done, independently of consequences). When John Stuart Mill (1962, first published 1859: ch. 3) talks about the sanction of morality as being a feeling in one's own mind, it seems to me that he is talking about the same phenomenon of experience as Kant when he speaks of reverence for the moral law, though he gives a different account of where this moral feeling comes from.

6 There is also the possibility of conceiving of oneself as a member of a wider than human (though still thoroughly natural) community. This can lead to a broadening of moral concern to take in other animals and aspects of the environment. In Kant's own theory there could be no moral obligation towards the environment or even towards other (non-rational) sentient beings.

7 This paper was first written for the Conference on Spiritual and Moral Education at the University of Plymouth, September 1993, then revised and extended for the present volume. Since then I have used some of the ideas in it, and some of the paragraphs, in Haydon (1997: chs 6–8).

References

Anscombe, G. E. M. (1970) 'Modern moral philosophy' (first published 1958), in G. Wallace and A. D. M. Walker (eds) *The Definition of Morality*, London: Methuen.

Baier, A. (1985) 'Secular faith', in *Postures of the Mind*, London: Methuen.

Blackburn, S. (1993) *Essays in Quasi-Realism*, Oxford: Oxford University Press.

Cupitt, D. (1980) *Taking Leave of God*, London: SCM Press.

—— (1985) *Only Human*, London: SCM Press.

Freeman, A. (1993) *God in Us: A Case for Christian Humanism*, London: SCM Press.

Gilligan, C. (1982) *In a Different Voice: Psychological Theory and Women's Development*, Cambridge, MA: Harvard University Press.

Haydon, G. (1997) *Teaching about Values: A New Approach*, London: Cassell.

Hume, D. (1888) *A Treatise of Human Nature* (first published 1739), Oxford: Oxford University Press.

Kant, I. (1948) *Groundwork of the Metaphysic of Morals* (first published 1785), tr. H. J. Paton (1948) *The Moral Law*, London: Hutchinson.

Kohlberg, L. (1981) *The Philosophy of Moral Development*, San Francisco, CA: Harper and Row.

MacIntyre, A. (1981) *After Virtue*, London: Duckworth.

Maclagan, W. (1961) *The Theological Frontier of Ethics*, London: Allen and Unwin.

Milgram, S. (1974) *Obedience to Authority*, London: Tavistock.

Mill, J. S. (1962) *Utilitarianism* (first published 1859), in M. Warnock (ed.) *Utilitarianism*, London: Fontana.

National Curriculum Council (1993) *Spiritual and Moral Development: A Discussion Paper*, York: NCC.

Noddings, N. (1984) *Caring: A Feminine Approach to Ethics and Moral Education*, Berkeley: University of California Press.

Scanlon, T. (1982) 'Contractualism and utilitarianism', in A. Sen and B. Williams (eds) *Utilitarianism and Beyond*, Cambridge: Cambridge University Press.

School Curriculum and Assessment Authority (1995) *Spiritual and Moral Development: SCAA Discussion Paper 3*, London: SCAA.

Tillich, P. (1964) *Morality and Beyond*, London: Routledge.

White, J. (1990) *Education and the Good Life*, London: Kogan Page.

Williams, B. (1985) *Ethics and the Limits of Philosophy*, London: Fontana.

14

WEAKNESS, WANTS AND THE WILL

Roger Straughan

The gap between moral beliefs and moral conduct

Moral education throws up a host of theoretical and practical problems, none of which is more fundamental than those concerned with the relationship between moral judgements, beliefs and decisions (on the one hand) and moral actions, behaviour and conduct (on the other). This relationship has long exercised educators and philosophers alike. John Dewey, a representative of both groups, claimed (1966: 360) that the most important problem of moral education concerns the relationship of knowledge and conduct, a subject of great interest to a much earlier educator and philosopher, Socrates.

The reasons why this relationship is so central to any discussion of moral education stem from the nature of both morality and education, and can be summarised briefly as follows. Morality is basically about what it is right to do and not to do and about what reasons may be given why something ought or ought not to be done. Education is primarily concerned with offering ways of thinking and understanding which again provide reasons why certain things ought to be believed and certain procedures followed. Both morality and education, then, contain a 'theoretical', reasoning element and a 'practical', doing element, so it would be surprising if the double-barrelled concept of moral education did not exhibit these features to an even more marked degree.

However, these features also suggest an inherent difficulty for morality, education and moral education arising from the relationship between the two elements. On the face of it at least, it appears quite possible and indeed likely that a gap or inconsistency may at times occur between thinking and doing, or, as Dewey put it, between knowledge and conduct. This phenomenon may be conceived of and described in various ways, for example: failing to do what one knows or believes one ought to do; failing to follow the dictates of reason; failing to translate theory into practice; or failing to act upon one's principles or convictions.

Such descriptions need not refer exclusively to what would normally be thought of as 'moral' contexts. Moral examples probably come most readily to mind, and 'moral weakness' has traditionally been and still is a major ethical issue that has fascinated moral philosophers. Yet the phenomenon appears to extend well beyond the boundaries of morality and into any area where disparities can occur between knowledge and conduct, and where one fails to do what one knows there are good reasons for doing.

'Non-moral' examples may be even more puzzling (though sometimes more trivial) than failures to live up to one's moral principles, and are thus potentially instructive. One may, for instance, know that there are good, prudential reasons for adopting a more healthy diet and lifestyle, yet fail to make any changes in practice. Or in a cricket match a batsman, knowing that it is important for his side to play defensively and not take unnecessary risks, suddenly attempts a highly ambitious stroke and gives an easy catch, thus throwing his wicket away while fully aware of his stupidity. Or in the garden one may find oneself behaving like this character in one of Nigel Balchin's novels:

> I remember seeing that one of the outdoor peaches had the usual slight attack of leaf curl. I knew quite well that half an hour's work would deal with it in that stage. I knew if it wasn't tackled then it would spread. I had plenty of time, and desperately wanted something to do. Yet I remember standing and looking at that tree, and in the end turning away and leaving it untouched . . .
>
> (Balchin 1951: 131)

Such cases may for convenience be labelled instances of 'weakness of will' to distinguish them from the specifically 'moral' cases of 'moral weakness'. Moral weakness constitutes a major problem for moral education, and the latter part of this chapter will focus upon this issue. However, the very nature of education, as has already been suggested, makes it peculiarly susceptible to non-moral instances of weakness of will. This is because educational methods are rational in the sense that they seek to develop within the learner an awareness that there are good reasons for believing and doing certain things rather than others, but this awareness may not in practice result in the mental or physical behaviour that reason dictates. The learning and practising of any skill, for example, must allow for this possibility if the teaching methods employed encourage the making of judgements and decisions rather than the inculcation of specific conditioned responses. Also the development of general intellectual virtues of a non-moral kind (such as carefulness, persistence and rigour) can easily fall prey to weakness of will: pupils may know that they ought to check their work for obvious mistakes, for example, and may appreciate that there are good reasons for this, yet still at times fail to do it. The classic cliché of the school report, 'Could do better', succinctly (if unimaginatively) encapsulates the intimate relationship that exists between education and weakness of will (Straughan 1989: 1–5).

The nature of specifically *moral* motivation and the Kantian notion of acting morally as a point of principle clearly have implications for moral education which need exploring, but the puzzle that lies at the heart of this present chapter is created by apparent failures to act as we think or believe or know that we have good reason (*of any kind*) to act. Apart from having general significance for education, this puzzle also has a wider application to *moral* education than does the Kantian issue, because of the great variety of reasons that children (and adults) can have for their moral beliefs and judgements. Kohlberg's lower stages of moral development, for instance, which cover the majority of school-age pupils, are characterised by reasons based upon such considerations as rewards and punishments, and the approval or disapproval of one's peers. These would not presumably qualify as 'moral' reasons or motives for Kant, yet they provide the foundations for why children believe it is right or wrong to behave in certain ways. Furthermore, whether or not such reasons are to be counted as 'moral', they may not always be acted upon. Children may 'know' that lying is wrong because it is punished or because their peers do not like liars, yet still on occasion tell lies. This is just as much of a problem for moral education as the student who at a more sophisticated level accepts that lying is wrong as a point of principle, yet who still on occasion tells lies.

Moral weakness can be seen, therefore, as a sub-set of weakness of will and need not be limited to instances involving one specific kind of reason or motivation. Possible explanations of moral weakness and weakness of will are clearly of interest to philosophers and psychologists, but before exploring further in that direction we can further illustrate the need for such exploration by highlighting a set of current educational and political concerns in this area which appear to call for urgent attention and clarification.

The failure of moral education to address the problem

Moral education in the UK and many other countries in recent years has attracted increasing public interest and political enthusiasm. The reasons for this development lie beyond the scope of this chapter, but the form in which the debate has been conducted is of extreme relevance to the issues we are considering here. What frequently happens in discussions about moral education is that the problem of moral weakness is bypassed or ignored, largely because of the language used by the participants. It is in fact fatally easy to talk about moral education in such a way as to wipe out the possibility of moral weakness and the practical problems it poses.

In the UK, for instance, moral education has recently been interpreted by politicians and the media as 'teaching children the difference between right and wrong', the implication being that such teaching will prevent various forms of antisocial behaviour. This approach, however, embodies a highly simplistic view both of teaching and of morality. What exactly constitutes 'teaching the difference between right and wrong'? Apart from the apparently unexamined assumption that right and wrong can always be clearly identified and differentiated in ways that would be agreed upon by all teachers and parents (which seems extremely unlikely), the nature of teaching itself and the logically distinct forms it can take are completely overlooked.

One can, for example, teach children that it is right to help blind people cross roads; one can teach them *how* to help blind people cross roads, and one can teach them *to* help blind people cross roads. But these three forms of teaching are logically distinct from each other and there is no guarantee or even likelihood that one will automatically spill over into another in practice. 'Teaching that', if successful, will produce 'knowledge that', and recipients of this teaching will be able to say that it is right to help blind people across roads. 'Teaching how', if successful, will produce 'knowledge how', and recipients of this teaching will acquire the skills needed to perform the task. 'Teaching to', if successful, will produce the right response in appropriate circumstances, and recipients of this teaching will consistently behave in this way. Yet it is entirely possible for 'teaching that' to take place without the acquisition of those skills needed to translate knowledge into conduct, and equally possible for both 'teaching that' and 'teaching how' to take place without any effect upon the learners' actual behaviour in a subsequent real-life situation (Straughan 1989: 74–90).

These distinctions represent another way of describing some cases of weakness of will, where knowledge of various kinds is not reflected in action. They can be applied to non-moral as well as to moral instances of teaching and learning: I can be taught when skiing that I ought to keep my body facing downhill and *how* to keep my body facing downhill, but this is not to be equated with being taught *to* keep my body facing downhill and certainly does not ensure (as any aspiring skier will testify) that I will always (or even normally) ski as I know I ought.

The exhortation to teach children the difference between right and wrong completely blurs these logical distinctions between different forms of teaching, for it assumes that if children are so taught, the 'right' behaviour (which has been differentiated from the 'wrong') will be automatically adopted. This naive assumption reveals the radical ambiguity of 'teaching the difference between right and wrong' and indeed of 'moral teaching' generally, for it is all-too easy for such teaching to degenerate into mere verbalism and to be credited with more significance and success than it deserves. Moral teaching that relies heavily upon verbal prescription is clearly vulnerable to moral weakness, which may prevent it from having any practical effect in terms of the learners' behaviour.

To draw attention in this way to the possible dangers of verbalism, however, is not to underestimate the importance of language in moral education. Learning moral concepts is a complex activity intimately connected with the acquisition of language. Learning to apply moral concepts to situations and experiences, and to appreciate the prescriptive and emotive overtones of such concepts, is a crucial element in the development of a moral agent, and one that may offer important clues to the relationship between moral knowledge and conduct (see Straughan 1982: 133–7). To acknowledge this point, though, is not to accept the validity of simplistic expectations that the problem of moral weakness will vanish if children are merely exposed to moral prescriptions and exhortations.

The nature of moral weakness and moral motivation

Accepting the existence of the problem and not allowing linguistic ambiguities to obscure it are necessary first steps before anything more positive can be attempted: but if moral education is to try to counter moral weakness, some explanation or interpretation of what is (on the face of it) a puzzling phenomenon needs to be sought. I have elsewhere explored a variety of such explanations and have argued for one particular interpretation that seems to do justice to the logical and psychological features of the phenomenon (Straughan 1982). Rather than repeat this detailed argument here, however, I shall very briefly sketch some of its outlines, indicate what I now see as its major strengths and weaknesses and, finally, speculate upon some possible implications for moral education.

My original argument placed considerable weight upon a distinction between different kinds of reason for action. The phenomenon usually labelled 'moral weakness' (and also the wider notion of 'weakness of will') reflects a conflict between two logically separate types of reason for action, which may be called 'justificatory' and 'motivational'. A justificatory reason for action is one a person appreciates as a valid reason for why he or she ought to behave in a certain way, and this 'ought' will be backed by a more general principle seen (or implicitly assumed) to have application to the particular situation. A motivational reason for action, on the other hand, is one that stems from the agent's wants or desires to achieve some end. In many (probably most) cases there may be no conflict between justificatory and motivational reasons despite their logical distinctness: I will often want to do what I believe I ought to do, perhaps simply *because* I believe I ought to do it. Yet it is always possible for tension to arise between these two sorts of reason, and I may then find that I want to do something else *more* than that which I believe I ought to do. It is always meaningful, as Frankena (1958: 44) puts it, to ask the question, 'Why should I do what I morally ought to do?'

Moral weakness and weakness of will, therefore, are somewhat misleading terms that in fact simply refer to situations where reasons conflict and one's actual priorities are not clearly acknowledged or spelt out. Thus, I fail to tell the police what I really witnessed at the scene of the crime, although I realise that I ought, because I do not want to risk reprisals from the offenders. That want weighs so heavily with me that it in fact takes priority over the justificatory reason why I ought to tell the truth, but I may well not wish to admit (either to myself or others) that priority explicitly, so my behaviour becomes interpreted as resulting from some 'moral weakness'. Similarly in a non-moral context, the batsman wants the satisfaction of achieving a spectacular if risky stroke rather than of playing safely and defensively as he knows he ought, though his behaviour would not normally be explained in such terms by himself or others, who might typically talk of a 'rush of blood to the head', implying weakness in the face of an overpowering urge.

This account of weakness of will and moral weakness, of which the above is a very sketchy synopsis, has attracted some further discussion and constructive criticism (see, for example, Suttle 1987 and Steutel 1988[1]), and I would now wish to restate parts of my original argument in certain respects. The basic distinction between justificatory and motivational reasons for action still seems to me valid and of central importance in understanding the problem of weakness of will. However, certain implications of that distinction need to be given a greater or a different emphasis than they earlier received.

Although inclination and obligation may often in practice coincide, justificatory reasons do not *necessarily* motivate. Ought-judgements logically contain a justificatory element, but only contingently a motivational one. But this raises the problem of what precisely is the function of an ought-judgement if it happens to lack motivational content and is not acted upon. What meaning can then be given to the claim that in sincerely making the judgement, one is accepting the validity of the justificatory reasons that back it, whether or not one acts upon it?

Two points need to be emphasised in responding to this objection, one of which featured in my earlier account and one of which did not:

1 Acting in conformity with one's ought-judgement is not the only way of establishing that that judgement was sincerely made and that the justificatory reasons backing it are accepted as valid. If one fails to act in accordance with one's ought-judgement, one may still demonstrate one's acceptance of its validity in a wide variety of ways, which I listed as follows:

> . . . lies about what one has done, attempted elaborate rationalisations, over-compensation for what appears a trivial error, unsolicited confessions, pleas for forgiveness and 'another chance', self-abasement or even self-sacrifice, embarrassment, hesitation, undue reticence or extreme bravado. Any of these might or might not be accompanied by pangs of remorse.
>
> (Straughan 1982: 80)

Some criterion of this kind, then, is needed to demonstrate the sincerity of an ought-judgement and its justificatory function, if that judgement is not in fact acted upon.

2   A closer link might be forged between justificatory and motivational reasons by drawing a distinction which I only hinted at in my earlier account. Ought-judgements can be formulated in either the active or the passive mode: I may, for example, judge either that I ought *to give* more to the poor or that the poor ought *to be given* more. It might then be argued that while the active version does not necessarily imply any personal desire to give more *myself*, the passive version does imply a desire (or wish) that more should be given, without specifying the donors. To say that I think more ought to be given but that I do not *want* more to be given sounds logically odd, whereas to say that I think I ought to give more but that I do not actually want to may call for further explanation but does not sound obvious nonsense.

This distinction could throw further light on explanations of weakness of will and moral weakness, for it is possible that instances of such apparent 'weakness' may often (or even always) involve a confusion on the part of the agent in forming or expressing the ought-judgement in the active form while really only accepting the implications of the passive form. The agent judges that the poor ought to be given more and wants them to be given more, but expresses this judgement actively in the form that he or she ought to give them more, which does not necessarily coincide with motivational priorities.

Such a confusion would represent another form of self-deception, which I have argued is a central element in cases of weakness of will. The most obvious way in which weakness of will involves self-deception is where the agent fails to acknowledge or make explicit the priorities in practice weighing most heavily with him or her. For example, I want to give the police a full account of the crime I have witnessed *less* than I want to avoid reprisals from the criminals, but I fail to spell out (publicly or privately) the priority I am assigning to these motivational reasons and make explicit only the justificatory reasons backing the ought-judgement, which then comes to be presented as my final assessment of the situation (which my 'weakness' prevents from being implemented), whereas my actual unacknowledged, final assessment is determined by motivational factors.

Self-deception of various kinds, therefore, can help to explain cases of weakness of will, though it represents only one of several interlinked factors. These I labelled earlier (Straughan 1982) as the *language factor*, whereby the agent fails for various reasons to be influenced by the prescriptivity of ought-judgements, and the *immediacy factor*, whereby more immediate features of the situation facing the agent (for example, in terms of time or distance) outweigh more remote features (*ibid.*: 133–45). These factors cannot be elaborated upon here, but even if we restrict ourselves to the forms of self-deception mentioned above, a number of interesting implications for moral education suggest themselves, to which we can now finally turn.

Implications for moral education

If the distinction between active and passive ought-judgements is a valid one, it would follow that moral education programmes should be sensitive to this distinction and should perhaps be wary of approaches which over-emphasise the passive mode by encouraging or allowing pupils to formulate ought-judgements predominantly in this mode. This has particular applica-tion to the treatment of current moral issues, such as inequalities between the developed and developing world, or issues of environmental responsi-bilities, for it is all-too easy for discussion of such topics to develop into a self-righteous consensus and a plethora of passive ought-judgements (for example, starving refugees ought to be given more food and medical care; tropical rain forests ought to be protected, and so on). Many 'green' causes featuring in moral education discussions and tending to attract the verbal support of young people can lead to the expression of well-meaning, gener-alised ought-judgements of this kind.

One strategy for teachers to adopt here would be to encourage pupils to translate passive ought-judgements into an active form and to examine the implications of this. For example, rather than remaining content with a conclu-sion such as 'The atmosphere ought not to be polluted by unnecessary exhaust fumes', pupils could be challenged to make this judgement active and specific: 'I ought not to make unnecessary car journeys that contribute to pollution.' This restatement of the ought-judgement brings the motivational issue to the fore, by forcing pupils to consider whether they might want the atmosphere not to be polluted but at the same time not want the incon-venience of making less use of car transport. Reflecting on such possible conflicts could be far more morally educative than a generalised discussion of global issues in non-personal terms.

This strategy would be one example of a broader educational approach that could be followed in an attempt to counter the kind of self-deception that seems central to moral weakness. If such so-called weakness involves wanting to do x rather than y (which one acknowledges is backed by justificatory reasons, because x is seen at the time as being more desirable and attractive), the failure to accept and admit this motivational weighting explicitly is in fact a sign of moral awareness rather than a total lack of it. This is because such conflicts presuppose an agent who is concerned about moral questions and ought-judgements – otherwise there could be no conflict and no apparent 'weakness'. Spelling out one's *overall* assessment of the situation declares (either to others or to oneself) one's actual situational priorities – that is, the greater priority one is allocating to non-moral considerations – but by making explicit only the moral ought-judgement, one can fall back on the apparently explanatory excuse of 'weakness', which carries with it certain causal connotations that seem to lessen one's moral culpability.

267

If moral education is to try to do anything about this problem, approaches that encourage an open and honest self-appraisal of pupils' wants and motives are likely to achieve more than either traditional verbal instruction or the currently fashionable discussion of global issues. Acknowledging what one's dominant wants and motives are in a particular situation does not of course necessarily lessen their influence or make it more likely that ought-judgements will be acted upon. However, such an acknowledgement is certainly a precondition of any re-examination or conscious modification of those wants and motives. It is then possible that by reflecting upon one's wants one may see alternative ways of satisfying them which do not conflict with the ought-judgement one has formed. This could often occur, for example, in cases where a pupil's dominant want is to gain or retain the approval of their peers and where there is a variety of ways of achieving this; some of these may clash with particular ought-judgements, but others may not. In such cases the role of moral education is best seen not as 'strengthening the will' but as encouraging a cool and detached review of various options. Much more investigation needs to be done into possible educational methods of tackling this task and the contexts in which they would be most effective, but this is not the place for a detailed consideration of these important practical questions (see Straughan 1982: chs 8–9).

Several different factors are probably operative in cases of moral weakness, and moral education will consequently need to try a combination of methods and approaches that do justice to the philosophical, psychological and educational complexities of the problem. This chapter has outlined only one dimension of that problem, which has been highlighted by current simplistic views of moral education and their uncritical reliance upon 'verbalistic' methods. To advocate a policy of 'teaching children the difference between right and wrong' on the assumption that this approach will at a stroke render moral education unproblematic is unlikely to achieve much, and one suspects that Socrates' reaction to such a policy would be identical to that which he expressed over two thousand years ago: 'When I see the subject in such utter confusion, I feel the liveliest desire to clear it up' (Plato 1956: 99).

Note

1 I would also like to acknowledge some particularly helpful verbal and written comments from Dr Barbara Applebaum of the Ontario Institute for Studies in Education.

References

Balchin, N. (1951) *A Way Through the Wood*, London: Fontana.
Dewey, J. (1966) *Democracy and Education*, New York: Macmillan.

Frankena, W. K. (1958) 'Obligation and motivation', in A. I. Melden (ed.) *Essays on Moral Philosophy,* Seattle: University of Washington.

Plato (1956) *Protagoras,* tr. W. K. C. Guthrie, Harmondsworth: Penguin.

Steutel, J. (1988) 'Learning the virtue of self-control', in B. Spieker and R. Straughan (eds) *Philosophical Issues in Moral Education and Development,* Milton Keynes: Open University Press.

Straughan, R. (1982) *I Ought to, but . . .: A Philosophical Approach to the Weakness of Will in Education,* Windsor: NFER.

—— (1989) *Beliefs, Behaviour and Education,* London: Cassell.

Suttle, R. R. (1987) Review article – 'I ought to, but . . .', *Educational Theory* 37(4): 477–86.

INDEX

60